P9-CEZ-096

# VEGAN
## Holiday Kitchen

*Also by Nava Atlas*

## COOKBOOKS

Vegan Soups and Hearty Stews for All Seasons

Vegan Express

The Vegetarian Family Cookbook

The Vegetarian 5-Ingredient Gourmet

Pasta East to West

Great American Vegetarian

Vegetarian Express

Vegetarian Celebrations

Vegetariana

## VISUAL NONFICTION

The Literary Ladies' Guide to the Writing Life

Secret Recipes for the Modern Wife

Expect the Unexpected When You're Expecting! (A Parody)

MORE THAN 200 DELICIOUS, FESTIVE

RECIPES FOR SPECIAL OCCASIONS

# VEGAN
# Holiday Kitchen

## NAVA ATLAS

PHOTOGRAPHS BY SUSAN VOISIN

STERLING
New York

STERLING
New York

An Imprint of Sterling Publishing
387 Park Avenue South
New York, NY 10016

ISBN 978-1-4027-8005-9 (hardcover)
ISBN 978-1-4027-9096-6 (Sterling epub)

Distributed in Canada by Sterling Publishing
c/o Canadian Manda Group, 165 Dufferin Street
Toronto, Ontario, Canada M6K 3H6
Distributed in the United Kingdom by GMC Distribution Services
Castle Place, 166 High Street, Lewes, East Sussex, England BN7 1XU
Distributed in Australia by Capricorn Link (Australia) Pty. Ltd.
P.O. Box 704, Windsor, NSW 2756, Australia

For information about custom editions, special sales, and premium and
corporate purchases, please contact Sterling Special Sales at 800-805-5489
or specialsales@sterlingpublishing.com

Book design by Christine Heun

Manufactured in the United States of America

2  4  6  8  10  9  7  5  3  1

www.sterlingpublishing.com

# CONTENTS

# INTRODUCTION

More than twenty years ago, I published *Vegetarian Celebrations*, a collection of holiday menus. I did this out of necessity—my own, as a longtime vegetarian, and that of friends and acquaintances who seemed to come to me regularly for ideas on what to serve the inevitable vegetarian guest or two at holiday meals, particularly Thanksgiving, Christmas, and Passover. Now, vegetarians at the table rarely cause a stir, and the bar has been set higher by the burgeoning vegan population. Neither vegans nor vegetarians want to feel like a footnote at the table; nor do they want to go back to the old way of celebrating holidays, which consisted of politely picking at side dishes and being made to feel guilty for not partaking of all the dishes for which our parents, grandparents, or aunts slaved over a hot stove.

We of the plant-based predilection want to celebrate holidays in style, without apologies, and enjoy every course of the meal, from appetizers to desserts. Vegan cuisine has blossomed into full glory, which doesn't include sacrifice. If it means we must make each animal-free course of the meal ourselves, we'll do so, and joyfully, at that. The irony is that lovingly, thoughtfully crafted vegan dishes made for celebratory occasions are the very ones that everyone else—no matter what their culinary bent—wants to try. My sister-in-law Anne often notes that on the many occasions when she is asked to bring a vegan dish to share (so that my brother, a vegan, but no cook himself, will have something substantial to eat) she has learned to make double of what she thinks will be needed, because everyone will want to try what Ron is eating.

Those of us who live on either the east or west coast of the United States have come to think of the vegan way of life as nearly (if not downright) mainstream. But it's not just a bicoastal phenomenon; almost any major city in the U.S. has a plethora of pleasures for vegans, from natural foods groceries to all-vegan restaurants to vegan-friendly ethnic eateries. Honestly, being a vegan today is easier than it was being a vegetarian twenty or twenty-five years ago. It

**Spring Vegetable Tart, see page 178**

wasn't that much of a leap when my own family (consisting of husband and two sons) went from vegetarian to vegan some years ago.

But having said all that, many vegans still feel as if they're living on a lonely outpost, especially if they don't live in a metropolitan area, or if they are a part of a family that's not vegan-friendly. Holidays can be particularly trying for vegans who aren't part of a wider circle of like-minded eaters. This book is dedicated to them—and to vegans of all stripes. That's one of the reasons why I've focused, as much as possible, on ingredients that are familiar and easily obtained almost anywhere. The other is that during the holidays there's a powerful pull of the past, for rituals and traditions that are familiar. So while many new traditions have emerged when it comes to holiday fare, I've tried to incorporate as many well-known ingredients, seasonings, and embellishments into the recipes and menus as possible.

If you are one of my longtime readers, you might wonder if this book is a revised and updated edition of *Vegetarian Celebrations*. For the most part, it is not, although I have included some of the more useful, relevant sections of *Vegetarian Celebrations*, such as the guides to grilling vegetables and protein foods. A number of my Thanksgiving favorites and Jewish holiday classics, such as sweet noodle kugel, latkes, and

matzo balls—which are already vegetarian, but need a bit of creativity to convert to vegan—have migrated here from *Vegetarian Celebrations* in new, dairy- and egg-free versions.

In this book, I also chose to focus more on major holidays for which people everywhere tend to cook. In *Vegetarian Celebrations* I covered Mother's Day, Father's Day, St. Patrick's Day, and the like. Mother's Day and Father's Day, for instance, are often occasions for going out (though you can easily tap into some of the ideas in this book if you'd like to cook for Mom or Dad, or choose one of the brunch menus on pages 264 to 265). St. Patrick's Day seems like the kind of holiday where people like to go out and, shall we say, imbibe, rather than stay home and make a classic cabbage and potato colcannon. Other, minor holidays similarly don't have "stay home and cook" written all over them. But Thanksgiving, Christmas, Easter, Independence Day, and the major Jewish holidays certainly do, so that's where I've devoted my attention in this new collection of recipes and menus. One additional chapter, the last, presents a selection of recipes for miscellaneous entertaining—a trio of brunch menus that can be used for all sorts of occasions (from feeding overnight guests to greeting the New Year), a selection of hot and cold appetizers, and an array of sturdy dishes suitable for transporting to potlucks or serving at home for casual buffets.

Another thing that has changed over the last couple of decades, I've noticed, is a greater awareness of food allergies. Even as an expanding number of soy-based dairy alternatives has made life easier and tastier for many vegans (as well as for anyone with dairy allergies), it has given rise to the awareness of soy allergies (and most likely, the cause of the allergies themselves). Fortunately, the selection of non-soy dairy alternatives is on the rise. Tree nut allergies are another serious consideration. But the food allergy that has garnered quite a bit of serious attention in the last few years is gluten sensitivity, which can result in celiac disease. As I was nearing the completion of the manuscript for this book, I noticed that many of the recipes were gluten-free, or could be made gluten-free, with minor adjustments—a development I hadn't planned on—but that was, perhaps, the result of my own evolving habits. Even though I don't follow a gluten-free regimen, I seem to be less inclined these days to eat bready sorts of foods. And if given a choice between bulgur and quinoa, I'm more inclined to choose the latter. As for pasta, I like my durum wheat, but there are plenty of good alternatives now for anyone on a gluten-free diet. To make it easier to tell which recipes in this book address

food sensitivities, I've identified them with gluten-free, soy-free, or nut-free labels. And of course all the recipes are dairy-free and egg-free, so just about every major food allergy is accounted for. May all be fed!

Finally, here are a few tips to help make it easier to plan, manage, and enjoy cooking in the vegan holiday kitchen:

⬤ Everyone is busy these days. Even though I'm no stranger to preparing four- to six-course meals for company, and as much as I've always liked to channel my inner Aunt Blanche (who was the ultimate hostess of the family when I was growing up), the thought of preparing an entire Thanksgiving feast for a crowd is overwhelming for me now. I've found that it's not only easier, but a lot more fun, to make a huge meal cooperatively. If everyone makes a dish or two, no one comes to the table already feeling frazzled—or broke!

⬤ If you're going to be the lone vegan at a holiday meal, or one of the few, offer to bring a main dish, at the very least. Bring plenty of what you'll be eating, because everyone will want some of what you're having. Look at this as a good thing: Is there a better way to promote a vegan diet than by showing how delicious it is?

• If you're the host, even if you're not making all the dishes, it's good to plan the event at least a week ahead of time to avoid last-minute panic. Plan the menu first, then see if other guests will be contributing to the meal. Follow up by making your shopping list. Even though we live in such a hurry-up, last-minute world, I would recommend shopping no less than three days before the date. This gives you a bit of leeway, should you need to make any last-minute changes, or if you want to get extra-fresh produce the day before.

• Plan to shop for ancillary needs such as beverages, napkins, candles, table seasonings, aluminum foil, baking parchment, trash bags, and storage containers for leftovers at least one week ahead of time, instead of saving it up for the big food shop.

• Make use of good-quality shortcuts such as prepared vegetable broth, all-purpose seasoning blend, canned beans, and pre-made pie crust, to free up your time for all the other dishes you'll need to prepare from scratch. As you'll see in the pages ahead, I've suggested some of my favorite time-savers.

• Serving sizes in this book are based on my own experience, although that's somewhat subjective. If your guests bring contributions to the meal, then each dish will go a longer way. If a bunch of high school– or college-age young men (or lumberjacks) show up at the last minute, this will skew the number of servings downward. In either case, I've tried to go for a median. If you're expecting a larger number of guests than the menus in this book typically serve (usually 8 to 10), doubling a couple of the recipes and/or adding another dish or two to the mix will ensure that there will be enough food to go around.

• I don't offer a lot of make-ahead tips in this book since, to my mind, most recipes just don't taste as good when they're made too far ahead of when they'll be used. I'll alert you to exceptions; many kinds of soups and stews, for example, benefit from extra time that allows flavors to mingle. Honestly, most of the recipes in this book are not so lengthy or complicated that they benefit from advance prep. However, there are some components of dishes that can be made ahead, saving time once it comes time to assemble them. Here are a few things you can do a day or two in advance (and feel very glad that you didn't save them for the day of the event!):

BAKE winter squashes for making pies, stuffed squash dishes, and the like (see baking tips for squashes on page 22).

**COOK,** bake, or microwave potatoes or sweet potatoes.

**COOK** grains, including brown rice, and even quinoa, which cooks quickly, simply because it's one less thing to do at the last minute when you're cooking for company.

**MAKE** any salad dressings or sauces that are part of a recipe; they can be made either earlier the same day, or a day ahead, then refrigerated.

**MAKE** breadcrumbs or croutons.

**ACCEPT** help when it's offered. Many of us, especially those of the female persuasion, tend to turn help away, with that inherent, self-sacrificing, "don't bother, I'll handle it" attitude. If someone asks what he or she can do to help with a holiday meal, assume that the offer is sincere, and give that person a task or a dish to make. And if no help seems to be forthcoming, enlist some! If you ask politely and sincerely, most people would love to be part of the holiday preparation.

When we gather together for holidays, it's a chance to reflect on our heritage, celebrate the unique splendor of the season, enjoy a respite from the everyday routine, revisit cherished rituals from our past, and simply rejoice. Food is central to nearly every important celebration. For vegans, any celebratory occasion is made even sweeter knowing that no harm came to any other living creature for the sake of our own pleasure.

# CHAPTER ONE

# THANKSGIVING

*A compassionate way to celebrate
the holiday everyone loves*

I start this book with Thanksgiving, because for many vegans and vegetarians, it's the Mother of All Holidays. It used to mean being relegated to eating side dishes (and being put on the spot about how rude it is to refuse Aunt Clarabelle's famous turkey and stuffing), but over the last couple of decades it has grown into a feast for full culinary expression. Though the holiday has a kind of all-American identity, let's not forget that Canadians celebrate Thanksgiving as well—it's in October, befitting a harvest festival. And that's exactly what Thanksgiving's original intent was—a feast of gratitude for the harvest's abundance.

The bounty of squashes, pumpkins, sweet potatoes, apples, pears, cranberries, nuts, greens, Brussels spouts, and other veggies typical of this holiday's theme gives vegans and vegetarians the ability to enjoy a full-scale feast. Still, Thanksgiving can be a trying time for the meatless crowd. That's because the holiday is so completely bound up with the concept of turkey. So much emphasis is placed on this hapless bird, from construction-paper turkeys fashioned by legions of schoolchildren each year, to the ostentatious annual "presidential pardon" of two turkeys by whomever is occupying the White House.

Vegans and vegetarians would prefer that all turkeys were pardoned from their ignominious fates, and that the holiday be returned to its original intent—from the 1621 proclamation of Governor

**Pumpkin Cheesecake with a Hint of Chocolate, see page 52**

William Bradford of Massachusetts to "render thanksgiving . . . for the abundant harvest of Indian corn, wheat, beans, squashes, and garden vegetables." Indeed, it's the "Three Sisters" of Native American lore—corn, beans, and squash—that were once the most honored components of the feast.

The beauty of Thanksgiving is that it's so inclusive—you need not be from any particular culture or creed, nor adhere to any denominational belief to partake of its pleasures. It's a holiday for everyone—a day for giving appreciation for the abundance that exists in our lives, and enjoying the bountiful foods of the season.

## MIX AND MATCH MENUS FOR THE THANKSGIVING TABLE

Since Thanksgiving is such a favored holiday in the vegan and vegetarian realms, I'm launching this book with the biggest and most plentiful chapter. Plant-based meals for Thanksgiving are sure to have their offbeat twists, but the ingredients emphasized here are those most closely associated with the holiday and its fresh, seasonal offerings. Corn, beans, squashes, sweet potatoes, apples, nuts, and cranberries figure prominently in these dishes. Mixing and matching the components of your Thanksgiving meal from these selections will keep you in good stead for years to come, whether you're the host or the guest.

Though none of the dishes here are terribly complicated, if you want to serve a dish from each of the categories from soups to desserts, you might consider doing this cooperatively with all participants making one or two dishes. That way everyone can enjoy a wonderful feast without feeling wiped out from a lot of preparation.

If you'd like to add any appetizers to the menu, consider the possibilities listed in the Holiday Appetizer Buffet (page 74) in chapter two, *Christmas*, or the listing of Easy Appetizers (page 277) in chapter six.

# THANKSGIVING ETIQUETTE

What do you do if you're a vegan or vegetarian invited to a traditional Thanksgiving gathering (or, for that matter, any holiday gathering at which you know that meat will be served)? If you're going to be in the veg minority, volunteer to bring a main dish that you can enjoy (and, possibly, a stuffing baked in a casserole) and that others can have as side dishes. Perhaps you're a non-veg reader consulting this book because you're hosting the meal and expecting a vegan or vegetarian or two. If that's the case, and your veg guests haven't volunteered to contribute anything (or if you'd like to try making something to impress the new vegan in the family), read on for plenty of alternative main dishes and stuffings. After all, that's exactly what this book is about.

# SOUPS & BREADS

Spiced Vegetable Peanut Soup

Coconut Butternut Squash Soup

Creamy Wild Mushroom Soup

Squash, Sweet Potato, and Corn Chowder

Sweet Potato Biscuits

Green Chili Corn Bread or Muffins

# Spiced Vegetable Peanut Soup

**GLUTEN-FREE**
**SOY-FREE**

## 8 OR MORE SERVINGS

*This rich soup is loosely based on an old recipe from the American South that was in turn inspired by an African recipe. Use enough cayenne or hot red pepper flakes to give the soup a pleasant heat. Pass around additional red pepper flakes for those who'd enjoy a spicier soup.*

2 tablespoons olive or other healthy vegetable oil

1 large onion, chopped

2 large celery stalks, finely diced

3 medium carrots, thinly sliced

2 tablespoons unbleached white flour

1 medium yellow summer squash, diced

1 medium red bell pepper, diced

1 teaspoon good-quality curry powder

2 teaspoons grated fresh or jarred ginger, or more, to taste

2 tablespoons lemon juice

⅔ cup natural smooth peanut butter

1½ to 2 cups rice milk

Dried hot red pepper flakes, to taste

Salt and freshly ground pepper to taste

2 good handfuls baby spinach leaves

¼ to ½ cup chopped fresh parsley, to taste

1. Heat the oil in a soup pot. Add the onion, celery, and carrots. Sauté over medium-low heat, stirring frequently, until the vegetables are golden. Sprinkle in the flour and continue to sauté, stirring constantly, until the entire mixture begins to turn a golden brown.

2. Add 4 cups water along with the squash, bell pepper, curry powder, ginger, and lemon juice. Bring to a gentle boil. Cover and simmer gently over low heat until the vegetables are tender, about 10 to 15 minutes.

3. Whisk in the peanut butter until it is well blended with the liquid. Stir in enough rice milk to give the soup a slightly thick consistency. Add red pepper flakes to give the soup some subtle heat. Season with salt and pepper. Simmer very gently for 10 minutes or so longer, stirring occasionally.

4. If time allows, let the soup stand off the heat for an hour or more to allow the flavors to blend, then heat through as needed. Stir in the baby spinach leaves and half the parsley, and use the rest to garnish each serving.

# Coconut Butternut Squash Soup

**GLUTEN-FREE**

**SOY-FREE**

**NUT-FREE (if coconut is safe for you)**

## 8 SERVINGS

*Once you've got the squash baked, this soup comes together quickly. The mellow flavors of squash, kale, and red onions synergize delectably and look gorgeous together as well.*

1 large butternut squash (about 1½ pounds)

2 tablespoons olive oil or other healthy vegetable oil

1 large yellow or sweet white onion, chopped

1 medium apple, any variety, peeled and diced

2 cups prepared vegetable broth, or 2 cups water with 1 vegetable bouillon cube

2 teaspoons good-quality curry powder

2 teaspoons grated fresh or jarred ginger, or more, to taste

Pinch of ground nutmeg or allspice

1 14-ounce can light coconut milk

Salt and freshly ground pepper to taste

### GARNISH

2 medium red onions, quartered and thinly sliced

1 good-size bunch kale (about 10 to 12 ounces)

**1.** To bake the squash, see the instructions in the sidebar on page 22.

**2.** Heat about half the oil in a soup pot. Add the onion and sauté over medium-low heat until golden, about 8 to 10 minutes.

**3.** Add the apple, squash, broth, and spices. Bring to a steady simmer, then cover and simmer gently until the apples are tender, about 10 minutes.

**4.** Transfer the solids to a food processor with a slotted spoon, in batches if need be, process until smoothly pureed, then transfer back to the soup pot. Or better yet, simply insert an immersion blender into the pot and process until smoothly pureed.

**5.** Stir in the coconut milk and return the soup to a gentle simmer. Cook over low heat for 5 to 10 minutes, until well heated through. Season with salt and pepper. If time allows, let the soup stand off the heat for an hour or two, then heat through as needed before serving.

**6.** Just before serving, heat the remaining oil in a large skillet. Add the red onions and sauté over low heat until golden and soft.

**7.** Meanwhile, strip the kale leaves off the stems and cut into thin shreds. Stir together with the onions in the skillet, adding just enough water to moisten the surface. Cover and cook over medium heat, stirring occasionally, until the kale is bright green and just tender, about 5 minutes.

**8.** To serve, ladle soup into each bowl, then place a small mound of kale and onion mixture in the center.

# Creamy Wild Mushroom Soup

**GLUTEN-FREE**

Can be made **SOY-FREE** by omitting the optional tofu

**NUT-FREE**

## 8 SERVINGS

*This flavorful soup gets its creamy thickness from a base of pureed white beans.*

2 tablespoons olive oil or other healthy vegetable oil

1 large onion, chopped

2 to 3 cloves garlic, minced

2 medium potatoes, peeled and diced

2 large celery stalks, with leaves, diced

1 32-ounce carton vegetable broth

½ teaspoon dried basil

½ teaspoon dried thyme

¼ cup dry white wine, optional

12 ounces baby bella or crimini mushrooms, stemmed, wiped clean, and sliced

4 to 6 ounces fresh shiitake mushrooms, stemmed, wiped clean, and sliced

1 15- to 16-ounce can white beans (cannellini), drained and rinsed

1 12.3-ounce package firm silken tofu, crumbled (optional, see Variation)

2 cups rice milk, or as needed

Salt and freshly ground pepper to taste

½ cup minced fresh parsley for garnish

1. Heat the oil in a large soup pot. Add the onions and sauté over medium heat until translucent. Add the garlic and continue to sauté until the onion is golden. Add potatoes, celery, broth, basil, thyme, and optional wine. Bring to a gentle boil, then cover, lower the heat, and simmer gently for 15 to 20 minutes, or until the vegetables are tender.

2. Meanwhile, combine both varieties of mushrooms in a small skillet or saucepan with enough water to keep the mixture moist. Cover and cook over medium heat for 10 minutes.

3. Add the beans and optional tofu to the soup. Puree the soup in batches in a food processor or blender, then return to the soup pot. Or, simply insert an immersion blender into the pot and process until smoothly pureed.

4. Stir in the cooked mushrooms and add enough rice milk to give the soup a slightly thick consistency. Season with salt and pepper. If time allows, let the soup stand for several hours or overnight.

5. Heat though before serving and adjust the consistency with more rice milk if too thick; adjust the seasonings as well. Ladle into soup bowls and sprinkle each serving with the parsley.

**VARIATION:** To make the soup soy-free, use two cans of white beans and omit the tofu.

# Squash, Sweet Potato, and Corn Chowder

**Can be made GLUTEN-FREE by using gluten-free bouillon cubes**
**SOY-FREE**
**NUT-FREE**

**6 TO 8 SERVINGS**

*Squash, corn, and sweet potato combine to make a hearty chowder that's perfect for this time of year. Do try to use fresh corn if it's still available where you live.*

1 medium butternut squash (about 1½ pounds)

2 tablespoons olive oil or other healthy vegetable oil

1 large onion, finely chopped

1 celery stalk, finely diced

1 large sweet potato, peeled and diced

1 32-ounce carton vegetable broth, or 4 cups water with 2 vegetable bouillon cubes (gluten- and soy-free, if need be)

2 bay leaves

2 teaspoons cumin

½ teaspoon dried basil

½ teaspoon dried thyme

2½ to 3 cups corn kernels, cooked fresh from about 3 medium ears or thawed frozen corn kernels

1 cup rice milk, or as needed

Salt and freshly ground pepper to taste

¼ cup minced fresh parsley, or more, to taste

**1.** With a sharp knife, cut the squash across the center of the rounded part. Remove the seeds and fibers. Slice the squash into ½-inch rings, then peel each ring and cut into small dice. If you don't have a knife (or the patience) for this task, partially bake the squash as directed in the sidebar on page 22 to make the cutting and peeling easier.

**2.** Heat the oil in a soup pot. Add the onion and celery and sauté over medium heat until the onion is golden. Add the squash and sweet potato dice and enough broth or water to cover all but about an inch of the vegetables. Bring to a simmer, then add the bay leaves and other seasonings. Simmer gently, covered, until the squash and potatoes are tender, about 25 to 30 minutes.

**3.** With a slotted spoon, scoop out 2 heaping cups of the solid ingredients, mash them well, and stir back into the soup. Or simply insert an immersion blender into the soup pot and puree a small portion of the ingredients—enough to give the base of the soup some thickness.

**4.** Add the corn and enough rice milk to give the soup a slightly thick consistency. Season with salt and pepper, then simmer over low heat for 10 to 15 minutes longer.

**5.** Serve at once, or let the soup stand for an hour or so before serving, then heat through as needed. Stir in the parsley just before serving. This may also be cooked a day ahead and refrigerated, since its flavor develops nicely overnight.

# Sweet Potato Biscuits

**MAKES 12 TO 16**

*Delightfully moist and slightly sweet, these biscuits are delicious served with seasonal soups.*

1   medium sweet potato

2⅓ cups spelt flour or whole wheat pastry flour

2   teaspoons baking powder

½   teaspoon salt

¼   cup Earth Balance or other non-hydrogenated margarine

¼   cup maple syrup

½   cup coarsely chopped walnuts or pecans

1. Cook, bake, or microwave the sweet potato until tender. When cool enough to handle, peel and cut it into large chunks, then mash well.

2. Preheat the oven to 375° F.

3. Combine the flour, baking powder, and salt in a food processor fitted with either the metal blade or the dough blade. Pulse on and off a few times.

4. Add the margarine and pulse on and off until it is evenly distributed in the flour.

5. Add the sweet potato and drizzle in the maple syrup. Process until the mixture holds together as a soft dough. Add the nuts and pulse on and off until they are evenly distributed in the dough.

6. Line a baking sheet with parchment paper. Pinch off sections of the dough (it will be slightly sticky, so flour your hands if you'd like) to form 2-inch balls (make slightly smaller if you'd like to have more to go around). Flatten lightly and arrange in rows on the baking sheet.

7. Place on the center rack in the oven and bake for 12 to 15 minutes, or until a knife inserted into the center of a biscuit tests clean and the bottoms are lightly brown. Transfer the biscuits to a plate and serve warm.

# Green Chili
# Corn Bread or Muffins

**Can be made SOY-FREE by using coconut yogurt and soy-free nondairy cheese**
**NUT-FREE (for those who aren't also allergic to coconut)**

**MAKES 1 DOZEN**

*Served warm out of the oven, green chili corn bread or muffins are great companions to harvest soups.*
*Nondairy cheese definitely adds a major "yum" factor, so do try it if you can.*

- 1 cup cornmeal, preferably stone ground
- 1 cup whole wheat pastry flour or unbleached white flour
- 1 teaspoon baking soda
- 1 teaspoon baking powder
- 1 teaspoon salt
- 1 6-ounce container plain soy yogurt or coconut yogurt
- ¼ cup extra-virgin olive oil
- ⅓ cup rice milk, or as needed
- 1 small fresh hot chili, seeded and minced, or one 4-ounce can chopped mild green chilies
- ½ cup frozen corn kernels, thawed, optional
- 1 cup grated nondairy cheese, optional

1. Preheat the oven to 400° F.

2. Combine the first 5 (dry) ingredients in a mixing bowl and stir together.

Make a well in the center of the dry ingredients. Pour in the yogurt, oil, and rice milk. Stir until well combined, adding more rice milk if needed, to make a smooth, slightly stiff batter. Stir in the chilies, optional corn kernels, and optional cheese.

3. Pour the batter into an oiled 9 x 9–inch baking pan, or divide among 12 foil-lined muffin tins. Bake for 20 to 25 minutes, or until the tops are golden and a knife inserted in the center of a muffin tests clean. Let cool slightly, then transfer the muffins to a serving plate, leaving them in the foil liners.

**NOTE:** A piece of this corn bread is depicted in the photo of Butternut Squash Soup on page xi.

# SALADS

Tri-Color Coleslaw

Sweet Potato–Poppy Seed Coleslaw

Mixed Baby Greens with Pears and Glazed Pecans

Massaged Kale Salad with Cranberries and Cashews

Jícama Salad with Fennel and Oranges

# Tri-Color Coleslaw

**GLUTEN-FREE**

**NUT-FREE (if seeds are safe for you, otherwise omit)**

**8 OR MORE SERVINGS**

*This easy slaw is an old standby for my holiday meals. Kale gives it a deeper flavor and additional color, not to mention a nice nutritional boost.*

2 cups thinly shredded red cabbage

2 cups thinly shredded white or Napa cabbage

2 cup thinly shredded kale

⅔ cup dried cranberries

¼ cup toasted pumpkin or sunflower seeds

⅔ cup vegan mayonnaise

1 to 2 tablespoons lemon juice, to taste

1. Combine all the ingredients in a serving bowl and mix thoroughly. Serve at once or cover and refrigerate until needed.

# Sweet Potato–Poppy Seed Coleslaw

**GLUTEN-FREE**
**SOY-FREE**

**4 TO 6 SERVINGS**

*A rich raw cashew dressing, lots of poppy seeds, and above all, the surprise of raw sweet potato combine to make a festive variation on classic coleslaw.*

½ cup raw cashews

1 medium sweet potato, peeled

1½ cups green cabbage, thinly sliced

½ cup red cabbage, thinly sliced

2 scallions, green part only, thinly sliced

2 tablespoons minced fresh dill, or ½ teaspoon dried

2 teaspoons black sesame seeds, chia seeds, or poppy seeds

Juice of ½ lemon, or more, to taste

½ teaspoon salt

Freshly ground pepper to taste

1. Place the cashews in a small bowl and pour ½ cup of boiling water over them. Let stand for 10 to 15 minutes.

2. Peel the sweet potato and cut into coarse chunks. In a food processor fitted with the grating blade, grate the sweet potato, then transfer to a serving bowl. Add the two cabbages, scallions, dill, and seeds. Stir together.

3. Rinse the food processor, then fit with the regular blade. Place the cashews and any unabsorbed water in the work bowl. Process until the mixture is fairly smooth. Add the lemon juice and salt and process until creamy.

4. Pour the cashew mixture over the slaw and stir together. Season with pepper. Let the slaw stand for a few minutes before serving, or up to an hour, to allow the flavors to blend.

# Mixed Baby Greens with Pears and Glazed Pecans

**8 SERVINGS**

*Here's a burst of color for the holiday plate that's nutritious and invigorating as well.*

---

**GLAZED PECANS**

- ¼ cup agave nectar
- Pinch of cinnamon
- Pinch of salt
- 1 cup pecan halves

**GREENS AND PEARS**

- 4 to 6 ounces mixed baby greens
- 2 good handfuls of baby spinach or arugula
- ½ medium head radicchio, thinly sliced
- 1 cup baby carrots, halved lengthwise if slender, quartered if thick
- 2 medium Bosc pears, cut into quarters lengthwise, cored, seeded, and diced
- 2 tablespoons extra-virgin olive oil
- 2 tablespoons lemon juice

1. Heat the agave nectar in a small skillet and sprinkle in the cinnamon and salt. When it just starts to get bubbly, stir in the pecans. Cook over low heat, stirring frequently, until the pecans are nicely glazed, 3 to 5 minutes.

2. Combine the remaining ingredients in a serving bowl and toss together. Just before serving, add the pecans and toss again.

# Massaged Kale Salad with Cranberries and Cashews

**GLUTEN-FREE**

Can be made **SOY-FREE** by using a soy-free vegan salad dressing

**6 TO 8 SERVINGS**

*This is a salad that my family enjoys pretty much all year round, save when tomatoes beckon in the summer. But I'll always associate it with Thanksgiving, because that is when I first encountered raw "massaged" kale in a salad at the home of our great friends Wendy and Harry. There are so many ways to vary this salad: You can toss in some slivered baby carrots, substitute another kind of nut, or add a bit of thinly shredded red cabbage for extra color or sliced celery or bok choy for extra crunch. Even in its simple form, as presented here, it's luscious and festive. I find it almost addictive; but I suppose that if one is going to be addicted to something, it may as well be kale!*

1 good-size bunch kale, washed and dried

Olive oil or other healthy vegetable oil, as needed

⅔ cup dried cranberries

½ cup crushed toasted cashews, or pumpkin seeds

½ cup vegan mayonnaise

1 to 2 tablespoons lemon juice, to taste

**1.** Strip the kale leaves off the stems. Cut into ribbons and place in a large bowl. With a little olive oil rubbed into your palms, massage the kale for a minute or so, until it becomes bright green and softens a bit.

**2.** Stir in the remaining ingredients and serve at room temperature.

**OPTIONAL ADDITIONS AND VARIATIONS:**

· Tiny orange sections

· Diced apple

· Diced pear

· Dried cherries or golden raisins in place of cranberries

· Toasted walnut or pecans in place of cashews

# Jícama Salad with Fennel and Oranges

**GLUTEN-FREE**

**SOY-FREE**

**NUT-FREE (if seeds are safe for you)**

## 8 OR MORE SERVINGS

*In the fall, jícamas are fairly easy to come by. My local supermarket, which isn't located in a sophisticated urban center, carries them at this time of year. I highly recommend getting acquainted with this offbeat veggie. Deceptively plain on the outside, it yields a burst of crisp, slightly sweet texture and flavor. If unavailable, substitute 2 to 3 medium turnips, and you've still got a lovely autumn salad.*

1 medium jícama, peeled and cut into narrow 1½-inch-long strips

3 to 4 clementines or other small seedless oranges, sectioned

1 fennel bulb, very thinly sliced

2 scallions, green parts only, thinly sliced

¼ to ½ cup chopped fresh cilantro, parsley, or dill, or a combination

4 ounces mixed baby greens

### DRESSING

Juice of ½ to 1 lime, to taste

2 tablespoons extra-virgin olive oil

1 tablespoon agave nectar

¼ cup toasted pumpkin seeds

1. Combine the first 6 ingredients in a serving bowl.

2. Combine the dressing ingredients in a small bowl and whisk until blended. Pour the dressing over the salad and toss together. Scatter the pumpkin seeds over the top and serve.

# WHAT ABOUT FAUX TURKEY?

For many years, I've been interviewed as an expert on vegetarian and vegan Thanksgiving meals. Invariably, I'm asked what I think about "tofu turkey" (though they aren't entirely made of tofu; often, gluten and beans are part of the mix), a product whose popularity has soared in recent years. "Well, I suppose it's preferable to the real thing," I reply tactfully. Personally, I'd rather focus on harvest produce for a truer sense of the holiday. Scouring local markets for the best of late-season crops becomes part of the celebration. To my mind, even a fake turkey is a diversion from the universal message of the Thanksgiving celebration.

Still, I very much understand why those who have given up meat would want to re-create a version of the famed holiday centerpiece. So much of what makes holiday meals appealing is ritual and nostalgia—dipping back into the past for the kind of continuity and familiarity that gives our crazy, hectic lives little islands of comfort and order. So if that's what makes your holiday table complete, I say, to each his or her own. There are even lots of turkey-style tofu or seitan roast—stuffing and all—recipes and videos on the Web, if you want to make the dish completely from scratch. It's quite a project, but for many, well worth the effort. This savory stuffed centerpiece, whether you buy it prepared (Tofurky and Field Roast are two popular brands) or make it via an online tutorial, is nearly equally popular for Christmas dinners as well.

# MAIN DISHES

Butternut Squash with Whole Wheat, Wild Rice, and Onion Stuffing

Quinoa and Lentil-Stuffed Golden Squashes

Rice and Pecan-Stuffed Squash

"Three Sisters" Stew

Pueblo Corn Pie

Baked Thanksgiving Risotto

Black Bean and Sweet Potato Tortilla Casserole

Ravioli with Sweet Potatoes and Sage

Hearty Vegetable Pot Pie

# Butternut Squash with Whole Wheat, Wild Rice, and Onion Stuffing

Can be made **GLUTEN-FREE** by using gluten-free bread

**SOY-FREE**

**NUT-FREE**

**8 SERVINGS**

*Here's one of my favorite holiday main dishes, which I adapted slightly from the original recipe in* Vegetarian Celebrations. *Instead of using dried sage, as in the earlier version, this recipe uses fresh sage leaves (which are so much nicer) plus a few other tweaks for deeper flavor. This satisfying dish makes a handsome centerpiece for a festive meal.*

4 medium-small butternut squashes (about 1 pound each)

¾ cup raw wild rice, rinsed

2 cups prepared vegetable broth, or 2 cups water with 1 vegetable bouillon cube

1½ tablespoons extra-virgin olive oil

1 large red onion, chopped

2 to 3 cloves garlic, minced

2½ cups firmly packed torn whole wheat bread

½ teaspoon dried thyme

5 or 6 fresh sage leaves, thinly sliced

2 to 3 teaspoons all-purpose seasoning blend (see sidebar on page 31), or to taste

1 cup fresh orange juice

1. Bake the squashes until tender but still firm enough to hold their shape, according to the directions in the sidebar on page 22.

2. Meanwhile, combine the wild rice with the broth in a saucepan. Bring to a gentle boil, then cover and simmer gently until the water is absorbed, about 40 minutes.

3. Heat the oil in a skillet. Add the onion and sauté until translucent. Add the garlic and continue to sauté until the onion is golden.

4. In a mixing bowl, combine the cooked wild rice with the sautéed onion and the remaining ingredients. When the squashes are cool enough to handle, scoop out the pulp, leaving firm shells about ½ inch thick. Chop the pulp and stir it into the rice mixture. Stuff the squashes, place in foil-lined baking dishes, and cover.

5. Before serving, place the squashes in a preheated 350° F oven. Bake for 20 to 30 minutes, depending on the size of the squashes, or until fork-tender and well heated through.

**VARIATION:** To add drama to this presentation, try this recipe with other squash varieties. Hubbard squash, delicata, sweet dumpling, and golden nugget are just a few of the stuffable squashes available.

# HOW TO BAKE WINTER SQUASHES OR SUGAR PUMPKINS

A number of recipes in this book call for baked winter squash, so rather than repeat the same directions, here are a few handy steps to follow each time:

1. Preheat the oven to 375° F.

2. Cut away large stems from squash or pumpkin, then cut it in half (you'll need a really good knife to do this!). Place the halves, cut side up, in a foil-lined, shallow baking dish and cover tightly with more foil.

3. Bake for 30 to 50 minutes, depending on the size of the squash and what you intend to do with it. If you ultimately need firm slices or chunks, or if you'll be stuffing and re-baking the vegetable, bake only until you can just pierce the flesh with a fork or knife. If you'll be pureeing the flesh, as for a pie or a soup, bake until easily pierced with a knife.

4. If you don't have a knife sharp enough to cut through a raw winter squash or sugar pumpkin, don't worry; prebaking partially makes squashes and pumpkins much easier to cut. Place the whole vegetable in the foil-lined baking dish. Cover loosely with foil and bake 15 minutes for smaller squashes, or 25 to 30 minutes for larger squashes and sugar pumpkins.

5. When cool enough to handle, remove the stem and cut the squash in half lengthwise.

6. Scoop out the pulp and seeds. Then proceed with directions given in individual recipes.

# Quinoa and Lentil-Stuffed Golden Squashes

**GLUTEN-FREE**

**SOY-FREE**

**NUT-FREE**

**8 SERVINGS**

*Here's a hearty rendition of stuffed squash. For a lovely visual effect, use red quinoa or a combination of red and regular quinoa.*

- 4 small winter squashes (carnival, golden acorn, delicata, or other small winter squash)
- 1 cup raw quinoa, rinsed
- 1½ cups prepared vegetable broth, or water with 1 vegetable bouillon cube
- 1½ tablespoons olive oil or other healthy vegetable oil
- 1 large red onion, finely chopped
- 2 cloves garlic, minced
- 1 medium red bell pepper, finely diced
- ⅓ cup orange juice, preferably fresh squeezed
- 2 teaspoons ground cumin
- ½ teaspoon ground turmeric
- 1 to 2 teaspoons grated fresh or jarred ginger, to taste
- 1 15- to 16-ounce can lentils, drained and rinsed
  Salt and freshly ground pepper to taste
- ½ cup minced fresh parsley

1. Bake the squashes until tender but still firm enough to hold their shape, according to the directions in the sidebar on page 22.

2. When the squashes are cool enough to handle, scoop out and discard the seeds. Scoop out the squash pulp, leaving a sturdy shell of about ½ inch all around. Chop the pulp finely.

3. Preheat the oven to 375° F.

Combine the quinoa with the broth in a small saucepan. Bring to a gentle boil, then lower the heat, cover, and simmer gently until the water is absorbed, about 15 to 20 minutes.

4. Heat the oil in a large skillet. Add the onion and sauté over medium heat until translucent. Add the garlic and bell pepper and sauté over medium heat until the onion is golden. Add the cooked quinoa, orange juice, and seasonings. Stir together and cook for 2 to 3 minutes longer, then gently stir in the lentils and half the parsley. Season with salt and pepper.

5. Stuff each squash half generously with the quinoa mixture. Sprinkle each with the remaining parsley. Bake for 20 to 25 minutes, then serve.

# Rice and Pecan-Stuffed Squash

Can be made **GLUTEN-FREE** by making crumbs from gluten-free bread
**SOY-FREE**

**8 SERVINGS**

*Squash and pecans make for a memorable duo when combined in this Creole-inspired recipe. The savory nut, bread, and rice stuffing, contrasted with the smooth sweetness of the butternut squash, makes for a perfect holiday main or side dish.*

4 medium golden acorn or delicata squashes

2 tablespoons olive oil or other healthy vegetable oil

1 large onion, finely chopped

¾ to 1 cup soft whole-grain breadcrumbs (see sidebar on page 30)

1½ cups cooked brown rice

⅔ cup finely chopped pecans

⅔ cup fresh orange juice, or as needed

2 tablespoons maple syrup

2 teaspoons fresh thyme leaves

½ teaspoon dried oregano

Salt and freshly ground pepper to taste

Pinch of nutmeg

Sprigs of fresh thyme for garnish

1. Preheat the oven to 375° F.

2. Bake the squashes according to the directions in the sidebar on page 22.

Meanwhile, heat the oil in a small skillet. Add the onion and sauté until it is golden brown. Combine the sautéed onion in a mixing bowl with the breadcrumbs, cooked rice, and pecans.

3. When the squash is done and cool enough to handle, discard the seeds, then scoop out the pulp, leaving a sturdy, ½-inch shell all around. Chop the pulp, and add it to the pecan mixture.

4. Add the orange juice, more or less as needed to moisten the mixture, followed by the syrup and herbs. Season with salt, pepper, and nutmeg, mix thoroughly, and stuff the squash shells. Bake for 20 to 25 minutes, then serve.

5. For butternut squashes, serve each squash half as a hearty main dish; or cut each half across to serve 8 as a smaller portion. For golden acorn or delicata, serve each half as a main dish portion.

# "Three Sisters" Stew

**GLUTEN-FREE**

**SOY-FREE**

**NUT-FREE**

**6 SERVINGS**

*Squash, corn, and beans are known as the "Three Sisters" in Native American mythology. In some legends, the sisters are also the daughters of the Earth Mother. These three crops were central to the first Thanksgiving feasts. This hearty dish is very much like a robust chili, with the addition of squash. It's delicious served with Sweet Potato Biscuits (page 10) or Green Chili Corn Bread or Muffins (page 11).*

- 1 small sugar pumpkin or 1 large butternut squash (about 2 pounds), peeled and cut into large dice
- 1 tablespoon extra-virgin olive oil
- 1 medium onion, chopped
- 2 to 4 cloves garlic, minced
- ½ medium green or red bell pepper, cut into short, narrow strips
- 1 14- to 16-ounce can diced tomatoes, with liquid
- 1 15- to 16-ounce can pinto or red beans, drained and rinsed
- 2 cups fresh corn kernels (from 2 large or 3 medium ears; substitute thawed frozen corn if fresh is unavailable)
- 1 or 2 small fresh hot chilies, seeded and minced, or one 4-ounce can chopped mild green chilies
- 2 teaspoons cumin
- 2 teaspoons chili powder
- 1 teaspoon dried oregano
- Salt and freshly ground pepper to taste
- ¼ cup minced fresh cilantro, or more, to taste

1. Bake the pumpkin or squash according to the directions in the sidebar on page 22.

2. Heat the oil in a soup pot. Add the onion and sauté over medium-low heat until translucent. Add the garlic and continue to sauté until the onion is golden.

3. Add the pumpkin or squash dice, 1½ cups water, and all the remaining ingredients except the last 2 and bring to a simmer. Simmer gently, covered, until all the vegetables are tender, about 20 to 25 minutes. Season with salt and pepper.

4. If time allows, let the stew stand for 1 to 2 hours before serving, then heat through. Just before serving, stir in the cilantro. The stew should be thick and moist but not soupy; add additional broth if needed. Serve in shallow bowls.

# Pueblo Corn Pie

**GLUTEN-FREE**

Can be made **SOY-FREE** by using a soy-free nondairy cheese

**NUT-FREE**

## 6 TO 8 SERVINGS

*This layered casserole, adapted from a Native American recipe, is another one of my old standbys for Thanksgiving. I love how the simple chili contrasts with the cheesy cooked cornmeal topping.*

- 1 tablespoon extra-virgin olive oil
- 1 large onion, chopped
- 2 cloves garlic, minced
- 1 medium green or red bell pepper, diced
- 1½ cups cooked fresh or thawed frozen corn kernels
- 2¼ cups canned or cooked pinto beans
- 2 cups chopped ripe tomatoes, or one 14- to 16-ounce can diced tomatoes, lightly drained
- 2 teaspoons chili powder, or to taste
- 1 teaspoon dried oregano
- 1 teaspoon ground cumin
- Salt to taste
- 1¼ cups cornmeal
- ½ teaspoon salt
- 1 cup grated cheddar-style nondairy cheese, optional

1. Heat the oil in a large skillet. Add the onion and sauté until translucent. Add the garlic and bell pepper and continue to sauté until the onion is golden brown.

2. Add the corn kernels, pinto beans, tomatoes, and seasonings. Stir well and simmer for 10 to 15 minutes. Season to taste with salt. Remove from the heat.

3. Bring 5 cups of water to a rolling boil in a heavy saucepan or double boiler. Slowly pour the cornmeal into the water in a thin, steady stream, whisking continuously to avoid lumping. Add the salt and cook over very low heat, covered, for 20 minutes, stirring occasionally.

4. Preheat the oven to 375° F.

5. Oil a shallow 1½-quart baking dish and line the bottom with half the cooked cornmeal. Pour the skillet mixture in and gently pat it in evenly. Sprinkle with the optional grated cheese. Top with the remaining cornmeal, patting it in smoothly.

6. Bake for 45 to 50 minutes, or until the cornmeal is golden brown and crusty. Let stand for 10 minutes, then cut into squares to serve.

# Baked Thanksgiving Risotto

**GLUTEN-FREE**
**SOY-FREE**
**NUT-FREE**

**8 SERVINGS**

*Creamy, comforting risotto is given a festive seasonal spin with the "Three Sisters" of the native harvest—corn, squash, and beans.*

1½ cups Arborio rice

1 32-ounce carton vegetable broth

3 to 4 cloves garlic, very finely minced

1 15- to 16-ounce can small red or pinto beans, drained and rinsed

2 tablespoons olive oil or other healthy vegetable oil

1 medium red onion, chopped

1½ cups peeled winter squash (butternut, delicata, or golden acorn), cut into ½-inch dice (see Note)

1 cup fresh or thawed frozen corn kernels

3 to 4 ounces baby spinach

Salt and freshly ground pepper to taste

⅓ cup minced fresh parsley

Cherry tomatoes or sun-dried tomato strips

**1.** Preheat the oven to 375° F.

**2.** Combine the rice with the broth, one additional cup of water, and the garlic in a deep 2-quart casserole dish. Cover and bake for 1 hour, stirring every 15 minutes. At the third stirring, stir in one more cup of water and the beans. When done, the rice should have a tender and creamy texture.

**3.** About halfway through the baking process, heat the olive oil in a large skillet. Add the onion and sauté until golden. Add the squash and a little water (enough to keep the skillet moist) and cover. Cook until the squash is tender but still firm. Add the corn kernels and cook until both they and the squash are done.

**4.** Add the spinach, then cover and cook just until it's wilted. Once the risotto is out of the oven, carefully transfer to a larger serving dish (a large, shallow casserole dish or a large, shallow pasta plate both work well). Stir in the vegetable mixture from the skillet, then season with salt and pepper.

**5.** Sprinkle the parsley over the top of the risotto followed by a scattering of fresh or dried tomatoes. Serve at once or cover and keep warm until serving.

**NOTE:** To make the squash easier to cut, partially prebake according to the directions in the sidebar on page 22.

# Black Bean and Sweet Potato Tortilla Casserole

**GLUTEN-FREE**

Can be made **SOY-FREE** by using a soy-free vegan cheese

**NUT-FREE**

## 12 SERVINGS

*There's something delectable about the harmony of black beans and sweet potatoes. Add spinach and tomatillo salsa to the mix and you've got gorgeous layers of color and lively contrasts of flavor.*

2 large sweet potatoes

1 15- to 16-ounce can black beans, drained and rinsed

1 16-ounce jar salsa verde (tomatillo salsa)

3 to 4 scallions, white and green parts, thinly sliced

¼ cup minced cilantro or parsley

10 to 12 ounces baby spinach, rinsed

10 to 12 corn tortillas

### CHEESY SAUCE

1½ cups rice milk

3 tablespoons cornstarch or arrowroot

2 cups grated cheddar-style nondairy cheese

Salt to taste

1. Cook, bake, or microwave the sweet potatoes until done but still firm. When cool enough to handle, peel and cut into ½-inch-thick slices.

2. Preheat the oven to 400° F.

3. In a mixing bowl, combine the beans, 1 cup of the salsa, scallions, and cilantro and stir together.

4. Place the spinach in a large skillet or small soup pot and cook over medium-high heat just until barely wilted down. Transfer to a colander and use the bottom of a bowl, fitted into the colander, to press excess liquid from the spinach.

5. Combine about ½ cup of the rice milk with the cornstarch in a small bowl. Whisk together until smoothly blended—no lumps!

6. In a small saucepan, heat the remaining rice milk. Sprinkle in 1½ cups of the cheese and set the remainder aside. Bring the sauce to a gentle simmer, then whisk in the dissolved thickener. Continue to cook, whisking almost constantly, until the cheese is melted and the sauce is smooth and thick. Add salt sparingly (you may not need much, depending on the saltiness of the cheese).

7. Oil a rectangular shallow 2-quart casserole dish. Layer as follows: half the tortillas, the black bean mixture, the sliced sweet potatoes, the spinach, the remaining salsa, half the cheese sauce, the remaining tortillas, the remaining cheese sauce. Finally, sprinkle the reserved cheese over the top.

8. Bake for 20 minutes, or until the cheese sauce is bubbly. Let the casserole stand for 10 minutes, then cut into squares to serve.

# Ravioli with Sweet Potatoes and Sage

**8 OR MORE SERVINGS**

*Hearty pasta, sweet potatoes, creamy sauce, crunchy crumbs, and aromatic sage come together in a dish that I can only describe as swoon-worthy.*

2 medium sweet potatoes

1 tablespoon extra-virgin olive oil

**CREAMY SAUCE**

2 tablespoons Earth Balance or other non-hydrogenated margarine

3 to 4 cloves garlic, minced

1 12.3-ounce container silken tofu

⅓ cup rice milk

1 teaspoon salt, or to taste

Pinch of nutmeg

Freshly ground pepper to taste

16 ounces vegan ravioli (see Note)

6 to 8 ounces baby spinach

½ to ¾ cup fresh breadcrumbs (see sidebar on page 30)

Small fresh sage leaves, as desired, to taste

**1.** Bake or microwave the sweet potatoes ahead of time until done but still nice and firm. When cool enough to handle, peel and cut into ½- to ¾-inch dice. Transfer to a mixing bowl, toss with the oil, and sprinkle lightly with salt.

**2.** Preheat the oven to 400° F.

**3.** Heat the margarine in a small skillet. Add the garlic and sauté over low heat until golden. Transfer to a food processor along with the tofu, rice milk, salt, nutmeg, and pepper. Process until the mixture is completely smooth.

**4.** Cook the ravioli in plenty of rapidly simmering water in a large cooking pot, according to package directions, until *al dente*. Just before draining the ravioli, plunge the spinach into the cooking water so that it wilts. Drain the ravioli and spinach mixture at once, then transfer it back to the cooking pot. Add the creamy sauce, and stir gently to coat the ravioli and spinach.

**5.** Transfer the ravioli mixture to an attractive, shallow, lightly oiled baking dish. Top with the diced sweet potatoes, then sprinkle evenly with the breadcrumbs. Scatter sage leaves over them.

**6.** Bake for 15 to 18 minutes, or until the sauce is bubbly and the crumbs are golden and crisp. Serve at once.

**NOTE:** Many brands of vegan ravioli are filled with tofu, which is fine and dandy, but even better, in my humble opinion, are veggie-filled ravioli. One good brand is Rising Moon Organics, which makes three vegan variations: Spinach Florentine, Garlic and Roasted Veggies, and Butternut Squash. Soy Boy also makes some wonderful vegan raviolis. You can find these in the freezer cases of natural foods stores.

## HOMEMADE BREADCRUMBS

Sure, you can buy prepared breadcrumbs, but if you have a food processor, using prepared breadcrumbs is one shortcut that isn't worth taking (and I am quite fond of shortcuts). Store-bought breadcrumbs are often dry and almost always overpriced, especially the ones called "panko." I mean seriously, they're just breadcrumbs! It takes less than a minute to make them at home, and it's also a great way to use up ends of bread.

There's nothing more to making breadcrumbs than tearing up a few slices of bread, putting them in the food processor, and letting it run until the bread is reduced to coarse crumbs. An average-size slice will yield ½ to ¾ cup of crumbs.

## A NOTE ON ALL-PURPOSE SEASONING BLENDS

Unlike prepared breadcrumbs, commercial seasoning blends are a staple in my kitchen. I think they're nifty and useful. Seasoning blends provide a flavor punch by combining anywhere from a dozen to two dozen herbs and spices in one bottle, which, to my mind, means economy of both time and money. Seasoning blends are an especially good way to season stuffings, and I make ample use of them in most of the recipes in this chapter. Spike Gourmet Natural Seasoning (be aware that this one isn't soy-free) and Simply Organic All-Purpose Seasoning are my favorites from the natural foods store; Mrs. Dash Table Blend is one I like from the supermarket.

Curry powder and chili powder are seasoning blends as well; no matter which kind you use, make sure they're fresh and good quality.

# Hearty Vegetable Pot Pie

**SOY-FREE (if seasoning blend is soy-free)**
**NUT-FREE**

## MAKES TWO PIES, 12 SERVINGS

*Watch your guests' faces light up when you serve this nostalgic classic. Using prepared whole-grain pie crusts makes pot pies a snap to prepare.*

8 medium potatoes

2 tablespoons extra-virgin olive oil

1 large onion, quartered and finely chopped

3 cups diced vegetables of your choice (choose 3 or 4 from among cauliflower, broccoli, leeks, peas, corn kernels, zucchini, yellow summer squash, mushrooms, kale, etc.)

2 tablespoons unbleached white flour

1 cup vegetable broth (homemade or store-bought)

¼ cup nutritional yeast (optional but highly recommended)

1½ tablespoons all-purpose seasoning blend (see sidebar on page 31)

1 teaspoon dried thyme

¼ cup minced fresh parsley

Salt and freshly ground pepper to taste

2 9-inch prepared good-quality piecrusts, preferably whole grain

1 cup fine whole-grain breadcrumbs (see sidebar on page 30)

Paprika for topping

1. Cook or microwave the potatoes in their skins until done. When cool enough to handle, peel them. Dice 4 potatoes and mash the other 4 coarsely. Set aside until needed.

2. Preheat the oven to 350° F.

3. Heat the oil in a large skillet. Add the onion and sauté over medium heat until golden. Add the vegetables of your choice, layering quicker-cooking vegetables like peas, corn, and zucchini over longer-cooking ones like cauliflower, broccoli, and leeks (although none of these are terribly long-cooking). Add a bit of water; cover and cook until the vegetables are tender but not overdone, about 5 minutes.

4. Sprinkle the flour into the skillet, then pour in the broth. Cook for a minute or two, stirring constantly until the liquid thickens. Stir in both the diced and mashed potatoes. Heat through gently. Stir in the nutritional yeast, seasoning blend, thyme, and parsley. Season with salt and pepper. Pour the mixture into the pie crust and pat in.

5. Sprinkle the breadcrumbs evenly over each pie, then top with a sprinkling of paprika. Bake for 35 to 40 minutes, or until the crust is golden. Let the pies stand at room temperature for 10 minutes or so, then cut into wedges and serve.

# STUFFINGS

Wild Rice Stuffing with Dried Cranberries

Whole Wheat Stuffing with Pine Nuts and Dried Fruit

Walnut-Apple Stuffing

Sauerkraut, Potato, and Apple Stuffing

Polenta, Sausage, and Mushroom Stuffing

# Wild Rice Stuffing with Dried Cranberries

**Can be made GLUTEN-FREE by making breadcrumbs from gluten-free bread**

**SOY-FREE (if seasoning blend is soy-free)**

**NUT-FREE**

## 6 OR MORE SERVINGS

*Wild rice adds a wonderful texture to this stuffing, and the dried cranberries make it simply delicious.*

2½ cups water or prepared vegetable broth

⅔ cup raw wild rice

1½ tablespoons olive oil or other healthy vegetable oil

1 medium red onion, chopped

2 large celery stalks, diced

3 cups whole-grain breadcrumbs (see sidebar on page 30)

⅓ cup dried cranberries

1 teaspoon ground cumin

1 teaspoon good-quality curry powder

½ teaspoon dried thyme

Salt and freshly ground pepper to taste

½ cup apple juice

1. Bring the water or broth to a simmer in a small saucepan. Stir in the wild rice, bring to a simmer, then cover and simmer gently until the water is absorbed, about 35 minutes. Once done, preheat the oven to 350° F.

2. Heat the oil in a medium skillet. Add the onion and celery and sauté over medium heat until both are golden.

3. Combine the onion-celery mixture with the cooked wild rice and all the remaining ingredients except the apple juice in a mixing bowl. Stir well to combine. Slowly drizzle in the apple juice, stirring constantly, until the mixture is evenly moistened.

4. Transfer the mixture to a lightly oiled, large shallow baking dish and bake for 25 to 30 minutes, or until the top begins to get slightly crusty. Keep warm until serving.

# Whole Wheat Stuffing with Pine Nuts and Dried Fruit

**Can be made GLUTEN-FREE by using gluten-free specialty bread**
**SOY-FREE (if seasoning blend is soy-free)**

## 6 TO 8 SERVINGS

*This versatile stuffing is good on its own or stuffed into winter squashes or green or red bell peppers.*

6 cups firmly packed diced whole-grain bread, or the soft inner bread from a large whole-grain Italian loaf

1½ tablespoons olive oil or other healthy vegetable oil

1 large red onion, finely chopped

3 scallions, white and green parts, thinly sliced

¼ cup chopped fresh parsley

½ teaspoon dried thyme

Leaves from 2 sprigs fresh rosemary, or 8 fresh sage leaves that have been thinly sliced

1 tablespoon all-purpose seasoning blend (see sidebar on page 31)

¼ cup toasted pine nuts

½ cup dark or golden raisins, or ⅔ cup sliced dried apricots

Salt and freshly ground pepper to taste

1 cup vegetable broth (homemade, see page 112, or prepared), or as needed

1. Preheat the oven to 350° F.

2. Place the diced bread on a baking sheet. Bake 10 to 12 minutes, or until dry and lightly browned.

3. Heat the oil in a large skillet. Add the onion and sauté over medium heat until golden.

4. Combine the bread cubes with the onion in a mixing bowl. Add all the remaining ingredients except the broth and toss together. Slowly drizzle in the broth, stirring, to moisten the ingredients evenly.

5. Transfer the mixture to a shallow, oiled 1½-quart baking pan, or stuff into bell peppers or winter squashes (see sidebar on page 22). Bake for 30 to 35 minutes, or until browned and still slightly moist. Stir once during the baking time.

# Walnut-Apple Stuffing

**Can be made GLUTEN-FREE by using gluten-free bread**
**SOY-FREE (if seasoning blend is soy-free)**

## 8 TO 10 SERVINGS

*This stuffing, lightly sweetened with apple, is one of my longtime favorites.*

6 cups firmly packed diced whole-grain bread

1½ tablespoons olive oil or other healthy vegetable oil

1 large sweet white onion, such as Vidalia

2 peeled, diced tart apples, such as Granny Smith

¼ cup chopped fresh parsley

½ teaspoon dried thyme

1 teaspoon dried tarragon

1 tablespoon all-purpose seasoning blend (see sidebar on page 31)

½ cup finely chopped walnuts or pecans

Salt and freshly ground pepper to taste

1 cup apple juice, or as needed

**1.** Preheat the oven to 350° F.

**2.** Place the diced bread on a baking sheet. Bake 10 to 12 minutes, or until dry and lightly browned.

**3.** Heat the oil in a large skillet. Add the onion and sauté over medium heat until golden. Add the apple and sauté for 5 minutes longer.

**4.** In a mixing bowl, combine the bread cubes with the onion and apple mixture. Add all the remaining ingredients except the apple juice and toss together. Drizzle in the apple juice slowly, stirring at the same time to moisten the ingredients evenly.

**5.** Transfer the mixture to an oiled shallow 1½-quart baking pan. Bake 30 to 35 minutes, or until the mixture is lightly browned and still slightly moist. Stir once during the baking time.

## SAVORY VEGAN STUFFINGS

Some years back—actually many years ago—there was a TV commercial in which a reporter accosted people in the street and asked whether they would prefer rice, potatoes, or stuffing for dinner, if given a choice. No one seemed to think this was a strange question; after all, these were actors. So, of course, the respondents invariably and emphatically chose stuffing. One young man exclaimed eagerly, "I'm going to call my mom right now and ask her to make some!"

To the all-American team of Mom and apple pie, we can also add stuffing. Though the latter doesn't usually cause as much culinary ecstasy as this commercial suggests, it does evoke comfort-food nostalgia. Stuffing is a good, sturdy sort of everyday dish. Although it's not often considered other than for holiday meals, it's a nice change of pace from other starch-based side dishes.

Many of us who no longer use stuffing for its original purpose still warmly welcome it as a side dish or as a filling for seasonal vegetables. Most of the stuffing recipes given here follow tradition by including bread cubes or breadcrumbs as a basic ingredient. For those of you who eat gluten-free, the good news is that there are several brands of gluten-free bread that can be used to make the bread cubes or breadcrumbs in these recipes. I've also included a polenta-based stuffing recipe—you don't have to be on a gluten-free regimen to love it.

# Sauerkraut, Potato, and Apple Stuffing

**Can be made GLUTEN-FREE by using gluten-free bread**
**SOY-FREE (if seasoning blend is soy-free)**
**NUT-FREE**

**8 SERVINGS**

*This recipe is inspired by a Slavic stuffing. Sweet apple contrasted with tart sauerkraut gives it a unique flavor twist.*

- 3 medium red-skinned or golden potatoes
- 2 tablespoons olive or other healthy vegetable oil
- 1 large red onion, chopped
- 2 large sweet apples, peeled, cored, and thinly sliced
- 1 8-ounce can or jar sauerkraut, lightly drained
- 1½ cups fresh breadcrumbs (see sidebar on page 30)
- 2 teaspoons all-purpose seasoning blend (see sidebar on page 31)
- 2 teaspoons paprika
- 1 teaspoon poppy seeds
- ½ teaspoon dried thyme
- Salt and freshly ground pepper to taste

1. Cook, bake, or microwave the potatoes until done but still firm. When cool enough to handle, peel and dice them.

2. Preheat the oven to 350° F.

3. Heat the oil in a skillet. Add the onion and sauté over medium-low heat until golden. In a mixing bowl, combine the onion with all the remaining ingredients and mix thoroughly. Pat into a lightly oiled 1½-quart casserole dish.

4. Bake for 40 to 45 minutes, or until the top is golden brown. Cover and keep warm until serving. This stuffing may be made ahead of time and then reheated before serving.

# Polenta, Sausage, and Mushroom Stuffing

**Can be made GLUTEN-FREE by using the variation**

**Can be made NUT-FREE by omitting the optional pine nuts**

**8 SERVINGS**

*Using prepared polenta makes for a nice change-of-pace stuffing. By using vegan sausages, it just misses being a gluten-free stuffing, but I do provide an all-polenta variation, which would indeed make it gluten-free.*

- 1 18-ounce tube polenta
- 1 14-ounce package Tofurky or Field Roast vegan sausages, sliced ½-inch thick
- 6 ounces cremini or baby bella mushrooms, sliced
- 3 tablespoons olive oil or other healthy vegetable oil
- 1 large onion, preferably red, quartered and thinly sliced
- 1 cup diced celery
- 2 sprigs rosemary leaves
- ¼ cup minced fresh parsley
- ½ teaspoon dried thyme
- 2 teaspoons all-purpose seasoning blend (see sidebar on page 31)
- 6 to 8 fresh sage leaves, thinly sliced, optional

  Salt and freshly ground pepper to taste
- ¼ to ½ cup vegetable broth
- ¼ cup toasted pine nuts for topping, optional

1. Preheat the oven to 400° F.

2. Cut the polenta into ½-inch-thick slices, then cut each slice into 8 little wedges. Combine with the sliced sausages and mushrooms in a large mixing bowl. Drizzle in half the oil and toss to coat. Spread evenly in a lightly oiled or parchment-lined roasting pan. Bake for 20 minutes, stirring after 10 minutes.

3. Meanwhile, heat the remaining oil in a medium skillet. Add the onion and sauté over medium heat until translucent. Add the celery and continue to sauté until both it and the onion are golden.

4. Once the polenta and sausage mixture has roasted for 20 minutes, stir in the onion and celery mixture; then stir in the rosemary leaves, parsley, thyme, seasoning blend, optional sage leaves, and salt and pepper. Drizzle in a bit of broth, just enough to moisten the mixture but not drench it. Bake for 10 minutes longer.

5. Remove from the oven, and transfer to a serving bowl or casserole dish. If using pine nuts, sprinkle over the top. Cover and keep the stuffing warm or serve at once.

**VARIATION:** For a gluten-free version of this stuffing use an additional 18-ounce tube of polenta in place of the sausages.

# SIDE DISHES AND SAUCES

Maple-Pecan Sweet Potatoes

Rosemary-Citrus Sweet Potatoes

Agave and Mustard-Glazed Brussels Sprouts or Green Beans

Red Wine–Roasted Brussels Sprouts

Smashed Potatoes with Mushroom Gravy

Red Quinoa Pilaf with Kale and Corn

Cranberry-Apple Sauce

Cranberry Chutney

# Maple-Pecan Sweet Potatoes

**GLUTEN-FREE**

**8 TO 10 SERVINGS**

*How lovely that one of the healthiest veggies around is so traditional at the Thanksgiving table. Here are two simple recipes that showcase sweet potatoes.*

4  large or 6 medium sweet potatoes (about 4 pounds), peeled and sliced ¼ inch thick

½  cup maple syrup

¼  cup Earth Balance or other non-hydrogenated margarine, melted

¼  cup orange juice, preferably fresh

¼  teaspoon cinnamon

½  teaspoon salt

½  cup pecans, coarsely chopped

   Leaves from 2 to 3 sprigs fresh rosemary

1. Preheat the oven to 375° F.

2. Arrange the sweet potato slices in overlapping rows in an oiled shallow 2-quart casserole. In a small bowl, combine the syrup, margarine, juice, cinnamon, and salt. Pour evenly over the potatoes.

3. Cover with lid or foil and bake, covered, for 25 to 30 minutes, or until readily pierced with a fork but still firm.

4. Scatter the pecans and rosemary leaves over the surface of the sweet potatoes. Bake for 20 to 25 minutes longer, uncovered, or until glazed and golden around the edges.

# Rosemary-Citrus Sweet Potatoes

**GLUTEN-FREE**

Can be made **SOY-FREE** by replacing margarine with olive oil or other healthy vegetable oil

**NUT-FREE**

## 6 TO 8 SERVINGS

*This is a variation on the classic recipe more often referred to as "candied yams." Did you know that calling sweet potatoes "yams" is actually a misnomer? Yams are rarely sold in this country, so quite often, what you're actually buying are sweet potatoes. I make this dish nearly every Thanksgiving dinner.*

2  tablespoons Earth Balance or other non-hydrogenated margarine, melted

Juice of 2 oranges (½ to ¾ cup)

⅓  cup agave nectar

1 to 2 teaspoons pumpkin pie spice, to taste

5  large sweet potatoes, peeled and sliced ¼ inch thick

Fresh rosemary leaves from 2 sprigs, or to taste

1. Preheat the oven to 375° F.

2. Combine the first 4 ingredients in a large mixing bowl and stir to blend. Add the sliced potatoes, toss gently, and transfer to a lightly oiled shallow 1½-quart round or 9 x 13–inch oblong baking dish.

3. Cover and bake until the sweet potatoes are just tender, about 40 minutes. Stir once or twice during that time to distribute the liquid over the potatoes.

4. Stir in the rosemary leaves, then bake, uncovered, until the glaze thickens, about 10 to 15 minutes. Cover and keep warm until ready to serve.

# Agave and Mustard-Glazed Brussels Sprouts or Green Beans

**GLUTEN-FREE**

**SOY-FREE**

Can be made **NUT-FREE** by omitting optional nuts

**8 OR MORE SERVINGS**

*This easy, sweet, and mustardy glaze is a fantastic way to add a burst of flavor to Brussels sprouts or green beans.*

¼ cup agave nectar

¼ cup yellow mustard

1 tablespoon extra-virgin olive oil

1½ pounds Brussels sprouts or green beans (see Note)

Pinch of salt

Toasted pine nuts, slivered almonds, or pumpkin seeds for garnish, optional

1. Combine the agave nectar, mustard, and olive oil in a small bowl and stir together.

2. If using Brussels sprouts, stem them and cut them in half. If using green beans, trim the tips.

3. Place the vegetables in a skillet with just enough water to keep moist. Steam until bright green and just tender-crisp, not a moment longer!

4. Pour in the agave-mustard mixture and a pinch of salt. Turn up the heat to medium-high and cook, stirring, until the vegetables are nicely glazed, about 2 to 3 minutes. Make sure they stay bright green! Remove from the heat, sprinkle with the optional nuts, and serve at once, straight from the skillet.

**NOTE:** Though clearly out of season in most areas, green beans are one of the traditional vegetables favored at the Thanksgiving table. Personally, I prefer to serve the other iconic green veggie of the holiday—Brussels sprouts. They are more seasonal for this time of year. If you do wish to serve green bean dishes, by all means do so if you can find good, fresh ones. If those elude you, I see nothing wrong with using whole organic frozen green beans. They'll save you a lot of work and they are consistently delicious.

# Red Wine–Roasted Brussels Sprouts

**GLUTEN-FREE**

**SOY-FREE**

**NUT-FREE**

**8 SERVINGS**

*The slightly sweet glaze gives Brussels sprouts and their companion veggies a rich flavor.*

1½ to 2 pounds Brussels sprouts, stemmed and halved lengthwise

1 medium red bell pepper, cut into narrow strips, about 2 inches long

1 cup baby carrots, halved lengthwise

2 to 3 cloves garlic, thinly sliced

⅓ cup dry red wine

3 tablespoons agave nectar or maple syrup, or to taste

1½ tablespoons reduced-sodium soy sauce, or to taste

½ teaspoon dried tarragon

¼ teaspoon dried thyme

Freshly ground pepper to taste

1. Preheat the oven to 425° F.

2. Combine all the ingredients in a large mixing bowl. Transfer to a foil-lined roasting pan. Roast for 30 minutes, stirring every few minutes, or until the vegetables are touched with brown spots here and there and nicely glazed.

3. Transfer to a serving bowl and keep warm until needed, or serve at once.

# Smashed Potatoes with Mushroom Gravy

**GLUTEN-FREE (if using optional nutritional yeast, make sure it's gluten-free)**
**SOY-FREE**
**NUT-FREE**

**MAKES AS MANY SERVINGS AS NEEDED (1 potato per serving)**

*Simple as the dish is, making mashed potatoes for a crowd is a considerable amount of work. Here, you get the same great flavors with a fraction of the work. Potatoes are baked, smashed, and topped with a delicious gravy.*

1 large baking potato per person, well scrubbed

**GRAVY**

1 tablespoon olive oil or other healthy vegetable oil

½ cup minced shallots or red onion

2 cups thinly sliced fresh mushrooms (about 2 to 3 ounces); try a combination of shiitake and baby bella or cremini

1½ cups prepared vegetable broth

2 tablespoons reduced-sodium soy sauce

3 tablespoons cornstarch or arrowroot

¼ teaspoon dried thyme

2 tablespoons nutritional yeast, optional (but highly recommended)

**1.** Preheat the oven to 375° F or 400° F, depending on what else you have in the oven. Either temperature works well for baking potatoes.

**2.** Line a baking dish with foil. Arrange the potatoes in it and cover snugly with more foil. Bake for 40 to 45 minutes, or until the potatoes are easily pierced with a knife. Potatoes can be made ahead.

**3.** Shortly before serving, prepare the gravy. Heat the oil in a large saucepan. Add the shallots and sauté over medium-low heat until golden and just beginning to brown.

**4.** Add the mushrooms, cover, and cook until the mushrooms have wilted down, about 8 minutes. Add the broth and soy sauce.

**5.** Combine the cornstarch or arrowroot with just enough water to dissolve in a cup or small container. When the liquid in the saucepan comes to a steady simmer, slowly whisk in the dissolved cornstarch, stirring constantly until the liquid is thickened.

**6.** Remove from the heat and whisk in the thyme and yeast. Transfer to a small pitcher or gravy boat for easy pouring.

**7.** Just before serving, reheat the potatoes if needed (either by returning to a hot oven for about 15 minutes, or in the microwave). Cut each potato in half and arrange on a serving platter, cut side up.

**8.** Using a potato masher, smash each potato half, flattening lightly and creating lots of indentations for the delicious gravy to pool into. Pour a little gravy over each potato half, then pass around additional gravy for individual use.

# Red Quinoa Pilaf with Kale and Corn

**GLUTEN-FREE**

**SOY-FREE (use a soy-free bouillon cube)**

**NUT-FREE**

**8 OR MORE SERVINGS**

*This nutrition-packed side dish is so hearty that, with the addition of some beans, it could be a simple entree. Black beans are a perfect fit for this.*

1½ cups red quinoa, rinsed in a
fine sieve

3 cups prepared vegetable broth
or 3 cups water with 1 vegetable
bouillon cube

1 bunch kale (about 8 ounces)

2 tablespoons extra-virgin olive oil

4 to 6 cloves garlic, minced

3 to 4 scallions, white and green
parts, thinly sliced

2 cups cooked fresh or thawed
frozen corn kernels

2 jarred roasted red peppers, cut
into strips, or ⅓ cup oil-packed
sun-dried tomatoes, cut into
strips

2 tablespoons lemon juice, or more,
to taste

1 teaspoon sweet paprika

1 teaspoon ground cumin

½ teaspoon dried rosemary

Salt and freshly ground pepper
to taste

1. Combine the quinoa with 3 cups broth in a medium saucepan. Bring to a rapid simmer, then cover and continue to simmer gently until the broth is absorbed, about 15 to 20 minutes. If the quinoa isn't quite done, add an additional ½ cup broth (or water) and continue to cook until absorbed.

2. Strip the kale leaves away from the stems. Discard the stems, or slice them very thinly. Cut the kale leaves into narrow strips. Rinse well and set aside.

3. Meanwhile, heat the oil in a large skillet or stir-fry pan. Add the garlic and sauté over low heat until golden.

4. Add the kale, stir together, and cover; raise the heat to medium and cook until wilted, about 2 to 3 minutes. Add the remaining ingredients and cook, stirring frequently for 4 to 5 minutes longer. Transfer to a serving bowl or casserole dish and serve at once, or cover until needed.

# Cranberry-Apple Sauce

**GLUTEN-FREE**
**SOY-FREE**
**NUT-FREE**

## 8 OR MORE SERVINGS

*Apples provide a sweet contrast to the tart cranberries in this lively rendition of the traditional holiday relish.*

1    12-ounce bag fresh cranberries

4    sweet apples, any variety, peeled and diced

½    cup natural granulated sugar

½    cup apple juice

½    teaspoon cinnamon

¼    teaspoon ground ginger

      Pinch of allspice or nutmeg

¼    cup golden or dark raisins

**1.** Combine all the ingredients except the raisins in a large saucepan. Stir together, bring to a simmer, then cover and continue to simmer gently until the cranberries have burst and the apples are tender, about 20 to 25 minutes.

**2.** Stir in the raisins and allow to cool, uncovered. Transfer to a serving bowl and serve at room temperature.

# Cranberry Chutney

**GLUTEN-FREE**

**SOY-FREE**

**NUT-FREE**

**8 SERVINGS**

*This spiced chutney is a perfect venue for cranberries.*

12 ounces fresh cranberries

1 cup peeled, finely diced apple or 1 cup finely diced fresh or canned pineapple

1 cup apple, orange, or pineapple juice

½ cup chopped dried apricots

2 teaspoons grated fresh or jarred ginger, or more, to taste

1 teaspoon ground cinnamon

½ teaspoon ground cloves

Dried hot red pepper flakes to taste

3 to 4 tablespoons agave nectar or maple syrup, to taste

**1.** Place all the ingredients except the agave nectar in a saucepan and bring to a simmer. Cover and simmer gently for 20 to 25 minutes, or until the most of the liquid is absorbed.

**2.** Add agave nectar to taste and simmer uncovered for 5 to 10 minutes longer, until thickened. Let the chutney cool to room temperature. Transfer to a serving bowl. If making ahead, transfer to a tightly sealed jar or container. Refrigerate until needed. Before serving, bring to room temperature.

# DESSERTS

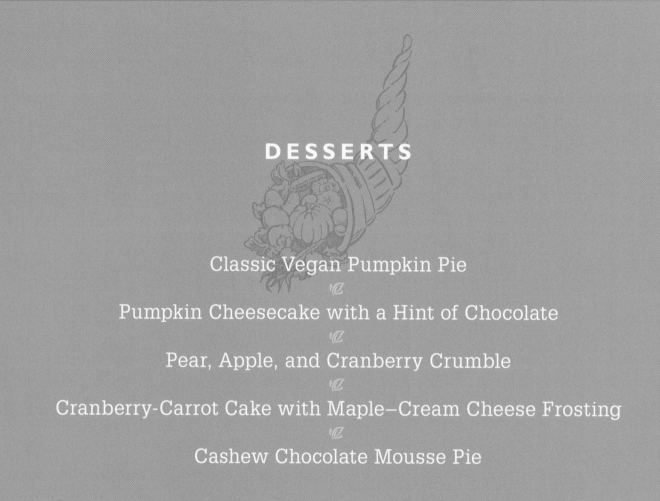

Classic Vegan Pumpkin Pie

❧

Pumpkin Cheesecake with a Hint of Chocolate

❧

Pear, Apple, and Cranberry Crumble

❧

Cranberry-Carrot Cake with Maple–Cream Cheese Frosting

❧

Cashew Chocolate Mousse Pie

# Classic Vegan Pumpkin Pie

**NUT-FREE**

**MAKES TWO 9-INCH PIES, 6 TO 8 SERVINGS EACH**

*Thanksgiving dinner without pumpkin pie is almost unimaginable to most people, no matter what their dietary bent. To that end, I present two versions of this iconic dessert. Still, though it's hard for us pumpkin pie fans to imagine, there are plenty of people who don't care for it. ("Je n'aime pas le citrouille," said the Parisian mother of my niece-by-marriage at a recent Thanksgiving gathering. My brother-in-law concurred, "I'm not a big pumpkin pie fan.") Since I have two pumpkin pie naysayers in my family, I'm sure there are others out there. For them, I've provided a trio of additional desserts to choose from.*

*This is just as good made with butternut squash as it is with sugar pumpkin. Once the pumpkin or squash is baked, which you can (and should) do ahead of time, the pie comes together quickly. It goes down very easily, which is why I recommend making two pies for practically the same effort as one.*

---

4 cups well-baked sugar pumpkin or butternut squash

1 12.3-ounce package firm silken tofu

1⅓ cups natural granulated sugar

2 teaspoons cinnamon

2 teaspoons pumpkin pie spice mix

2 9-inch good-quality natural pie crusts (pastry or graham cracker)

1. Preheat the oven to 350° F.

2. Combine the prebaked pumpkin or squash pulp in a food processor with the next 4 ingredients and process until velvety smooth. If you have a small or medium-size processor, you may need to do this with half the ingredients at a time.

3. Pour the filling into the crust. Bake for 40 to 45 minutes, or until the mixture is set and the crust is golden. Let the pies cool to room temperature. Cut into 6 or 8 wedges to serve.

**VARIATION:** If you need a major shortcut, use a 15- to 16-ounce can of pureed pumpkin. It's not as good as fresh, but a shortcut pumpkin pie is better than no pumpkin pie at all! Use organic canned pumpkin, which tends to be more flavorful than other commercial varieties.

# Pumpkin Cheesecake with a Hint of Chocolate

**Can be made NUT-FREE by slightly increasing chocolate chips and omitting walnuts**

**MAKES ONE 9-INCH PIE, 6 TO 8 SERVINGS**

*Here's a cheesecake-like version of pumpkin pie that offers a subtle chocolate twist with each bite (see photo on page xii).*

½ cup chocolate chips

¼ cup walnuts

1 9-inch good-quality natural pastry crust, preferably whole grain

1 12.3-ounce container extra-firm silken tofu

½ cup vegan cream cheese

⅔ cup natural granulated sugar

1½ cups well-baked, coarsely mashed sugar pumpkin or butternut squash (see sidebar on page 22 for baking tips)

½ teaspoon cinnamon

½ teaspoon pumpkin pie spice, or more, to taste

½ cup chocolate chips for optional chocolate drizzle

Vegan whipped cream for garnish, optional

1. Preheat the oven to 350° F.

2. Combine the chocolate chips and walnuts in a food processor and pulse on and off until finely chopped.

3. Scatter the chocolate chip–walnut mixture evenly over the bottom of the piecrust and set aside.

4. Combine half the tofu, half the cream cheese, and half the sugar in a food processor and process until smoothly pureed. Pour into the piecrust and smooth down with a cake spatula.

5. Combine the pumpkin or squash pulp in the food processor with the remaining tofu, cream cheese, and sugar, along with the cinnamon and pumpkin pie spice. Process until smoothly pureed, then pour into the pie crust over the plain tofu layer. Smooth down with a cake spatula.

6. Bake for 40 to 45 minutes, or until the mixture is set and the crust is golden. Let the pie cool to room temperature. Cut into 6 or 8 wedges to serve.

7. If you'd like to garnish each slice of pie with chocolate drizzle, melt the chocolate chips in a heatproof bowl in the microwave (start with 45 seconds) or in the top of a double boiler. Transfer the melted chips to a pastry piping bag or, less fancy but almost as effective, a Ziploc bag. If using the latter, snip a tiny hole in one corner. Gently squeeze the melted chocolate over each wedge of pie in an attractive zigzag pattern.

# Pear, Apple, and Cranberry Crumble

**Can be made SOY-FREE by using a soy-free frozen dessert (such as one based on coconut)**

**8 SERVINGS**

*Though pies are a more traditional finale for the Thanksgiving meal, crumbles are more about the fruit than the pastry. That's especially true for this one, with a trio of the season's favorite fruits.*

1   cup fresh cranberries

3   medium Bosc pears, cored and thinly sliced

2   large crisp apples, peeled, cored, and thinly sliced

½   cup maple syrup

1   teaspoon cinnamon

¼   teaspoon ground nutmeg or allspice

1   teaspoon vanilla extract

**TOPPING**

½   cup whole wheat pastry flour

¼   cup wheat germ

½   cup sliced almonds

¼   cup natural granulated sugar

½   teaspoon cinnamon

2   tablespoons safflower oil

Frozen dessert for topping, optional

1. Preheat the oven to 350° F.

2. Place the cranberries in a food processor. Pulse on and off until coarsely chopped.

Combine the cranberries, pears, and apples with the syrup, cinnamon, nutmeg, and vanilla. Stir together until evenly coated. Pour into a lightly oiled 9 × 13–inch baking pan.

3. Combine the first 5 topping ingredients in a small bowl and stir together. Drizzle in the oil and stir until the dry ingredients are evenly moistened. Sprinkle the topping evenly over the fruit mixture.

4. Bake for 40 minutes, or until the fruits are soft and the topping is golden. Serve warm, topping each serving with a dollop of frozen dessert such as coconut ice cream, if desired.

# Cranberry-Carrot Cake with Maple–Cream Cheese Frosting

**Can be made SOY-FREE by omitting the frosting**

**Can be made NUT-FREE by omitting the walnuts**

## 8 SERVINGS

*This cake is festive and luscious, but with a minimum of fat and a plethora of fresh fruit (and a vegetable!) in the batter—not the least bit guilt-inducing. Using a springform pan makes it easier to release this cake in a lovely, intact round, but the same can be achieved with a flexible silicone pan.*

8 to 10 ounces fresh cranberries

⅓ cup natural granulated sugar

1¾ cups whole wheat pastry or spelt flour

2 tablespoons ground flaxseeds, optional

1 teaspoon baking powder

½ teaspoon baking soda

½ teaspoon ground ginger

½ teaspoon cinnamon

½ cup applesauce

⅓ cup maple syrup

2 tablespoons safflower or other light oil

1 teaspoon vanilla extract

1 cup grated carrot

Maple–Cream Cheese frosting (see following recipe)

⅓ cup finely chopped walnuts

1. Preheat the oven to 350° F.

2. Place the cranberries in a food processor and pulse on and off until evenly and finely chopped. Transfer to a bowl. Add the sugar, stir well, and set aside.

3. In a large mixing bowl, combine the flour, optional flaxseeds, baking powder, baking soda, ginger, and cinnamon. Stir to combine thoroughly.

4. Make a well in the center and add the applesauce, syrup, safflower oil, and vanilla. Stir until the wet and dry ingredients are completely combined, but don't overmix.

5. Stir the cranberries and carrots into the batter. Pour into a lightly oiled 9-inch round cake pan or springform pan (see recipe introduction). Bake for 30 to 35 minutes, or until a knife inserted into the center tests clean.

6. If using the walnuts, toast them in a small dry skillet over medium heat until they brown lightly. Once the cake has cooled to room temperature, release from the pan if you've used a springform or other easy-to-release pan and spread the frosting over the top evenly, allowing it to drip fetchingly over the sides. Otherwise, leave the cake in the pan and simply frost the top.

7. Sprinkle evenly with the optional walnuts, then cut into wedges to serve.

# Maple–Cream Cheese Frosting

**GLUTEN-FREE**

**NUT-FREE**

**MAKES ABOUT ¾ CUP, enough to frost one average-size cake**

*I love this simple frosting on fruit- or vegetable-based baked goods, especially those containing carrots or pumpkin.*

½ cup vegan cream cheese

2 to 3 tablespoons maple syrup, to taste

2 tablespoons rice milk or other plain or vanilla vegan milk

**I.** Combine the ingredients in a food processor. Process until creamy and smooth. Use a flexible cake spatula to remove from the work bowl. Spread on cakes or cupcakes once they've cooled to room temperature.

# Cashew Chocolate Mousse Pie

**MAKES ONE 9-INCH PIE, 6 TO 8 SERVINGS**

*If you've had your fill of pumpkins, squashes, and other orange vegetables, ending the meal with a chocolaty dessert is a good alternative. Even though this pie is rich, it disappears quickly, no matter how full everyone claims to be. And depending on how many you are serving, you may want to make two.*

1 cup raw cashews

1 12.3-ounce package firm silken tofu

¾ cup semi-sweet chocolate chips, preferably cane juice sweetened

⅓ cup pure maple syrup, or to taste

1 prepared 9-inch piecrust (pastry crust or graham cracker)

1. Place the cashews in a small heatproof bowl. Pour 1 cup boiling water over them; cover and let stand for 30 to 60 minutes, then pour off the water.

2. Preheat the oven to 350° F.

3. Place the cashews in a food processor and process until they begin to hold together like butter. Add the tofu and process until completely smooth. Transfer to a small saucepan and add the chocolate chips. Cook over medium-low heat, stirring often, until the chocolate chips have melted. Stir in the maple syrup.

4. Pour the mixture into the crust and bake for 30 minutes, or until the top of the filling feels fairly firm to the touch. Allow the pie to cool completely, then refrigerate for at least an hour, preferably two, before serving.

# CHAPTER TWO

# CHRISTMAS AND THE HOLIDAY SEASON

*Festive fare for holiday parties and dinners,
plus sweets to give and share*

Though it's a central holiday to Christianity, Christmas has been repositioned, in large part, as a cultural celebration that goes beyond the boundaries of specific faith. Come December, Christmas is in the air, and it's everywhere. Of course, it retains its religious meaning for many; but for others, it's part of the annual "holiday season," into which many traditions from the melting pot are stirred. It's a time for parties and celebrations that light up the shortest, darkest days of the year (at least in the Northern Hemisphere) with treats for the spirit and senses.

Those who grew up celebrating Christmas say that its flavors and aromas create sense memories that are indelible. Cinnamon- or nutmeg-scented hot beverages, sweet-spiced cookies, and savory dishes seasoned with rosemary and sage are culinary touchstones of the holiday. Bountiful holiday dinners and buffets often incorporate much of the same late-fall harvest that's abundantly used for

**Gingered Winter Fruit Medley, see page 103**

celebrating Thanksgiving. In fact, the big meal of the holiday, Christmas dinner, often so closely follows Thanksgiving traditions in North America, that for vegetarians and vegans, it can also pose the same challenges. Turkey is often the centerpiece, with its requisite stuffing and gravy. Traditional Christmas menus from around the world are likewise replete with animal foods.

It's easy enough to avoid the meat, but for vegans, buttery cookies and eggnog are out, along with all manner of creamy dairy dishes from soups to desserts.

But rather than focusing on what's no longer feasible to use in holiday fare, vegans have started new traditions that make lavish use of all the fresh seasonal foods, including nuts, cool-weather vegetables (sweet potatoes and other root veggies, Brussels sprouts, and greens), pumpkins and squashes, nourishing grains, and winter fruits. Feasting with family and friends, so central to this beloved holiday, is made all the merrier when the compassion of the vegan kitchen is paired with the abundance of the season.

## TIPS FOR HEALTHY HOLIDAY EATING

The holiday season can be a challenging time for health-conscious eaters as well as vegans and vegetarians, who often find themselves at the fringe of celebrations that are centered on high-fat meals and guilt-inducing sweets. It can also be stressful for those of us who don't like the idea of gaining the dreaded weight—as much as seven pounds!—the average American puts on between Thanksgiving and New Year's Day. I wonder if this is one of those urban myths that has been repeated so many times it's been accepted as the truth. But even if it is an exaggeration, it's become so emblazoned in our consciousness that just the fear of those extra pounds makes it a force to be reckoned with.

It doesn't have to be this way, of course. Better to adopt the exuberant attitude toward food and celebration that many global cultures share, by focusing on organic produce, grains, legumes, whole-grain flours, healthy sweeteners, and an array of herbs and spices. For anyone who wants to reduce food-related angst, here are some tried-and-true ideas for eating heartily yet healthfully during the holiday season. Take a handful of these tips, season them with plenty of thanks for the blessings in your life, add your family and friends, and stir well. Serve in a relaxing, inviting, and joyous atmosphere. Yield: Many happy and healthy celebrations!

⬤ Start with an abundance of cool-weather vegetables—preferably organic—including a variety of squashes, pumpkins, apples, pears, sweet and white potatoes and other root vegetables, cruciferous vegetables (cabbage, broccoli, cauliflower), and dark leafy greens. Add winter fruits—pears, apples, cranberries, and citrus—to the mix.

⬤ When planning a holiday meal, or any festive meal, I like to ask guests beforehand if they have any dietary restrictions. It's surprising, for example, how many people have gone gluten-free. Being able to accommodate everyone is gratifying, and I like everyone to leave the table happy.

⬤ If you're invited to a gathering where you suspect there will be limited food choices for you, volunteer to bring a festive and delicious dish to share, whether an appetizer, a main dish, or a low-fat dessert. You'll ensure your own satisfaction while sharing your good food choices with others. And as I mentioned in the previous chapter, make plenty. Everyone always seems to want what we (and by we, I mean the vegans and vegetarians) are eating!

⬤ Holidays are a perfect time for a bit of indulgence, but going overboard doesn't feel so good. Don't be afraid to break with tradition. Just because your grandmother made a favorite dish or cake with two sticks of butter, that doesn't mean you have to. There are many easy ways to substitute healthier ingredients for fatty ones. One of my personal favorites is substituting applesauce for some of the fat in baked goods.

⬤ The best thing I've done for myself recently is to switch to a smaller dinner plate. Portion sizes have gone haywire over the last few decades, thanks to the oversized plates that restaurants have gotten everyone used to. Did you know that dinnerware was about 25% smaller in the 1950s? Just think: four or five bites of something really delicious is just as good as ten or twelve, if you slow down and really savor each bite.

⬤ This is no time to undo good exercise habits you've (hopefully) gotten into. In fact, exercise will not only help you burn off the inevitable extra calories, it helps regulate the metabolism, and is a great cure for the winter doldrums. It doesn't have to be anything fancy—grab a few of your holiday guests, bundle up, and take a nice long walk!

# SWEETS FOR GIVING AND SHARING

Gingered Chocolate and Pear Mini-Loaves

Banana Chocolate-Chip Mini-Loaves

Multi-Seed Crispies

Pumpkin or Squash Mini-Loaves

Chocolate Nut Cookies

Chocolate Mint Bars

Fruit and Nut Chocolate Clusters

Ginger Cookies

Skinny Figgy Bars

# Gingered Chocolate and Pear Mini-Loaves

**Can be made SOY-FREE by using coconut yogurt**

**Can be made NUT-FREE by using soy yogurt**

**MAKES 3 MINI-LOAVES, 6 TO 8 SLICES EACH**

*I start this section with a trio of miniature quick breads. I love making these little breads because they're so adorable, and much easier to get out of the pan than regular-size loaves. You can find mini-loaf pans in the kitchen supply aisle at well-stocked supermarkets. The small slices just look so fetching on a plate. In this one, chocolate, ginger, and pear harmonize sweetly.*

1½ cups whole wheat pastry flour

⅓ cup cocoa powder

1½ teaspoons baking powder

1 teaspoon baking soda

¼ teaspoon ground nutmeg

½ cup natural granulated sugar

¾ cup (6 ounces) nondairy vanilla yogurt (soy or coconut)

2 tablespoons safflower oil

2 teaspoons vanilla extract

2 tablespoons rice milk, or as needed

1 cup Bosc pears, cored and cut into ¼-inch dice

⅓ cup sliced crystallized ginger, or more, to taste

1. Preheat the oven to 350° F.

2. In a mixing bowl, combine the first 6 (dry) ingredients and stir together.

3. Make a well in the center of the dry ingredients and add the yogurt, oil, and vanilla. Stir together until the dry ingredients are evenly moistened, adding a small amount of rice milk to loosen the batter for easier stirring, but allow it to remain stiff. Mix in the diced pear and ginger.

4. Divide the batter among three oiled mini-loaf pans. Bake for 20 to 25 minutes, or until a knife inserted in the center of each loaf tests clean. Allow the loaves to cool until just warm in the loaf pans, then loosen around the edges with a knife and cool them completely on a rack or plate. Cut into ½-inch-thick slices to serve.

# Banana Chocolate-Chip
# Mini-Loaves

**SOY-FREE**

**MAKES 3 MINI-LOAVES, 6 TO 8 SLICES EACH**

*What's a book on entertaining without a good banana bread recipe? I've often had a problem with regular-size loaves of banana bread—the outside of the bread is done long before the inside. Making small loaves solves this dilemma nicely—the outside is golden and the inside is done (but still moist and delicious) at the same time.*

1½  cups whole wheat pastry flour

1½  teaspoons baking powder

½  teaspoon baking soda

⅓  cup natural granulated sugar

¼  teaspoon ground nutmeg

2  large very ripe bananas, well mashed

2  tablespoons safflower oil

1  teaspoon vanilla extract

2  tablespoons rice milk, or as needed

1  cup dairy-free chocolate chips, preferably mini-chips

⅓  to ½ cup finely chopped walnuts

1. Preheat the oven to 350° F.

2. Combine the first 5 (dry) ingredients in a mixing bowl and stir together.

3. Make a well in the center of the flour mixture and pour in the mashed bananas, oil, and vanilla. Stir together until the dry ingredients are evenly moistened, adding a small amount of rice milk to loosen the batter for easier stirring, but allow it to remain stiff. Mix in the chocolate chips and walnuts.

4. Divide the batter among three oiled mini-loaf pans. Bake for 20 to 25 minutes, or until a knife inserted in the center tests clean. Allow the loaves to cool until just warm in the loaf pans, then loosen around the edges with a knife and allow them to cool completely on a rack or plate. Cut into ½-inch-thick slices to serve.

# Multi-Seed Crispies

**SOY-FREE**

**MAKES ABOUT 40**

*Filled with healthy, crunchy seeds, these little cookies might be rich, but not in the way that induces guilt! If you like "salty sweets" use salted sunflower or pumpkin seeds. Tahini lends a delicious background flavor.*

2 cups whole wheat pastry flour

⅔ cup unhulled sesame seeds

⅔ cup sunflower seeds

⅔ cup pumpkin seeds or pepitas

1 teaspoon baking soda

1 teaspoon salt

1 teaspoon cinnamon

¼ cup ground flaxseeds or hemp seeds, optional

½ cup applesauce

½ cup sesame tahini

1 cup maple syrup or brown rice syrup

1 cup dried blueberries, cherries, or cranberries

1. Preheat the oven to 350° F.

2. Combine the first 7 (dry) ingredients plus the optional flaxseeds in a mixing bowl and stir together.

3. Make a well in the center of the dry ingredients and add the applesauce, tahini, and syrup. Stir together until the wet and dry ingredients are completely mixed, then stir in the dried fruit.

4. Form into balls not larger than 1 inch in diameter; flatten each and arrange on a parchment-lined baking sheet.

5. Bake for 10 to 12 minutes, or until the bottoms are lightly browned. Let stand for a minute or two. With a spatula, carefully transfer the cookies to plates until cool.

# Pumpkin or Squash Mini-Loaves

**SOY-FREE**

**Can be made NUT-FREE by omitting optional nuts**

**MAKES 3 MINI-LOAVES**

*This seasonal treat makes a nice gift to bring when you visit friends and relatives; it's also an easy everyday treat, full of nutritious ingredients, to make and enjoy at home. A mug of hot cocoa is the very best companion for this.*

1½ cups whole wheat pastry flour

½ cup natural granulated sugar

1 to 2 teaspoons ground ginger, to taste

2 teaspoons cinnamon

2 teaspoons baking powder

½ teaspoon baking soda

1 cup smoothly pureed cooked sugar pumpkin or winter squash (see Note)

2 tablespoons unsulfured blackstrap molasses or maple syrup

2 tablespoons safflower oil

2 tablespoons orange or apple juice, or as needed

⅔ cup raisins or currants

⅓ cup finely chopped walnuts or pecans, optional

1. Preheat the oven to 350° F.

2. Combine the first 6 (dry) ingredients in a mixing bowl and stir together.

3. In another bowl, combine the pumpkin puree, molasses, and oil and whisk together until smooth. Make a well in the center of the dry ingredients and pour in the wet mixture. Stir together until completely mixed. If the batter is too stiff to mix, add a very small amount of juice to loosen it a bit, but it should remain thick. Stir in the raisins or currants and the optional walnuts.

4. Divide the batter among three lightly oiled mini-loaf pans. Bake 20 to 25 minutes, or until a knife inserted into the center tests clean.

**NOTE:** If you're baking sugar pumpkin or squash—butternut is the best for this—for another purpose, save a cupful to puree and add it to the batter. See instructions on baking winter squash in the sidebar on page 22. Otherwise, organic canned pumpkin works well and is quite a time-saver.

# Chocolate Nut Cookies

**MAKES ABOUT 4 DOZEN**

*These have a nice crackle top highlighted by the use of sugar. If you need a big batch of easy little cookies, these are a good choice.*

½  cup Earth Balance or other non-hydrogenated margarine

½  cup dry unsweetened cocoa powder

1  cup firmly packed natural light brown sugar

½  cup rice milk

2  cups whole wheat pastry flour

1½  teaspoons baking powder

¼  teaspoon salt

2  teaspoons cinnamon

½  teaspoon ground nutmeg or allspice

½  cup very finely chopped walnuts

1  cup semisweet chocolate chips

Powdered or granulated sugar for topping

1. Preheat the oven to 350° F.

2. Melt the margarine in a small saucepan. Add the cocoa powder, sugar, and rice milk. Whisk together until the mixture is a smooth syrup. Remove from heat.

3. Combine the flour with the baking powder, salt, cinnamon, and nutmeg. Make a well in the center and pour in the chocolate syrup. Work together, first with a spoon, then with clean hands, to make a stiff batter. Work in the walnuts and chocolate chips.

4. Form into balls no larger than 1 inch in diameter. Arrange on two parchment-lined baking sheets, flattening each ball lightly with your palm (or bake one batch at a time). Bake for 10 minutes, or until the bottoms are just starting to turn golden. Don't overbake, as these crisp up as they cool.

5. Sprinkle the cookies with powdered sugar. Allow to stand for 10 minutes on the baking sheet. With a spatula, carefully transfer the cookies to plates until cool.

# Chocolate Mint Bars

**MAKES 2 DOZEN BARS**

*I adapted these delightfully minty bars from a friend's mom's recipe. I replaced some of the fat with applesauce, but left the spirit of the recipe intact. It's still quite rich, but these small bites go a long way.*

4  squares unsweetened baking chocolate

½  cup Earth Balance or other non-hydrogenated margarine

½  cup applesauce

1  cup natural granulated sugar

½  teaspoon salt

1  teaspoon peppermint extract

2  teaspoons vanilla extract

1  cup unbleached white flour

½  cup finely chopped walnuts

### GLAZE

½  cup vegan semisweet chocolate chips

2  tablespoons coconut or soy cream (plain or vanilla)

¼  teaspoon peppermint extract

Powdered sugar

1. Preheat the oven to 350° F.

2. Melt the chocolate and Earth Balance in a small saucepan or the top of a double boiler over low heat. Once the chocolate starts melting, stir continuously. Remove from the heat as soon as the mixture is smoothly blended.

3. In a large mixing bowl, combine the applesauce, sugar, salt, and the peppermint and vanilla extracts. Whisk in the flour, chocolate mixture, and chopped nuts.

4. Pour into a parchment-lined or lightly oiled nonstick 9 x 13–inch pan. Bake for 20 minutes, or until a knife inserted in the center tests clean. Remove from the oven and let stand until just cooled to the touch.

5. For the glaze, combine the chocolate chips, cream, and extract in the same small saucepan or double boiler used earlier. Cook over low heat until the chocolate chips are melted, then whisk until smooth. Spread over the top of the cake, then sprinkle generously with the powdered sugar.

6. Let stand until the glaze is cooled completely and cut into small squares, no larger than 1½ inches. Arrange on a plate to serve.

# Fruit and Nut
# Chocolate Clusters

**GLUTEN-FREE**
**SOY-FREE**

**MAKES 32 TO 36**

*If you need a quick, easy, and truly delectable treat, but don't feel like baking, these might be just what you're looking for. You can use unsalted nuts if you prefer, but I think it's the salty twist that makes them as good as they are.*

2 cups semisweet chocolate chips

¾ cup chopped salted nuts (peanuts, cashews, pistachios, or a combination)

1 cup dried fruit (cranberries, cherries, sliced apricot, sliced mango, finely diced pineapple, or a combination)

**1.** Melt the chocolate chips in the top of a double boiler. Remove from the heat and stir in the nuts and fruits. Allow the mixture to stand for 5 minutes or so.

**2.** Scoop the mixture out by heaping tablespoons and drop onto parchment- or wax paper–lined plates. Refrigerate for at least two hours, then remove the parchment, arrange on plates, and serve.

# Ginger Cookies

**SOY-FREE**

**NUT-FREE**

**MAKES ABOUT 2 DOZEN**

*This spicy cookie is the perfect companion for tea or vegan hot cocoa.*

2 cups whole wheat pastry flour

½ cup natural granulated sugar

1 teaspoon baking soda

½ teaspoon salt

2 teaspoons ground ginger

1 teaspoon cinnamon

½ teaspoon pumpkin pie spice

⅔ cup applesauce

2 tablespoons safflower oil

2 tablespoons molasses or barley malt syrup

½ cup raisins or currants

1. Preheat the oven to 350° F.

2. Combine the first 7 (dry) ingredients in a mixing bowl and stir together.

3. Make a well in the center and add the applesauce, oil, and molasses. Stir together until the wet and dry ingredients are completely mixed, then stir in the raisins.

4. With well-floured hands, pinch off pieces of the dough to form 1-inch balls. Arrange them on a lightly oiled baking sheet. Flatten slightly with your palm.

5. Bake for 10 to 12 minutes, or until the cookies begin to turn golden brown. Remove from the oven and let stand for a minute or two. With a spatula, carefully transfer the cookies to plates until cool.

# Skinny Figgy Bars

**GLUTEN-FREE**
**SOY-FREE**
Can be made **NUT-FREE** by omitting optional nuts

**MAKES 16 BARS**

*Susan Voisin contributed this recipe, which she associates closely with Christmas. It was inspired by her husband's grandmother's recipe, which he looked forward to every year. Once he and Susan went vegan, his grandmother baked an egg-free batch just for them. Here is Susan's low-fat interpretation of that family favorite.*

**FILLING**

1 8-ounce package dried figs

4 ounces pitted dates

2 tablespoons slivered or chopped almonds, optional

2 drops anise extract, optional

1 tablespoon agave nectar or other liquid sweetener

1 tablespoon lemon juice

¼ teaspoon cinnamon

⅛ teaspoon ground ginger

**CRUST**

1 cup quick oats, uncooked (not instant oatmeal)

1 teaspoon baking powder

¼ teaspoon salt

4 ounces unsweetened applesauce

3 tablespoons agave nectar or other liquid sweetener

**1.** Preheat the oven to 375° F.

**2.** Snip off the fig stems and put the figs, dates, optional almonds, and 2 tablespoons of water into the food processor. Grind to a coarse paste. Stir in the remaining filling ingredients and process until mixed, but don't puree. Set aside.

**3.** Combine the dry ingredients in a mixing bowl. Stir in the wet ingredients, along with ¼ cup water. Stir to combine. Press half the crust mixture into the bottom of an oiled, 8-inch square cake pan (use a wooden spoon or your hands).

**4.** Spread the fig mixture evenly over the crust. Smooth the remaining crust mixture over the filling. Bake for about 30 minutes, or until lightly browned. Cool completely before cutting into bars.

**VARIATION:** For an optional icing, mix about 3 tablespoons powdered sugar with a little water; start with ½ teaspoon until it has a medium-thick consistency. Add vanilla or almond extract to taste (just a few drops). Drizzle or pipe over tops of bars before cutting.

# HOLIDAY APPETIZER BUFFET

Sweet and Spiced Pecans

❧

Garlic and Rosemary Roasted Mushrooms

❧

Kale and Carrot Strudel

❧

Creamy Cracked-Pepper Cheez

❧

Hot Artichoke and White Bean Spread

## HOLIDAY BEVERAGES

Hot Spiced Apple Cider

❧

"Vegg" Nog

❧

New World Wassail

# Sweet and Spiced Pecans

**GLUTEN-FREE**
**SOY-FREE**

**MAKES 2 CUPS**

*Nicely glazed and spiced pecans are a tasty finger food.*

⅓  cup agave nectar or maple syrup

½  teaspoon cinnamon

½  teaspoon chili powder

¼  teaspoon ground ginger

½  teaspoon salt

   Pinch of nutmeg

2  cups pecan halves

½  cup dried cranberries

1. Preheat the oven to 250° F.

2. Combine the agave in a medium mixing bowl with the cinnamon, chili powder, ginger, salt, and nutmeg. Whisk together. Add the pecans and stir to coat.

3. Spread the pecans in a foil-lined 9 x 9–inch baking pan. Bake for 20 minutes, or until nicely glazed and toasted. Let the nuts cool, then break them apart and transfer to a serving dish. Add the cranberries and toss together.

# Garlic and Rosemary Roasted Mushrooms

**SOY-FREE**

**8 SERVINGS**

*This recipe is slightly updated from one of my appetizer favorites from* Vegetarian Celebrations. *The original recipe, which I've tinkered with ever since, was given to me once upon a time by Pat Reppert, widely known as the Garlic Queen in the Hudson Valley region of New York.*

2 pounds large fresh brown mushrooms (baby bella or cremini)

1½ tablespoons extra-virgin olive oil

1 tablespoon dark sesame oil

4 cloves garlic, minced

2 tablespoons reduced-sodium soy sauce

¼ cup dry white or red wine

Freshly ground pepper to taste

Leaves from 2 sprigs fresh rosemary, or more to taste

Curly parsley for garnish

1. Preheat the oven to 375° F.

2. Wipe the mushrooms clean and trim off the stems.

3. Combine the mushrooms in a mixing bowl with the remaining ingredients except the rosemary and parsley. Toss together. Transfer to a shallow baking dish.

4. Bake for 15 minutes, then stir in the rosemary leaves. Bake for 15 minutes longer, or until the mushrooms are tender and any liquid is reduced.

5. Transfer the mushrooms to a serving platter. Garnish the perimeter with parsley. Serve warm or at room temperature.

## HOLIDAY APPETIZERS

Sometimes I wonder whether holiday appetizers and desserts are the culprits that lead to extra pounds, rather than the meals themselves. In everyone's desire to celebrate and be generous, the snacks and appetizers served before the main meal—and the sweets served afterward—are often enough to be a meal in themselves.

I've dealt with this by drastically reducing the amount of food I serve before any festive meal—two nicely presented appetizers are quite sufficient. An exception to this would be a gathering that focuses entirely on appetizers and finger foods in place of a meal. This can be a nice theme for a festive holiday open house, where an array of tempting treats could certainly be justified. Here is one such menu, offering a handful of seasonal delicacies that can be teamed with one or two of the holiday beverages in this section. The appetizers here may be somewhat rich (with the exception of the mushrooms) but they're filled with healthy nuts, veggies (even kale!), and beans. If you have some help with the preparation, serving a few savory appetizers with two or three desserts makes for a wonderful holiday celebration. Who needs dinner?

If you're planning a gathering where appetizers and holiday beverages will be the stars of the show, you can make all five of the recipes here (they are designed to harmonize), or choose three and serve one or two additional store-bought appetizers like hummus and pita chips. Or feel free to explore additional appetizers on pages 277–291 to swap with one or two of these.

# Kale and Carrot Strudel

**NUT-FREE**

**MAKES 16 PIECES**

*It almost doesn't matter what veggies you roll into this strudel, the puff pastry makes the result festive and delicious, and it's so easy to do. Start with this as a template, then make the recipe your own by varying the vegetable you use. It's nice to combine at least two. Many brands of puff pastry are vegan. Read the label to be sure. It's not exactly a healthy, low-fat food, but as an occasional indulgence, it's not off the charts. Healthy veggies inside provide the balance!*

2  sheets frozen puff pastry

1½  tablespoons olive oil or other healthy vegetable oil

1  large red or yellow onion, minced

4  cloves garlic, minced

1  good-size bunch of kale, about 10 ounces

½  cup grated carrot

¼  cup minced fresh parsley

2  tablespoons minced fresh dill or rosemary leaves, or a few sliced sage leaves, more, or less to taste

Salt and freshly ground pepper to taste

½  cup grated vegan cheese, any variety, optional

1. Allow the puff pastry to thaw for 45 minutes to an hour. You need to time this pretty precisely—too little and it won't unfold; too much and it will stick to itself. Turn the sheets of puff pastry out onto a parchment-lined baking sheet.

2. Preheat the oven to 375° F.

3. Heat the olive oil in a medium skillet. Add the onion and sauté over medium-low heat until translucent. Add the garlic and continue to sauté until the onion is golden and just beginning to turn brown.

4. Strip the kale leaves from their stems. Slice them into strips. Add to the skillet, cover, and sauté for a minute or two, until the leaves are starting to turn bright green, then stir in the grated carrot. Sauté until the kale and carrot are just tender, about 2 to 3 minutes longer. Stir in the parsley and other fresh herbs. Season with salt and pepper and remove from the heat.

5. Place one sheet of puff pastry on a parchment-lined baking sheet and fold out. Sprinkle the surface with half of the optional vegan cheese. Spread half the vegetable mixture down the length of the center of the puff pastry sheet. Fold one side over the veggies, then the other, then tuck in the ends.

6. Cut the pastry roll into 12 sections crosswise. Repeat with the second sheet of puff pastry. Bake for 20 to 25 minutes, or until the pastry is puffed and golden. Cool until just warm or at room temperature, then transfer to a platter to serve.

# Creamy Cracked-Pepper Cheez

**GLUTEN-FREE (make sure the brand of nutritional yeast used is gluten-free)**

**8 TO 10 SERVINGS**

*I find this treat completely addictive. The basic, spreadable recipe is wonderful, but do try the sliceable variation that follows; it will knock your (and your guests') socks off!*

- 1 cup raw cashews
- ¾ cup rice milk
- ¼ cup vegan cream cheese
- ¼ cup vegan mayonnaise
- ¼ cup nutritional yeast flakes
- 2 to 3 tablespoons lemon juice, to taste
- 1 teaspoon prepared yellow mustard
- 1 teaspoon salt, or to taste
- ½ teaspoon coarsely ground pepper, plus more for topping

**1.** Combine the cashews with the rice milk in a small saucepan. Bring to a slow boil, then cover and simmer gently for 5 minutes.

**2.** Transfer the mixture to a food processor along with the remaining ingredients and process until very smooth. Stop the machine and scrape down the sides with a rubber spatula from time to time. It takes a good few minutes to make this smooth.

**3.** Transfer to a small serving crock and grind additional pepper over the top. Cover the crock and refrigerate for several hours before serving. Serve with flat breads, a thinly sliced baguette, or raw vegetables.

**VARIATIONS:**

Add a tablespoon or so of horseradish when combining all the ingredients in the food processor for a fabulous flavor twist.

For a cheese-like delicacy that you can actually slice, increase the amount of rice milk to 1 cup and add ¼ cup agar flakes to the saucepan. Continue as directed above, but instead of transferring to a crock, as directed in step 3, transfer to a lightly oiled loaf pan or two mini-loaf pans. Refrigerate until cool. Just before serving, run a knife around the edges of the loaf pan and unmold the *"Boursin."* Cut into slices and arrange on a small platter to serve.

**NOTE:** If making this a few hours or a day ahead of when you will serve it, make sure to cover the loaf pan once the mixture has cooled down.

# Hot Artichoke and
# White Bean Spread

**GLUTEN-FREE (make sure to have gluten-free accompaniments on hand)**
**NUT-FREE**

**MAKES 2 CUPS**

*Hot artichoke dips are classic appetizer offerings. Serve with bread (such as an array of crisp breads, flat breads, and toasted baguette slices), baby carrots, spoon-size chunks of red bell pepper, and Belgian endive leaves.*

1 tablespoon olive oil or other healthy vegetable oil

1 medium onion, chopped

2 cloves garlic, minced

1 15- to 16-ounce can cannellini beans, drained and rinsed

½ cup vegan cream cheese

1 14-ounce can artichoke hearts, drained

1 cup baby spinach, arugula, or watercress leaves

2 tablespoons fresh dill (preferred), or 1 teaspoon dried dill

½ teaspoon dried thyme

Salt and freshly ground pepper to taste

½ cup grated mozzarella-style nondairy cheese, optional

Paprika for topping

1. Preheat the oven to 375° F.

2. Heat the oil in a small skillet. Add the onion and garlic and sauté over medium-low heat until the onion is golden and just beginning to brown.

3. Transfer the onion mixture to a food processor, along with the beans and cream cheese. Process until smooth.

4. Add the artichoke hearts, spinach, dill, thyme, salt, and pepper. Pulse on and off until the artichokes and spinach are finely and evenly chopped but not pureed. Transfer the mixture to a small ovenproof container. Top with the optional nondairy cheese. Bake for 20 to 25 minutes, or until the cheese is melted and the top is golden.

5. Sprinkle the top with paprika. Serve hot or warm with a small spreading knife or a spoon.

# Hot Spiced Apple Cider

**GLUTEN-FREE**

**SOY-FREE**

**NUT-FREE**

**MAKES 8 CUPS**

*If you're serving a really large crowd, you can easily double this recipe if you have a large soup pot.*

2 quarts apple cider, preferably organic

Generous pinch of ground nutmeg

2 cinnamon sticks

6 whole cloves

1 medium orange, preferably organic, with peel, cut into eighths.

1. Pour the cider into a large soup pot. Add the nutmeg.

2. Cut a large double-layer square of cheesecloth. Place the cinnamon sticks, cloves, and orange slices in the center. Fold up and tie securely with string. Place in the soup pot.

3. Bring the cider to a rapid simmer, then lower the heat. Cover (with the lid slightly ajar) and simmer gently for 15 to 20 minutes longer. Serve hot, using a ladle to scoop the cider into mugs.

**VARIATIONS:**

**CRANBERRY-APPLE CIDER:** Use 1 quart each apple cider and cranberry juice. Add ¼ cup natural granulated sugar, or to taste.

**SPIKED CIDER:** Add 1 cup or so of rum or apple brandy. If using rum, add ¼ cup natural granulated sugar, or to taste.

**MORE SPICES:** Experiment with other whole spices, such as allspice berries and cardamom pods; slices of fresh ginger are welcome, too.

# "Vegg" Nog

**GLUTEN-FREE**
**SOY-FREE**

**8 SERVINGS**

*The Internet is filled with vegan nog recipes made with lots of tofu, but somehow, the thought of tofu in something other than a smoothie seems odd to me (and truth be told, I don't much care for tofu in smoothies, either). For a more elegant version, cashew butter gives a little body to the beverage without being overly filling.*

½ cup cashew butter

2 32-ounce containers vanilla almond milk

¼ cup agave nectar or maple syrup

2 teaspoons vanilla extract

¼ teaspoon ground nutmeg, or to taste

1 cup rum, optional

1. Combine the cashew butter in a blender with two cups of the almond milk (reserving the rest), agave nectar, vanilla, and nutmeg. Process until smoothly blended.

2. Divide the mixture between two pitchers, then divide the remaining almond milk between them. If using rum, divide between the two pitchers. Stir well. Serve at room temperature.

# New World Wassail

**GLUTEN-FREE**
**SOY-FREE**
**NUT-FREE**

**MAKES 2½ QUARTS, ABOUT 10 SERVINGS**

*Photographer Susan Voisin contributed this recipe for the most traditional of holiday beverages, and with it, some musings and memories:*

*"Most of the holiday food traditions in my family seem to involve oranges. October through January is citrus season in southeastern Louisiana, or at least in my parents' garden, so both Thanksgiving and Christmas are celebrated with plenty of citrusy dishes like ambrosia, cranberry relish (with raw orange peel included), lemon pies, and wassail. During the holidays my mother often brews up a pot of wassail, and I grew up hearing the word and associating it with both her hot, spiced tea and orange drink and with the first line of the carol, 'Here We Go A-wassailing.'*

*"I call my version of wassail 'New World,' because instead of wine or ale, I've used fruit juices, including juice from cranberries, a North American ingredient that wasn't available in Europe until the early 1800s. I've left out the tea that my mother uses—as well as the generous amount of sugar that she adds to sweeten it—and stuck to 100 percent juice: apple juice or nonalcoholic cider and a cranberry juice blend that does not contain added sugar. A handful of cranberries brightens up the color, and long simmering brings out the spices, while a little brandy added at the end, if you like, carries on the tradition of wassail as an alcoholic drink."*

1½ quarts apple cider or apple juice

1 quart natural cranberry blend drink (no sugar added)

4 cinnamon sticks

8 whole cloves

10 allspice berries

1 quarter-size slice ginger

1 orange, peeled and sliced

¼ cup cranberries, optional

½ to 1 cup brandy, optional

Additional cinnamon sticks, as needed

1 to 2 oranges, thinly sliced, for serving

**1.** Place all ingredients except the brandy in a large, nonreactive pot or crockpot and bring to a gentle boil. Reduce the heat to the lowest setting and cover. Simmer for at least 2 hours (may be kept in a crockpot for 4 hours).

**2.** If using brandy, stir it in about 15 minutes before serving, and continue to simmer on low heat.

**3.** Strain out the spices and fruit and serve with cinnamon sticks and fresh slices of orange.

# A PAIR OF CHRISTMAS DINNER MENUS

Roasted Root Vegetable Salad

Gingered Carrot Soup

Wild Rice Pilaf–Stuffed Peppers

Glazed Onions and Brussels Sprouts

Sweet and Savory Rosemary Baked Squash

Spiced Pears and Fresh Figs in Red Wine

Rosemary Roasted Sweet Potato Soup

*

Mixed Greens with Green Apples, Beets, and Pistachios

*

Hearty Lentil and Mushroom Shepherd's Pie

*

Black Rice with Corn and Cranberries

*

Sautéed Broccoli Rabe

*

Gingered Winter Fruit Medley

# Roasted Root Vegetable Salad

**GLUTEN-FREE**

**SOY-FREE**

**NUT-FREE**

**8 SERVINGS**

*Root vegetables are so abundant this time of year and come in so many earthy hues. Roasting roots in a hot oven is the best way to bring out their mellow, slightly sweet flavors. Since they taste just as good at room temperature as they do hot, they're presented here in an altogether appetizing salad.*

5 to 6 cups peeled and diced root vegetables (choose 3 or 4 from among parsnips, turnips, sweet potatoes, daikon radish, red or golden beets, black radish)

1 diced red apple

1 small or medium fennel bulb, sliced, optional

2 tablespoons extra-virgin olive oil

1 tablespoon maple syrup or agave nectar

½ teaspoon dried thyme

½ teaspoon dried basil

Salt and freshly ground pepper to taste

3 to 4 ounces mixed baby greens

Citrus Dressing (see page 171), as needed

¼ cup toasted pumpkin seeds

1. Preheat the oven to 425° F.

2. Dice or slice the root vegetables fairly evenly and not too thinly. If you are using parsnip or daikon radish, slice them into pieces about ½ inch thick; cut other vegetables into ¾-inch dice.

3. Combine the cut vegetables with the apple and optional fennel in a large mixing bowl. Add the olive oil, syrup, thyme, and basil and stir together.

4. Transfer the mixture to a lightly oiled large roasting pan (line it with foil first if you'd like). Bake for 25 to 35 minutes, stirring every 10 minutes or so, or until the vegetables are just tender and golden brown in spots. Remove from the oven and allow to cool to room temperature. Season lightly with salt and pepper.

5. When ready to serve, combine the roasted vegetables with the greens in a serving bowl. Drizzle in enough dressing to moisten the salad and toss gently. Scatter the pumpkin seeds over the top and serve.

# Gingered Carrot Soup

**8 TO 10 SERVINGS**

*A warming soup with the cheering color of carrots and the zesty flavor of citrus. Using baby carrots saves a lot of cutting and peeling.*

2 tablespoons olive oil or other healthy vegetable oil

2 large onions, chopped

2 large celery stalks, diced

2 pounds baby carrots

1 cup orange juice, preferably fresh

1 to 2 tablespoons minced fresh or jarred ginger, to taste

1 tablespoon curry powder or garam masala

½ teaspoon grated fresh nutmeg or pinch of ground nutmeg

1 32-ounce container vegetable broth

1½ cups plain rice milk, or as needed

Salt and freshly ground pepper to taste

Vegetable garnish (see Note)

**1.** Heat the oil in a large soup pot. Add the onions and celery and sauté over medium heat until golden.

**2.** Add the carrots, juice, spices, and broth. Bring to a gentle boil, then cover and simmer until the vegetables are tender, about 20 minutes.

**3.** Transfer the soup to a food processor or blender in batches and puree until smooth, then return to the pot. Or, simply insert an immersion blender into the soup pot and process until smoothly pureed.

**4.** Return to low heat and stir in enough rice milk to give the soup a medium-thick consistency. Season with salt and pepper. If time allows, let the soup stand for an hour or two at room temperature, then reheat as needed before serving.

**NOTE:** For the garnish, steam two cups of finely chopped cauliflower, broccoli, or kale, or any combination of these veggies until tender-crisp. Mound a small portion of the garnish in the center of each serving of soup.

# Wild Rice Pilaf–Stuffed Peppers

**GLUTEN-FREE**

**SOY-FREE**

Can be made **NUT-FREE** by omitting the pecans

**12 SERVINGS**

*Stuffed peppers have endured as a perennially popular meatless main dish—without becoming a culinary cliché—simply because they're so satisfying, tasty, and healthy.*

⅔ cup wild rice, rinsed

1 vegetable bouillon cube

⅔ cup long-grain brown rice, rinsed

2 tablespoons extra-virgin olive oil

1 large red onion, finely chopped

½ cup finely diced celery

2 medium tart apples, such as Granny Smith, peeled, cored, and diced

⅓ cup orange juice (from 1 large orange)

2 scallions, green parts only, thinly sliced

Pinch each: cinnamon and nutmeg

Salt and freshly ground pepper to taste

¼ to ½ cup minced fresh parsley

½ cup finely chopped pecans

6 medium red bell peppers

6 medium orange or yellow bell peppers (see Note)

1. Combine the wild rice and the bouillon cube with 3¾ cups of water in a medium saucepan. Bring to a gentle boil, then lower the heat and simmer for 5 minutes. Stir in the brown rice, return to a slow simmer, then cover and cook until the water is absorbed, about 35 minutes.

2. Heat the oil in a large skillet. Add the onion and celery and sauté until the onion is golden. Add the apple and sauté 5 minutes longer. Stir in the cooked rice mixture along with the juice, scallions, cinnamon, and nutmeg. Season with salt and pepper.

3. Sauté over low heat, stirring frequently, another 5 minutes. Stir in the parsley and pecans.

4. Preheat the oven to 350° F.

5. Cut the peppers in half lengthwise. Remove the stems, seeds, and fibers. Arrange on a parchment-lined baking sheet or roasting pan (or two shallow pans). Stuff the pepper halves generously with the wild rice mixture. Cover loosely with foil and bake for 40 to 50 minutes, or until the peppers are tender but still retain their shape. Serve at once.

**NOTE:** Of course, you can use peppers all of one color, or 4 each of red, orange, and yellow.

# Glazed Onions and Brussels Sprouts

**GLUTEN-FREE**

**SOY-FREE**

**NUT-FREE**

**8 SERVINGS**

*Slow-baked onions (especially those that start out with a bit more natural sugar than ordinary yellow onions) have a mellow, sweet flavor that partners beautifully with Brussels sprouts.*

6 large onions (try Vidalia, red, or pure white onions)

1 cup vegetable broth (homemade, see page 112, or store-bought)

⅓ cup agave nectar or maple syrup

2 tablespoons olive oil or other healthy vegetable oil

½ teaspoon dried tarragon

¼ teaspoons dried thyme

1 pound Brussels sprouts, stemmed and halved

Salt and freshly ground pepper to taste

1. Preheat the oven to 375° F.

2. Cut the onions in half crosswise; trim away stem ends. Cut each half into quarters.

3. Combine the onions in a mixing bowl with the broth, agave nectar, oil, tarragon, and thyme. Stir together. Transfer to a foil-lined roasting pan. Cover with more foil.

4. Bake for 30 minutes, then uncover and stir in the Brussels sprouts. Bake for 20 to 30 minutes longer, or until the onions are tender when pierced with a fork. Once or twice during this time, spoon some of the liquid from the bottom of the pan over the onions. By the end of the baking time, most of the liquid should be absorbed and the vegetables should be nicely glazed.

5. Season with salt and pepper; transfer to a covered serving dish. Serve at once or keep warm until needed.

# Sweet and Savory
# Rosemary Baked Squash

**GLUTEN-FREE (make sure your brand of soy sauce is gluten-free)**
**NUT-FREE**

**8 SERVINGS**

*This works well with almost any orange winter squash except for acorn, which is too ridged to peel—you'd lose a lot of the flesh along with the peel in the process.*

3 to 4 pounds small winter squash (carnival, delicata, small butternut, very small sugar pumpkin, or other)

2 tablespoons reduced-sodium soy sauce, or more, to taste

3 to 4 tablespoons maple syrup, to taste

1 tablespoon olive oil or other healthy vegetable oil

Pinch each of cinnamon and nutmeg

Leaves from 2 sprigs rosemary

1. Partially prebake the squashes according to the directions in the sidebar on page 22.

2. Let the squashes cool. When cool enough to handle, scoop out and discard the seeds. Peel the squashes and cut into half-circles. Arrange in a parchment-lined roasting pan.

3. Combine the soy sauce, syrup, and oil in a small bowl and stir together. Drizzle over the squash, then stir in the cinnamon and rosemary leaves.

4. Heat the oven to 425° F, and roast the squashes for 20 to 30 minutes, stirring every 10 minutes, or until nicely glazed and tender.

# Spiced Pears and Fresh Figs in Red Wine

**GLUTEN-FREE**

**SOY-FREE**

**NUT-FREE**

**8 OR MORE SERVINGS**

*Pears and fresh figs are a dream team. Figs are often available during the holiday season, but if you can't find them, see the variation that uses dried figs.*

8 large, firm, ripe Bosc pears

⅓ cup red wine

½ cup pear nectar

1 small cinnamon stick, broken in half

8 whole cloves

¼ teaspoon ground allspice

1 tablespoon cornstarch dissolved in ¼ cup water

8 to 10 fresh figs, stemmed and halved lengthwise (see Variations)

1. Stem the pears and cut them into quarters lengthwise. Core them and divide the quarters in half again lengthwise.

2. Combine the pears, wine, pear nectar, cinnamon, cloves, and allspice in a large skillet. Bring the mixture to a gentle simmer. Cover and simmer over low heat for 15 to 20 minutes.

3. Stir in the dissolved cornstarch and let the mixture bubble until it's thickened. Stir in the figs. Remove from the heat and allow to cool to room temperature. Serve in individual shallow bowls, topped with whipped cream, if you'd like.

**VARIATIONS:**

If you can't find fresh figs, use dried figs. Trim away the tough stem end, cut the figs in half lengthwise, and add them to the skillet at the same time as the pears so they can tenderize.

If you don't care for regular figs, use mission figs instead. Since they're not as intense as regular figs, you can use as many as you'd like. Stem and cut them in half before adding them to the dissolved cornstarch.

# Rosemary Roasted Sweet Potato Soup

**GLUTEN-FREE**

Can be made **SOY-FREE** by omitting option of sour cream

Can be made **NUT-FREE** by omitting option of cashew cream

## 8 OR MORE SERVINGS

*Roasting the sweet potatoes gives this soup a deep flavor that's slightly smoky, an effect that's enhanced if you use smoked paprika. The end result is a rustic soup that's partially pureed, somewhat chunky, and appealing.*

4 pounds sweet potatoes

4 tablespoons olive oil or other healthy vegetable oil

2 large leeks, white parts only, chopped and well rinsed

2 cloves garlic, minced

3 large celery stalks, diced

1 32-ounce container vegetable broth or 4 cups water with 2 vegetable bouillon cubes

2 cups rice milk, plus more, as needed

Handful of celery leaves

½ teaspoon dried thyme

¼ teaspoon ground or freshly grated nutmeg

1 teaspoon smoked paprika, optional

2 tablespoons fresh rosemary leaves

¼ cup minced fresh parsley, plus more for garnish

Salt and freshly ground pepper to taste

Vegan Sour Cream (homemade, see page 96, or store-bought), or Cashew Cream (see page 96), for garnish (optional)

1. Preheat the oven to 425° F.

2. Peel the sweet potatoes and cut into ½-inch-thick slices. Place in a large bowl and toss with 3 tablespoons of the olive oil. Arrange in a single layer on a parchment-lined baking sheet or roasting pan.

3. Roast the sweet potato slices for 20 minutes, or until just turning brown on the undersides, then flip with a spatula and roast for 15 minutes longer, or until tender.

Meanwhile, heat the remaining oil in a soup pot. Add the leeks, garlic, and celery, and sauté over low heat until all are golden.

4. Transfer the roasted sweet potatoes to the soup pot, then add the broth, rice milk, celery leaves, thyme, nutmeg, and optional smoked paprika. Bring to a rapid simmer, then lower the heat.

5. With a potato masher, break up the sweet potato slices into bite-size chunks. Cover and simmer gently for 10 minutes.

6. Transfer half the solid ingredients to a food processor, and process until smoothly pureed. Return to the soup pot, or simply insert an immersion blender into the pot and puree about half the solid ingredients.

7. Stir in the rosemary leaves and parsley. If the soup is too thick, stir in additional rice milk. The soup should be slightly thick.

8. Season with salt and pepper. Serve at once, or, if time allows, let stand off the heat for an hour or two. Heat through before serving.

9. Garnish each serving with a sprinkling of additional minced parsley and a dollop of sour cream or cashew cream if desired.

# VEGAN SOUR CREAM
# AND CASHEW CREAM

Several recipes in this book call for vegan sour cream. This is usually tofu-based, and you can either make it at home or pick it up from the store. I love Follow Your Heart vegan sour cream, which I think tastes amazingly authentic, but if it's not available, or I don't have any on hand, I rely on one of these simple formulas. For those who avoid soy, the new kid on the block is cashew cream, which is a wonderful alternative, and serves the same purpose.

**vegan sour cream:** Combine about a cup of crumbled silken tofu with lemon juice and salt to taste (use 1 tablespoon of lemon juice and ½ teaspoon of salt as a guideline, more or less to taste) in a food processor. Process until smoothly pureed, stopping to scrape down the sides of the work bowl as needed. Add a tablespoon or two of rice milk or soy creamer if you need to thin the consistency a bit. To serve, transfer to a small serving bowl.

**cashew cream:** Place about a cup of raw cashews in a small, heatproof bowl and cover them with boiling water. Let stand for at least 30 minutes, or up to an hour, preferably. Drain and transfer to a food processor with 2 tablespoons of rice milk and 1 tablespoon of lemon juice, and ½ teaspoon salt. Process until smoothly pureed, stopping to scrape down the sides of the work bowl as needed. Add a little more rice milk if you need to thin the consistency a bit. To serve, transfer to a small serving bowl.

# Mixed Greens with Green Apples, Beets, and Pistachios

**GLUTEN-FREE**

**SOY-FREE**

Can be made **NUT-FREE** by omitting pistachios

## 8 OR MORE SERVINGS

*A red-and-green salad provides a refreshing contrast to hearty shepherd's pie.*

2 medium beets

4 to 5 ounces mixed baby greens (or a combination of baby greens with baby spinach or arugula)

2 Granny Smith apples, cored and diced

2 medium carrots, peeled and sliced diagonally

½ medium cucumber, halved lengthwise, seeded if desired, and thinly sliced

½ cup shelled toasted pistachios

⅓ cup dried cranberries

3 tablespoons lemon juice, more or less to taste

3 tablespoons extra-virgin olive oil, more or less to taste

1. Cook or microwave the whole beets until just tender. When cool enough to handle, peel and dice them.

2. Combine the beets with the remaining ingredients in a serving bowl and toss well. Serve at once.

# Hearty Lentil and Mushroom Shepherd's Pie

**Can be made GLUTEN-FREE by making breadcrumbs from specialty gluten-free bread**

**Can be made SOY-FREE by replacing margarine with olive oil**

**NUT-FREE**

## 8 OR MORE SERVINGS

*There are no words to describe this recipe other than "a deep dish of absolute comfort."*

- 8 large or 10 medium potatoes
- 2 tablespoons Earth Balance or other non-hydrogenated margarine
- ½ cup rice milk
- Salt to taste
- 2 tablespoons olive oil
- 1 large onion, finely chopped
- 2 cloves garlic, minced
- 6 ounces cremini or baby bella mushrooms
- 2 15-ounce cans lentils, drained but not rinsed
- 2 tablespoons dry red wine, optional
- 1 to 2 tablespoons reduced-sodium soy sauce or Bragg's Liquid Aminos
- 2 to 3 teaspoons all-purpose seasoning blend (see sidebar on page 31)
- ½ teaspoon dried thyme
- Freshly ground pepper to taste
- 3 tablespoons cornstarch or arrowroot
- 8 to 10 ounces baby spinach or arugula leaves
- 1 cup fresh breadcrumbs (see sidebar on page 30)

1. Peel and dice the potatoes. Place in a large saucepan with enough water to cover. Bring to a simmer, then cover and continue to simmer until tender, about 20 minutes. Drain and transfer to a small mixing bowl.

2. Stir the margarine into the potatoes until melted, then add the rice milk and mash until fluffy. Season with salt, cover, and set aside until needed. Preheat the oven to 400° F.

3. While the potatoes are cooking, heat the oil in a medium skillet. Add the onion and sauté over medium heat until translucent. Add the garlic and mushrooms and continue to sauté until the onion is golden.

4. Add the lentils and their liquid and bring to a slow simmer. Stir in the optional wine, soy sauce, seasoning blend, thyme, and pepper. Cook gently for 5 minutes. Combine the cornstarch with just enough water to dissolve in a small bowl. Stir into the lentil mixture.

5. Add the spinach or arugula, a little at a time, cooking just until it's all wilted down. Remove from the heat, taste, and adjust seasonings to your liking.

6. Lightly oil a 2-quart (preferably round) casserole dish, or two deep-dish pie plates. Scatter the breadcrumbs evenly over the bottom. Pour in the lentil mixture, then spread the potatoes evenly over the top. If using two pie plates, divide each mixture between them.

7. Bake for 30 to 35 minutes, or until the potatoes begin to turn golden and slightly crusty. Let stand for 5 to 10 minutes, then cut into wedges to serve.

# Black Rice with Corn and Cranberries

**GLUTEN-FREE**

**SOY-FREE**

**NUT-FREE**

**8 SERVINGS**

*The first time I came up with this recipe, I thought I'd better cut the recipe in half so my family of four wouldn't be eating it for the rest of the week. What a mistake—we tore through it in no time. We liked it so much that I felt compelled to make it again, from scratch, the next day to see if the results weren't a fluke—was my family extra-hungry the previous night? Happily I got the same results from the second go-around with this delectable grain dish, and I have been sure to make the full recipe ever since. While it's a festive eyeful, it's too good to save for only special occasions, and too simple not to make for everyday meals.*

1 cup black rice (see Note) or wild rice

3 tablespoons olive oil or other healthy vegetable oil

3 to 4 cloves garlic, minced

3 to 4 scallions, green and white parts, thinly sliced

2 cups thawed frozen corn kernels

¼ cup lemon or lime juice, or to taste

¼ to ½ cup chopped cilantro leaves, to taste

2 teaspoons ground cumin

½ teaspoon dried oregano

¼ teaspoon dried thyme

½ cup dried cranberries

Salt and freshly ground pepper to taste

¼ cup toasted pumpkin seeds for topping

1. If using black rice, combine in a saucepan with 2 cups water. Bring to a rapid simmer, then lower the heat, cover, and simmer gently until the water is absorbed, about 30 minutes. If you'd like a more tender grain, add ½ cup additional water and cook until absorbed. If using wild rice, combine with 3 cups of water and cook as directed above.

2. Just before the rice is done, heat half the oil in a large skillet. Add the garlic and sauté over low heat until golden. Add the scallions and corn kernels and sauté just until warmed through.

3. Transfer the cooked rice to the skillet. Turn the heat up to medium-high, then add the lime juice, cilantro, cumin, oregano, thyme, cranberries, and remaining oil. Gently stir the mixture, then season to taste with salt and pepper.

4. To serve, transfer to an attractive serving platter and sprinkle the pumpkin seeds over the top.

**NOTE:** Look for black rice in the specialty grains section of natural foods stores and well-stocked supermarkets, sometimes labeled Forbidden Rice.

# Sautéed Broccoli Rabe

**GLUTEN-FREE**
**SOY-FREE**
**NUT-FREE**

**8 TO 10 SERVINGS**

*I was given this recipe many years ago by an Italian chef who told me that it had always been a standard for his family's Christmas Eve dinner. Keep in mind that while many people consider broccoli rabe a delicacy, others may be put off by the slightly bitter flavor. If you're unsure of your guests' tastes, substitute ordinary broccoli or broccolini.*

2 tablespoons extra-virgin olive oil

3 to 4 cloves garlic, minced

¼ cup dry white wine

1½ pounds broccoli rabe or broccoli, trimmed and cut into large bite-size pieces

Salt and freshly ground pepper to taste

1. Heat the oil in an extra-large skillet or a wok. Add the garlic and sauté over moderate heat for 1 minute, or until golden. Add the wine. Stir the broccoli rabe or broccoli in quickly. Sauté, stirring frequently, until bright green and tender but still firm. Season to taste with salt and pepper.

# Gingered Winter Fruit Medley

**GLUTEN-FREE**

**Can be made SOY-FREE by using coconut yogurt**

**NUT-FREE if you aren't also allergic to coconut**

**8 OR MORE SERVINGS**

*This simple and pretty fruit combination is a refreshing finish to a hearty meal (see photo on page 58).*

2 pears, any variety, or two different types, including Asian pears, cored, seeded, and diced

2 Granny Smith apples, cored, seeded, and diced

2 small oranges, such as clementines, peeled and sectioned, or 2 small blood oranges, peeled and diced

1 20-ounce can unsweetened pineapple rings, drained

½ cup dried cranberries

¼ cup sliced crystallized ginger, or more or less to taste

2 6-ounce containers piña colada or vanilla nondairy yogurt (soy or coconut)

Ground cinnamon or freshly grated nutmeg

1. Combine all the ingredients except the yogurt in a serving bowl and mix together.

2. Serve in small dessert cups, preferably glass. Top serving with a dollop of yogurt and a sprinkling of cinnamon or nutmeg.

# CHAPTER THREE

# JEWISH HOLIDAYS: PASSOVER, ROSH HASHANAH, AND HANUKKAH

## *Celebrating the major festivals with a blend of nostalgia and updated traditions*

ven for nonreligious Jews (like my extended family), the holidays and traditional foods play an important role in our cultural identity. Those of us who grew up with Ashkenazic (Eastern European) traditions might shake our heads at the blandness of our mothers' or grandmothers' cooking, but there's an undeniable, often inexplicable pull of nostalgia that makes it so gratifying to revisit familiar dishes.

Recipes from the Sephardic Jewish cultures are quite different from their Eastern European counterparts. Drawing from Mediterranean and Middle Eastern cuisines, Sephardic cookery reflects the influence of those regions and their emphasis on vegetables, fruits (fresh and dried), grains, and legumes. The array of herbs and spices is far more varied than what's used in Ashkenazic cooking as well. It's easy to find many plant-based pleasures in a cuisine that is already so veg-friendly.

**Sweet Potato Tzimmes, see page 148**

Jewish holidays (other than the reflective Yom Kippur) are a time of rejoicing, made for gathering at the table to celebrate familiar, comforting rituals with family and friends. Food plays a central role at these festivities, of course, not only for the pleasure it confers, but for the symbolic ingredients used in each holiday meal. It's impossible, in a book of this length, to include all the Jewish holidays, so I've settled on three of the most widely celebrated ones. Interestingly, it was the dairy products used so lavishly in the Jewish repertoire that presented more of a challenge than did removing meat and fish from the recipes in this section. Brisket, roast chicken, and gefilte fish are easy to dispense with altogether. But how does one make matzo balls, latkes, and challah without eggs, noodle kugel without dairy, or for that matter, honey cake without honey? These are the challenges that test one's vegan mettle, but I think the plant-based versions in this chapter come through with flying colors. What's left to say but "Oy! Let's eat!"

## PASSOVER

The central event of this holiday, the seder, is a feast as well as a religious service, during which celebrants gather around the table and recount the story of the Exodus as told in the Haggadah (Passover ceremony book). Sampling many symbolic foods and drinking red wine play a large role in this ritual. Matzo (unleavened bread) is perhaps the most important of the symbolic foods, representing the bread the Jews hastily made as they fled Egypt thousands of years ago.

Commemorating the exodus of ancient Hebrews from slavery in Egypt, Passover lasts for eight days and most often falls in April. The seder service often mentions the concept of freedom. So even those of us who aren't fully engaged with the religious nuances of the holiday can appreciate that, at its heart, the holiday embraces the universal struggle for freedom.

During Passover week, Jews traditionally remove anything that is considered *hametz* from their homes—bread, any products made from wheat and other grains, and legumes. Soy products are considered *hametz*, since they are, after all, made from beans. Unlike Ashkenazic Jews, Sephardic Jews continue to use most grains, other than wheat, as well as legumes, during the holiday week.

If you observe Passover strictly, please note that in all cases of packaged products called for in the recipes, you will want to use those that are certified kosher for Passover.

# THE PASSOVER TABLE
## AND SEDER PLATE

During the seder and the meal that follows the reading of the first portion of the Haggadah, a plate of matzos is served and replenished as needed, along with plenty of Passover wine. Central to the table is the seder plate, a round dish with designated spots for the symbolic foods that are sampled during the reading of the Haggadah. These foods are not eaten from the seder plate— instead, everyone gets to sample them from separate platters.

*karpas:* A mild green vegetable or herb, such as celery or parsley, symbolizing the new growth of spring. A small leaf of romaine lettuce or other mild green might be used on the Sephardic Passover plate. It is sometimes dipped into salt water or vinegar as a reminder of the tears shed by enslaved Hebrews.

*maror:* A bitter herb, usually horseradish, for Ashkenazic Jews, or a bitter green such as escarole or endive for Sephardic Jews. This represents the bitterness of slavery suffered by the Hebrews in Egypt.

*haroset:* This mixture of nuts, wine, and apples, as Ashkenazic Jews make it, or nuts, wine, and dried fruits, as Sephardic Jews make it, has a bricklike color to symbolize the bricks used by the Hebrew slaves to build Pharaoh's cities.

*hazeret:* Another bitter herb or green, such as watercress or chicory. Some believe that two bitter herbs should be tasted, though this component of the seder plate is optional.

*zeroa:* the shank bone, and *beytzah,* a hard-boiled egg, are two components of the seder plate that vegans obviously skip or replace. To fill all the spots in the vegan Passover plate, the former is sometimes replaced with a roasted beet, and the latter with a boiled potato (more for their shapes than any symbolic similarity).

To paraphrase one of the Four Questions asked at the Passover table, "Why is this seder different from traditional seder menus?" Traditional Eastern European–style seder meals feature gefilte fish, matzo balls in a chicken broth, and meat—either brisket or some sort of fowl—along with salads and spring vegetables. The Passover menu in this book focuses on the fresh produce of the new season and incorporates new Passover traditions (including the use of quinoa), while giving nostalgia some due.

## HANUKKAH

Hanukkah, otherwise known as the Festival of Lights, is as eagerly awaited by Jewish children the world over as is Christmas by Christian children. This December holiday is celebrated with candles, songs, dreidl games, foil-wrapped chocolate coins, and gifts. In other parts of the world, gifts aren't emphasized as much as they are in North America—that's the influence that its proximity to Christmas has had on the holiday.

As far as food goes, Hanukkah is all about latkes. I never think of them as part of a meal, but the meal itself (not a very balanced one, to be sure). I do make a salad, at least, which is often summarily ignored on this occasion. Hanukkah doesn't have as wide an array of symbolic dishes as some other Jewish holidays do, but the most typical are fried foods—notably the aforementioned latkes, as well as deep-fried desserts like doughnuts. The symbolic ingredient for this holiday is simply oil. The holiday commemorates the victory of the Jewish Maccabees over their oppressors many centuries ago. When the Maccabees returned to rededicate their temple, they found only enough oil to last one day for the lighting of their menorah. The supply, as legend has it, lasted for eight days, and that's the Hanukkah miracle that is celebrated.

Oil-laden foods aren't exactly the healthiest fare, and though many celebrants forgo doughnuts, Hanukkah without latkes is unthinkable! If you'd like a Jewish dessert in place of doughnuts, Rugelach (see page 157) fits very nicely into the mix, or just serve Hanukkah chocolates and fresh fruit.

I gave some thought to what might go well with latkes, and in keeping with the spirit of the holiday, I thought a Middle Eastern–themed meal would be quite appropriate. Everything other than the latkes can be made ahead; the latkes are made just before or just as the guests arrive.

## ROSH HASHANAH (JEWISH NEW YEAR)

For many of us, the onset of fall feels like a time of renewal. A new school year begins, a sense of getting back to reality sets in, after the easier pace of summer; there's a renewed vigor as the air turns cooler. While some are figuratively turning a page in their year, for millions of Jews around the world, the early fall is truly the beginning of a new year. Though it's a joyous time, Rosh Hashanah is also the first of the Ten Days of Awe, a period of spiritual reflection and repentance that culminates in Yom Kippur, the Day of Atonement.

As with almost every sacred and ancient celebration, food plays a central role and is laden with symbolism. When making challah bread, for example, the baker might pinch off a bit of dough and burn it in the oven as a symbolic sacrifice. Serving carrots at Rosh Hashanah symbolizes one's wish for prosperity in the coming year; the Yiddish word for "carrots" also means "to increase."

The foods served emphasize the holiday's optimistic spirit. The choice of produce used for a Jewish New Year meal will differ somewhat, depending on whether one is of Ashkenazic or Sephardic descent. Ashkenazic dishes feature apples, carrots, sweet potatoes, beets, and other foods traditionally used in Eastern Europe cuisine; Sephardic dishes feature all those plus apricots, dates, pumpkins, and turnips. In both cases, the foods used to create holiday fare symbolize abundance, prosperity, and sweetness.

# AN ASHKENAZIC SEDER MENU

Mock Chopped Liver

Simple Vegetable Soup with Vegan Matzo Balls

Vegan Matzo Balls

Traditional Haroset

Spectacular Spring Salad

Spinach, Leek, and Potato Matzo Gratin

Quinoa Pilaf

Sautéed Asparagus and Broccolini

Passover Fruit Crisp (page 131)
OR
Chocolate Matzo Brittle (page 132)
OR
Coconut-Almond Macaroons (page 133)

# Mock Chopped Liver
# (Cashew, Onion, and Mushroom Pâté)

**GLUTEN-FREE**
**SOY-FREE**

**MAKES ABOUT 2 CUPS**

*This look-alike (though not taste-alike) of the classic Jewish pâté is very often favored over "the real thing" as an appetizer. Serve it with raw vegetables and matzo crackers.*

2 tablespoons olive oil or other healthy vegetable oil

1½ cups chopped onions

1 cup sliced baby bella or cremini mushrooms

⅔ cup toasted cashews

1 tablespoon lemon juice, or to taste

Salt and freshly ground pepper to taste

Paprika

Finely minced fresh parsley for garnish

1. Heat the oil in a small skillet. Sauté the onions slowly over medium-low heat, stirring frequently until nicely browned. Add the mushrooms and continue to sauté briefly until wilted.

2. Combine the onion mixture with the cashews and lemon juice in a food processor. Process until smoothly pureed, scraping down the sides of the work bowl as needed. Season with salt and pepper and additional lemon juice if desired, and pulse on and off to work into the mixture.

3. Transfer to a serving dish and cover until needed. If making ahead of time, store in the refrigerator and bring to room temperature before serving. Just before serving, sprinkle the top with paprika and parsley.

# Simple Vegetable Soup
# with Vegan Matzo Balls

**GLUTEN-FREE (by omitting matzo balls)**

**SOY-FREE**

**NUT-FREE**

**8 SERVINGS**

*The soup served at traditional Passover seders is very much akin to this one, except that it's made with chicken broth. In truth, the Passover soup course functions primarily as a venue for the matzo balls.*

2 tablespoons olive oil or other healthy vegetable oil

1 large onion, finely chopped

3 celery stalks, diced

1 32-ounce carton vegetable broth

6 medium potatoes, peeled and finely diced

6 to 8 medium carrots, sliced

Handful of celery leaves

1 tablespoon all-purpose seasoning blend (see sidebar on page 31, or use a Kosher for Passover brand)

¼ cup chopped fresh dill, or to taste

Salt and freshly ground pepper to taste

Vegan Matzo Balls (see page 115)

1. Heat the oil in a large soup pot. Add the onion and celery and sauté over medium heat until golden.

2. Add the broth, potato, carrots, celery leaves, seasoning blend, and 2 cups of water. Bring to a rapid simmer, then cover and simmer gently for 15 to 20 minutes, or until the vegetables are tender.

3. Stir in the dill, then season with salt and pepper. If time allows, let the soup stand for several hours off the heat to develop flavor. It can also be made a day in advance.

4. Just before serving, bring to a simmer. Adjust the consistency with more water if need be, and taste to adjust seasonings. Add warmed matzo balls to individual servings of soup.

## MATZO BALLS, QUINOA, AND PASSOVER

The Web is filled with vegan matzo ball recipes made with tofu. For many Ashkenazic Jews, even nonreligious ones, this isn't acceptable, as beans and bean products (such as tofu) are not consumed during Passover week. Cooked oats are a great binder (I've long used them for latkes—see the recipe on page 159)—but they aren't allowable on Passover, either. I was discussing this dilemma with Seth Branitz, co-owner and chef of Karma Road (a wonderful vegan café in the Hudson Valley region of New York State), and he suggested trying cooked quinoa flakes. I did, and they work like a charm.

Quinoa, though it is an ancient grain, is being touted as the "new" go-to grain for Passover, during a week when many (if not most) grains and grain products aren't used. Why quinoa is acceptable and, say, oats, aren't has a complicated answer, which I'm not equipped to give. Reading online articles such as one titled, I kid you not, "Quonfused about Quinoa" only muddles the subject further. Suffice it to say that quinoa is now just as welcome at the Passover table as it is at any other meal of the year.

# Vegan Matzo Balls

**SOY-FREE**

**NUT-FREE**

**Can be made GLUTEN-FREE using the gluten-free option**

**MAKES ABOUT 24**

*These are not going to be like your Bubbe's big, fluffy matzo balls. But neither are they cannonballs. They're easy to make and quite tasty. Cooked quinoa flakes are what binds them together. A lot of the vegan matzo ball recipes out there use silken tofu as a binder, which, for many Jews, is not an allowed Passover food. The trick here is to bake them at a low temperature rather than boiling them. Without egg as a binder, vegan matzo balls are more likely than not to fall apart in water.*

*These go very quickly and everyone usually wants more, so if you're increasing the amount of soup to accommodate a larger crowd, or serving more than 8 people, you would do well to double this recipe. Good news! If you need a gluten-free option, this recipe offers just that. By using only quinoa flakes (instead of the quinoa flakes/matzo meal combo), technically there's nothing "matzo" about the gluten-free variation, but truth be told, I think they're even better that way.*

1 cup quinoa flakes

2 cups boiling water

1 cup matzo meal (see gluten-free variation, below)

¼ cup light vegetable oil (such as safflower)

¼ teaspoon salt

A few grindings of black pepper

Pinch each of onion and garlic powder, optional

1. In a large mixing bowl, cover the quinoa flakes with the water. Let stand for 2 or 3 minutes.

2. Stir in the matzo meal along with the oil, and mix until well blended. Cover the bowl and refrigerate for at least 15 minutes.

3. Just before baking, preheat the oven to 275° F.

4. Roll the matzo meal mixture into approximately 1-inch balls; don't pack them too firmly. Arrange on a parchment-lined baking sheet.

5. Bake for 20 to 25 minutes, carefully turning the matzo balls after 10 minutes, until firm to the touch; don't let them brown.

6. If making ahead of time, let the matzo balls cool completely, then cover until needed. Warm them briefly in a medium oven and distribute them among the soup bowls, allowing 3 or 4 matzo balls per serving.

**VARIATION:** To make these gluten-free, substitute 1¼ cups quinoa flakes for the matzo meal. Don't add them to the original quantity of quinoa flakes; this is a separate measure to use dry. A bit more is needed than the quantity of matzo meal for the purpose, as the quinoa flakes are less dense.

# Traditional Haroset

**GLUTEN-FREE**
**SOY-FREE**

**MAKES ABOUT 2 CUPS**

*Eastern European-style* haroset *is always made of essentially the same few ingredients, though proportions may vary, depending on taste.*

2 large sweet apples, peeled, cored, and diced

⅔ cup walnuts

¼ cup sweet Passover wine

1 to 2 teaspoons honey, to taste

1 teaspoon cinnamon

Pinch each: nutmeg, allspice

1. Combine all the ingredients in a food processor. Process until coarsely pureed. Store in an airtight container until needed.

# Spectacular Spring Salad

**8 SERVINGS**

*This beautiful salad highlights fresh spring flavors and colors.*

1  bunch watercress leaves

2  good handfuls baby arugula

½  head radicchio, thinly sliced

1  cup baby carrots, halved

1  medium-firm, ripe avocado, pitted, peeled, and cut into small dice

4  to 6 radishes, thinly sliced

1  cup or so sprouts, preferably pea shoots or other large green sprouts

3  small seedless oranges, peeled and sectioned

¼  cup toasted sunflower seeds

2  tablespoons extra-virgin olive oil, or more, to taste

2  tablespoons lemon juice, or more, to taste

Salt and freshly ground pepper to taste

1. Combine all the ingredients in a serving bowl and toss together.

**117**

# Spinach, Leek, and Potato Matzo Gratin

**SOY-FREE**

**8 TO 10 SERVINGS**

*This dish closely resembles the layered matzo casseroles, called* minas, *which are commonly served at Sephardic seders. They consist of layered matzos, vegetables, and cheese. With optional Daiya cheese, or no cheese at all, it's a tradition well worth adopting (and adapting) for a vegan Passover seder.*

8 medium potatoes

1 cup raw cashews

1 fairly ripe avocado, pitted, peeled, and cut into large chunks

Juice of 1 lemon

2 tablespoons extra-virgin olive oil

2 large or 3 medium leeks, white and palest green parts only, chopped and well rinsed

10 to 12 ounces baby spinach, rinsed

2 tablespoons minced fresh dill, or 1 teaspoon dried

¼ cup matzo meal or quinoa flakes

Salt and freshly ground pepper to taste

6 matzos

1 cup grated Daiya cheese, optional

⅓ cup pine nuts for topping, optional

1. Cook, bake, or microwave the potatoes in their skins until just tender. When cool enough to handle, peel and cut into ¼-inch-thick slices.

2. Cover the cashews with 1 cup boiling water in a heatproof bowl and let stand for at least 15 minutes. Drain the cashews, then combine with the avocado and lemon juice in a food processor. Process until smoothly pureed; drizzle enough water through the feed tube while the processor is running to give the mixture a thick, creamy texture.

3. Preheat the oven to 350° F.

4. Heat the oil in a large skillet. Add the leeks and sauté over medium-low heat until golden. Add the spinach in batches, covering and cooking until wilted to make room for all of it. Stir in the cashew cream, dill, and matzo meal. Season with salt and pepper.

5. Break each matzo in half, and place in a shallow dish or bowl. Cover matzos with room-temperature water until slightly pliable (don't let them get mushy!), about 2 minutes; drain. Lightly oil a 9 x 13–inch casserole dish.

6. Layer the casserole as follows: line the bottom with a layer of matzos, using two matzos per layer. Follow with a layer of potato slices, half the spinach mixture, half the optional cheese, and another layer of matzos. Repeat, ending with a layer of matzo.

7. Bake for 30 to 40 minutes, or until top is golden with spots of brown. If using pine nuts, sprinkle them over the top about 10 minutes before removing from the oven. Let stand for 10 minutes, then cut into squares to serve.

# Quinoa Pilaf

**GLUTEN-FREE**

**SOY-FREE**

**NUT-FREE**

**8 TO 10 SERVINGS**

*This pilaf, contributed by a longtime reader of mine, Barbara Pollack, is especially attractive, made with a combination of red and white quinoa, but either color can be used on its own to great effect. This pilaf is a veggie-filled way to celebrate quinoa's acceptance as standard Passover fare.*

1½ cups quinoa, rinsed

3 cups prepared vegetable broth

3 tablespoons olive oil or other healthy vegetable oil

2 medium yellow or red onions, or 1 of each, quartered and thinly sliced

4 to 6 cloves garlic, minced

1 16-ounce bag shredded coleslaw cabbage

2 medium carrots, sliced

2 cups finely chopped broccoli florets

1 cup sliced cremini or baby bella mushrooms

2 teaspoons minced fresh ginger, or to taste

½ teaspoon dried basil

½ teaspoon dried thyme

2 tablespoons lemon juice, or to taste

Salt and freshly ground pepper to taste

½ cup minced fresh parsley

¼ cup minced fresh dill, more or less to taste

1. Combine the quinoa with the broth in a large saucepan. Bring to a rapid simmer, then lower the heat, cover, and simmer gently until the water is absorbed, about 15 minutes. Test to see if the quinoa is done to your liking; if needed, add another ½ cup water and simmer until absorbed.

2. Meanwhile, heat the oil in a large skillet or stir-fry pan. Add the onions and sauté over medium-low heat until translucent. Add the garlic and continue to sauté until the onion is golden.

3. Add the cabbage, carrots, broccoli, mushrooms, ginger, basil, thyme, and lemon juice. Turn the heat up to medium-high and stir-fry until the cabbage is tender-crisp, about 5 minutes.

4. Stir in the cooked quinoa, then season to taste with salt and pepper. Stir in the parsley and dill, remove from the heat, and serve.

# Sautéed Asparagus and Broccolini

**GLUTEN-FREE**

**SOY-FREE**

**NUT-FREE**

**8 SERVINGS**

*Here's a simple side dish to add more green to the holiday plate.*

10 to 12 ounces slender asparagus

2 tablespoons extra-virgin olive oil

1 bunch broccolini (6 to 8 ounces)

1 yellow bell pepper, cut into long, narrow strips

¼ cup chopped pitted black olives, preferably cured (such as Kalamata), or sliced sun-dried tomatoes, or more, as desired

1 tablespoon lemon juice

Salt and freshly ground pepper to taste

1. Trim any woody bottoms from the asparagus, and peel the bottom halves of the spears if needed.

2. Heat the oil in a medium skillet. Add the asparagus, broccolini, and bell pepper. Sauté over medium heat, covered, for 5 to 7 minutes, stirring frequently, until the vegetables are tender-crisp to your liking.

3. Stir in the olives and lemon juice. Season with salt and pepper and serve.

# A SEPHARDIC-STYLE SEDER MENU

Sephardic-Style Date Haroset

Moroccan-Style Vegetable Soup with Vegan Matzo Balls

Green Salad with Artichokes, Oranges, and Pickled Beets

Eggplant Matzo Mina

OR

Spinach, Leek, and Potato Matzo Gratin (page 119)

Moroccan Carrots

Sephardic Stewed Green Beans

Passover Fruit Crisp (page 131)

OR

Chocolate Matzo Brittle (page 132)

OR

Coconut-Almond Macaroons (page 133)

# Sephardic-Style
# Date Haroset

**GLUTEN-FREE**

**SOY-FREE**

**8 TO 10 SERVINGS**

*Sephardic* harosets *vary widely according to culture and use a far greater variety of ingredients than the Eastern European counterpart. One of the hallmarks is the use of dried fruits. This recipe is an amalgam from several cultures.*

1 cup pitted dates

½ cup dried apricots

⅓ cup walnuts

⅓ cup almonds

1 teaspoon cinnamon

¼ teaspoon ground ginger

⅓ cup orange juice

2 tablespoons sweet Passover wine

1. Combine all the ingredients in a food processor. Process until finely chopped. Pat into a serving bowl, then cover until needed.

# Moroccan-Style Vegetable Soup with Vegan Matzo Balls

**Can be made GLUTEN-FREE by omitting matzo balls**
**SOY-FREE**
**NUT-FREE**

**8 TO 10 SERVINGS**

*This isn't specifically a Sephardic soup, though it amply uses some of the favored ingredients and flavorings of that cuisine, including leeks, carrots, cumin, turmeric, and lots of fresh herbs. Matzo balls aren't always a part of the Sephardic tradition, but a Turkish friend remembers them from his childhood seders. They'd be sorely missed at most seders, so do include them with this flavorful vegetable soup.*

2 tablespoons olive oil or other healthy vegetable oil

2 large or 3 medium leeks, white parts only, quartered lengthwise, chopped, and well rinsed

2 medium potatoes, peeled and diced

2 medium turnips, peeled and diced

3 medium carrots, sliced

3 medium celery stalks, diced

6 to 8 ounces white, cremini, or baby bella mushrooms, chopped

6 cups vegetable broth (homemade, see page 112, or store-bought)

1 14- to 16-ounce can diced tomatoes

1 teaspoon ground cumin or more, to taste

¼ teaspoon turmeric

Salt and freshly ground pepper to taste

½ cup minced fresh parsley

¼ cup minced fresh dill

Vegan Matzo Balls (see page 115)

1. Heat the oil in a large soup pot. Add the leeks and sauté over medium heat until golden.

2. Add the potatoes, turnips, carrots, celery, mushrooms, broth, tomatoes, cumin, and turmeric. Bring to a gentle boil, then lower the heat, cover, and simmer gently until the vegetables are tender, about 30 minutes. Season with salt and pepper.

3. If time allows, let the soup stand off the heat for several hours to develop flavor. Just before serving, stir in the parsley and dill. Add water if the soup is too dense. Serve with Vegan Matzo Balls (see page 115).

# Green Salad with Artichokes, Oranges, and Pickled Beets

**GLUTEN-FREE**

**SOY-FREE**

Can be made **NUT-FREE** by using the pumpkin seed option (if seeds are safe for you)

## 8 SERVINGS

*Artichokes are a favorite Sephardic vegetable, and make for a lively spring salad in tandem with oranges and beets.*

- 1   10-ounce package frozen artichoke hearts, completely thawed and quartered

- 2   medium red or golden beets, cooked, peeled, and diced

- 3   small oranges, such as clementines, peeled and sectioned

- 1   medium crisp cucumber, thinly sliced

- 3   to 4 ounces mixed baby greens, or a combination of greens with baby arugula

- 2   tablespoons extra-virgin olive oil

- 2   tablespoons lemon juice, or more, to taste

    Minced fresh dill, to taste

    Salt and freshly ground pepper to taste

- ¼   cup toasted pumpkin seeds or pine nuts, optional

1. Combine all the ingredients in a mixing bowl. Toss together and serve.

# Eggplant Matzo Mina

**Can be made SOY-FREE by using a soy-free vegan cheese**
**NUT-FREE**

## 8 TO 10 SERVINGS

*Many variations of this matzo pie are made by Sephardic Jews of various cultures. This one is Italian-influenced, and came my way via a resident of Bologna. This will remind you of an eggplant lasagna. As an alternative to this dish, you might also consider Spinach, Leek, and Potato Matzo Gratin on page 119, which is, in effect, a mina-inspired recipe.*

2 medium eggplants, about 2 pounds total

2 tablespoons olive oil, or other healthy vegetable oil, divided

1 medium onion, finely chopped

2 cloves garlic, minced

1 15-ounce can tomato sauce

1 14- to 16-ounce can diced tomatoes, lightly drained

2 to 3 tablespoons minced fresh parsley

½ teaspoon each: dried oregano, dried basil, and paprika

Salt and freshly ground pepper to taste

6 matzos

12 ounces mozzarella-style nondairy cheese, grated (see Note)

1. Preheat the broiler.

2. Cut the eggplants into ½-inch slices and peel. Brush lightly with some of the oil and broil on each side until tender.

3. Heat the remaining oil in a deep saucepan. Add the onion and garlic and sauté until golden. Add the tomato sauce, tomatoes, parsley, and seasonings. Bring to a simmer and cook over low heat, covered, for 15 minutes.

4. Break each matzo into three strips. Fill a shallow casserole dish with cold water. Place the matzo strips in it for 2 minutes, until pliable but not mushy. Drain the water off.

5. Preheat the oven to 350° F.

6. Lightly oil a large, shallow casserole dish and layer as follows: a thin layer of sauce, a layer of eggplant, a layer of matzo, and a layer of cheese. Repeat. Bake for 35 to 40 minutes, or until the cheese is lightly browned.

**NOTE:** The use of soy or rice cheese is allowed here, unlike in the previous Passover menu. Many Sephardic cultures continue to use beans during Passover, whereas the Ashkenazic tradition does not. Another good choice is Daiya cheese, made from tapioca flour, though it's not specifically kosher for Passover.

# Moroccan Carrots

**GLUTEN-FREE**

**SOY-FREE**

Can be made **NUT-FREE** by omitting almonds or pine nuts

**8 TO 10 SERVINGS**

*Thanks to mon ami Jean-Luc Botbol for introducing me to this very tasty, traditionally Moroccan way of preparing carrots.*

¼ cup slivered or sliced almonds, or pine nuts

3 tablespoons extra-virgin olive oil

3 to 4 cloves garlic, minced, or more for garlic lovers

2 pounds carrots, thinly sliced

Juice of ½ to 1 lemon, to taste

1 teaspoon grated organic lemon zest, optional (but highly recommended)

2 to 3 tablespoons minced chives (substitute scallion if need be)

¼ to ½ cup minced fresh parsley, to taste

Salt and freshly ground pepper to taste

1. Toast the almonds or pine nuts in a large, dry skillet over medium heat until very lightly browned. Remove to a plate and set aside.

2. Heat the oil in the same skillet. Add the garlic and carrots and sauté over medium heat, stirring frequently, until the carrots are tender-crisp and beginning to turn golden, about 10 to 15 minutes. If the skillet begins to turn dry, sprinkle in small amounts of water.

3. Add lemon juice to taste along with the optional zest. Sprinkle in the chives and half the parsley and toss.

4. Transfer to a serving dish, top with the remaining parsley and the toasted nuts, then serve at once.

# Sephardic Stewed Green Beans

**GLUTEN-FREE**

**SOY-FREE**

**NUT-FREE**

## 8 SERVINGS

*Green beans are a much-loved vegetable in Sephardic cuisine, often used in simple side dishes like this one. While this vegetable isn't an allowed Ashkenazic Passover food, it isn't similarly forbidden in the Sephardic tradition.*

1½ to 2 pounds fresh green beans (see Note)

2 tablespoons extra-virgin olive oil

1 medium onion, quartered and thinly sliced

2 cloves garlic, minced

4 medium tomatoes, diced

1 tablespoon lemon juice, or to taste

1 teaspoon natural granulated sugar, to taste

2 tablespoons minced fresh dill

Salt and freshly ground pepper to taste

1. Trim the tips from the green beans and cut them in half.

2. Heat the oil in a deep skillet. Add the onion and sauté over medium-low heat until translucent. Add the garlic and continue to sauté until the onion is golden.

3. Add the green beans, tomatoes, lemon juice, and sugar, and about ¼ cup water. Bring to a gentle simmer, then cook until the green beans are tender, but haven't quite lost their appealing green color, about 10 to 15 minutes.

4. Stir in the dill and season with salt and pepper. Add more lemon juice and sugar if you'd like a more pronounced sweet/sour flavor. Transfer to a covered serving dish and serve warm.

**NOTE:** Green beans may be in season in warm climates in the Middle East, Spain, and Morocco, where this dish is customary, but in North American climates, where spring is just beginning, not so much. If you'd like to try this dish but can't get good, fresh green beans, use whole frozen organic baby green beans.

## A NOTE ABOUT THE
## SEPHARDIC-STYLE RECIPES

The recipes in this section may not hew closely to any specific traditional Sephardic seder, since I've mixed traditions within this style of cuisine to create a vegan-friendly menu. The Sephardic tradition, unlike the Ashkenazic, allows rice, legumes, corn, and green beans to be eaten during Passover. Still, I've used only green beans in the recipes to allow for the mingling of cultures, should you like to mix and match menus.

# PASSOVER SWEETS AND TREATS

Passover Fruit Crisp

Chocolate Matzo Brittle

Coconut-Almond Macaroons

Passover Granola

Vegan Matzo Brei

# Passover Fruit Crisp

**Can be made GLUTEN-FREE by using quinoa flakes**
**SOY-FREE**

## 8 SERVINGS

*Few desserts are easier to adapt for the Passover seder than a fruit crisp, since you can use matzo cake meal or quinoa flakes to satisfy the holiday's dietary criteria.*

6 cups peeled, thinly sliced pears or apples, or a combination

¼ cup maple syrup or agave nectar

1 teaspoon cinnamon

1 teaspoon vanilla extract

### TOPPING

½ cup matzo cake meal or quinoa flakes

½ cup very finely chopped or ground walnuts

3 tablespoons natural granulated sugar

½ teaspoon cinnamon

2 tablespoons safflower oil

1. Preheat the oven to 350° F.

2. Combine the fruit with the syrup, cinnamon, and vanilla in a mixing bowl. Stir together, then pour in to a lightly oiled 9 x 13–inch baking dish or cake pan.

3. Combine the first 4 topping ingredients in a small bowl. Drizzle in the oil and stir until the dry ingredients are evenly moistened. Sprinkle the topping evenly over the fruit.

4. Bake for 30 to 35 minutes, or until the fruit is tender and the topping is golden and turning crisp. Allow to cool until just warm, then serve.

# Chocolate Matzo Brittle

**SOY-FREE**

**8 TO 10 SERVINGS**

*This dessert is very rich, but it's an excellent way to use a surplus of matzo—a little goes a long way.*

1 cup chocolate chips

2 tablespoons agave nectar or maple syrup

Pinch of cinnamon

2 matzos, broken into pieces slightly larger than bite-size

⅓ to ½ cup lightly toasted nuts (see Variations)

½ cup dark or golden raisins, dried cranberries, or chopped dried fruit (see Variations), or any combination

**1.** Line two large plates with wax paper or parchment.

**2.** Combine the chocolate chips, agave nectar, and cinnamon in a medium saucepan. Cook over low heat until smoothly melted. Remove from the heat.

**3.** Add the broken matzo; stir to coat evenly with the chocolate. Spread in a more or less single layer onto the plates. Sprinkle the nuts and raisins over the top. Refrigerate for at least an hour before serving.

**4.** Just before serving, break up into large chunks and transfer to a serving platter.

**VARIATIONS:**

For the nuts, use sliced or slivered almonds, or chopped walnuts, pecans, or pistachios. If you like "salty sweets," you'll love this with chopped salted pistachios. You can use two different types of nuts, of course.

For the dried fruit, other than the raisins or cranberries, consider dried sliced apricot or mango, or finely chopped dried pineapple.

# Coconut-Almond Macaroons

**Can be made GLUTEN-FREE by using potato starch option**
**SOY-FREE**

**MAKES ABOUT 3 DOZEN**

*Macaroons are classic Passover treats, but don't limit the use of these chewy little cookies to Passover only. When making them at other times, you can use regular flour instead of potato starch or matzo cake meal.*

1 cup lightly toasted almonds

1 cup shredded unsweetened coconut

½ cup matzo cake meal or potato starch

½ teaspoon cinnamon

¼ cup unsweetened cocoa powder, optional

½ cup vanilla almond milk

½ cup maple syrup or agave nectar

2 teaspoons vanilla extract

1. Preheat the oven to 325° F.

2. Place the almonds in a food processor and process until they resemble a coarse meal.

3. Add the almonds to a mixing bowl with the coconut, matzo cake meal, cinnamon, and optional cocoa powder and stir together. Make a well in the center and add the almond milk, syrup, and vanilla and stir until the mixture is well blended.

4. Drop by tablespoonfuls onto a parchment-lined baking sheet. Bake for 10 to 12 minutes, or until the edges are golden. Allow to cool on the baking sheet for 10 minutes, then remove carefully with a spatula and set on plates. The cookies are soft at first, but will become crisp when they're cool.

# Passover Granola

**SOY-FREE**

**MAKES ABOUT 6 CUPS**

*This granola, another terrific Passover idea contributed by Barbara Pollack, is wonderful for breakfast, served with almond milk, during the Passover week. It's also perfect for snacking.*

4 cups matzo farfel

½ cup chopped walnuts or pecans, or slivered almonds, or a combination

½ cup shredded coconut, optional

½ cup agave nectar or maple syrup

¼ cup vegetable oil, such as safflower

2 teaspoons vanilla extract

1 cup dark or golden raisins, dried cranberries, or sliced apricots, or a combination

1. Preheat oven to 325° F.

2. Mix farfel, nuts, and optional coconut in a large mixing bowl.

3. Combine the agave nectar or syrup, oil, and vanilla in a small bowl and whisk together. Drizzle into the dry mixture and stir together until the dry mixture is evenly coated.

4. Spread the mixture in a shallow layer on a parchment-lined baking sheet or roasting pan. Bake for 20 to 30 minutes, until golden and fragrant, stirring often to prevent over-browning.

5. Remove from oven and stir in the dried fruit. Cool and store in an airtight container.

# Vegan Matzo Brei

**NUT-FREE**

**I SERVING**

*Matzo brei, a kind of omelet made with crushed matzo and egg, is a beloved Passover week breakfast. As in the recipe for Vegan Matzo Balls, page 115, quinoa flakes provide the appropriate "glue" that holds the matzo brei together. It's easiest to make this dish, one serving at a time, in a small skillet; for more servings, repeat the recipe as needed.*

1½ matzos, crumbled

Pinch of salt, plus more for serving, to taste

¼ cup quinoa flakes

1 tablespoon Earth Balance or other non-hydrogenated margarine

Maple syrup, optional

1. Combine the crumbled matzos and quinoa flakes in a heatproof bowl. Pour 1 cup boiling water over them, add a pinch of salt, and stir together. Let stand for 2 to 3 minutes while the skillet heats up.

2. Melt the margarine in a preheated 7- to 8-inch skillet. Once it's sizzling, pour in the matzo mixture and pat in evenly with a spatula. Cover and cook over medium-high until the bottom is golden brown and crisp.

3. Slide the matzo brei out onto a plate about the same size as the skillet. Holding the bottom of the plate with one hand, invert the skillet over the plate with the other and then flip right-side up quickly. Cook the other side of the matzo brei until golden brown.

4. Slide onto a serving plate. Serve with the optional maple syrup, or sprinkle additional salt over the top.

# A ROSH HASHANAH MENU OF MIXED TRADITIONS

## STARTERS

Vegan Challah

Apple Slices with Agave Nectar or Maple Syrup

Beet Borscht

Multi-Mushroom Barley Soup
OR
A simple, seasonal green salad

## MAIN DISHES

Seven-Vegetable Couscous

Vegan Cholent

Moroccan-Flavored Tofu with Apricots and Olives

## SIDE DISHES

Sweet Potato Tzimmes

🍂

Sweet Noodle Kugel

🍂

Turkish Eggplant Stew

🍂

Summer Squash Provençal

## DESSERTS

Just-as-Sweet-as-Honey Cake

🍂

Apple-Pumpkin Delight

🍂

Apple and Pear Strudel

🍂

Rugelach

# Vegan Challah

**SOY-FREE**

**NUT-FREE**

**MAKES 2 LOAVES**

*It's not your mom's (or grandmother's) challah, but it comes close enough. It's delicious fresh and warm, spread with agave nectar or Earth Balance. While round challah breads are more traditional for Rosh Hashanah, many still like to make and serve the braided kind. Both options are here.*

1 package active dry yeast

2 tablespoons natural granulated sugar

⅓ cup safflower or other light vegetable oil

2 tablespoons agave nectar

5 cups unbleached white flour, plus more, as needed

2 teaspoons salt

1 cup well-cooked, pureed winter squash (any golden-orange variety, or from completely thawed frozen butternut squash)

Poppy or sesame seeds for topping

**1.** In a medium bowl, combine the yeast with ½ cup of warm water and the sugar. Let stand for 5 to 10 minutes, or until dissolved. Stir in the oil, agave nectar, and 1 cup of warm water.

**2.** Combine the flour and salt in a large mixing bowl. Make a well in the center and pour in the wet mixture and squash puree. Work together, first with a wooden spoon, then with your hands. Add additional flour until the dough loses its stickiness.

**3.** Turn the dough out onto a well-floured board. Knead for 6 to 8 minutes. Place in a floured bowl, cover with a tea towel, and put in a warm place to rise until doubled in bulk, 1½ to 2 hours (the longer you can let it rise, the better). I like to turn the oven on, and just as it starts to heat up, turn it off. This seems to be a perfect spot for letting the dough rise.

**4.** Punch the dough down and divide into two parts. If you'd like to make round challahs, simply shape into two round loaves. If you'd like to make braided breads, divide each part into three parts. Make long strands, about 1½ inches in diameter, from each part. Attach three strands at one end by pinching together. Braid the strands and pinch together at the bottom. Place on a parchment-lined baking sheet and let rise until doubled in bulk again, about 1½ hours.

**5.** Brush the tops of the braids with a tiny amount of water and sprinkle with sesame or poppy seeds. Bake in a preheated 350° F oven for about 35 to 40 minutes, or until the tops are golden and the loaves feel hollow when tapped. Cool on a rack.

# APPLE SLICES WITH AGAVE NECTAR OR MAPLE SYRUP

One of the signature food rituals of this holiday is serving a platter of apple slices with a bowl of honey for dipping, usually before the meal, to symbolize the hope that the year ahead will be a sweet one. Since vegans generally don't use honey, agave nectar and pure maple syrup are each good substitutes. Of the two, agave nectar more closely resembles honey.

# ODE TO A VEGAN CHALLAH

It's hard to imagine a Jewish New Year celebration without challah. For many of us, a fresh loaf is more enticing than any sort of cake. Spreading honey on slices of this tender bread and eating it, along with the honey-dipped apple, are central to the celebration. Obviously, this part of the ritual needs tweaking for committed vegans.

Making vegan challah is quite a challenge, since it's the egg in this traditional Jewish Sabbath and holiday bread that gives it a pale golden color and a tender, pull-apart texture. My first couple of attempts fell flat; I simply left out the egg, and was left with a not-bad but not-challah result. For my next attempt, I thought I was being clever by adding garbanzo flour, which, I thought, might give the bread an egg-y color and consistency. Wrong. It made for an even denser loaf that was not challah-esque at all.

Then I remembered a recipe for Tender Squash Dinner Rolls by Alisa Fleming, in her book *Go Dairy-Free!*, which extols their soft, pull-apart texture. So a big thanks goes to Alisa for inspiring my most successful attempt at vegan challah. Admittedly, it's not exactly like egg bread, but this version comes closer to the original than any vegan versions I've tried, and is beautiful to behold.

# Beet Borscht

**GLUTEN-FREE**
Can be made **SOY-FREE** by omitting vegan sour cream
**NUT-FREE**

## 8 SERVINGS

*This gorgeous soup of Russian origin is filled with produce favored on this holiday for its subtle sweetness. A Russian proverb says, "Borscht and bread will make your cheeks red." Serve this soup with slices of fresh Vegan Challah (see page 138) and see if it's true. I don't recommend making beet borscht unless you have a food processor with a grating blade. Of course, you could do this with a hand grater, but you'd never forgive me.*

6 medium beets, peeled and cut into large chunks

4 medium carrots, peeled and cut into large chunks

1 large sweet apple, peeled, cored, and cut into chunks

1 large onion, cut into large chunks

Juice of 1 lemon, or more to taste

¼ cup natural granulated sugar or agave nectar, more or less to taste

Salt and freshly ground pepper to taste

¼ cup minced fresh dill

Vegan sour cream (homemade, see page 96, or store-bought), optional

1. Grate the beets, carrots, apple, and onion in a food processor fitted with the grating blade. As the work bowl gets filled, transfer the grated ingredients to a large soup pot.

2. Add enough water to cover the grated ingredients in the pot, then add the lemon juice and sugar. Bring to a gentle boil, then lower the heat, cover, and simmer gently until everything is tender, about 30 minutes.

3. Adjust the consistency with more water if the vegetables are too densely packed. Season with salt and pepper and stir in the dill. Taste and add more lemon juice and/or sugar to adjust the sweet and tangy balance to your liking.

4. This is a good soup to make ahead of time. If you'd like to serve it chilled (which is how it really shines), let it cool to room temperature, then refrigerate, covered, until chilled. To serve hot, heat through as needed before serving.

5. If desired, top each serving with a dollop of sour cream.

# Multi-Mushroom Barley Soup

**SOY-FREE**

**NUT-FREE**

**8 OR MORE SERVINGS**

*In its basic form, mushroom-barley soup is a great favorite in Jewish fare. Using a variety of mushrooms adds interest to this comfort soup without tampering too much with a classic.*

2 tablespoons olive oil or other healthy vegetable oil

1 large onion, chopped

2 cloves garlic, minced

1 cup raw pearl barley

3 large celery stalks, finely diced

1 large carrot, finely diced

1 32-ounce carton vegetable broth

2 bay leaves

½ teaspoon dried thyme

2 teaspoons paprika

12 to 16 ounces mushrooms, stemmed and sliced (use a combination of any two or three of cremini, shiitake, baby bella, and white mushrooms)

2 cups rice milk, or more or less as needed

¼ cup minced fresh dill

¼ cup minced fresh parsley

Salt and freshly ground pepper to taste

1. Heat the oil in a soup pot. Add the onion and sauté over medium heat until translucent. Add the garlic and continue to sauté until the onion is golden.

2. Place barley, celery, carrot, vegetable broth, and 2 cups water in a soup pot. Bring to a gentle boil, then lower the heat and add the bay leaves, thyme, and paprika. Cover and simmer gently for 30 minutes.

3. Stir in the mushrooms and simmer for about 30 minutes longer, or until the barley and vegetables are tender.

4. Add enough rice milk to give the soup the consistency you like—I like it slightly thick. Stir in the dill and parsley, and season with salt and pepper.

5. If time allows, let the soup stand for an hour or so off the heat. Just before serving, heat the soup through. Add more rice milk as needed, and adjust the seasonings.

# Seven-Vegetable Couscous

**Can be made GLUTEN-FREE by substituting quinoa for the couscous (less authentic, but still delicious!)**
**Can be made SOY-FREE by substituting olive oil for Earth Balance**

## 8 SERVINGS

*Seven is a lucky number in Jewish tradition, so a soup or stew featuring seven vegetables is a New Year's favorite among Sephardic Jews. A bountiful, colorful tribute to the harvest, you need not save this treat for holidays only. Don't be put off by the long list of ingredients. It's as easy as can be.*

1½ cups couscous

1 tablespoon Earth Balance

1 teaspoon turmeric

1 teaspoon salt

2 tablespoons extra-virgin olive oil

2 medium onions, chopped

1 cup finely shredded white cabbage

1 medium turnip, peeled and diced

1 medium yellow summer squash, halved lengthwise and thinly sliced

1 medium zucchini, halved lengthwise and thinly sliced

1 15- to 16-ounce can chickpeas, drained and rinsed

1½ cups diced ripe tomatoes

2 teaspoons grated fresh or jarred ginger, or more, to taste

1 teaspoon ground cumin

½ teaspoon ground coriander

Dried hot red pepper flakes to taste, optional

Salt and freshly ground pepper to taste

### GARNISHES

½ cup golden raisins

⅓ cup minced fresh parsley

1. Combine the couscous and 3 cups boiling water in a heatproof bowl. Cover and let stand until the water is absorbed, about 15 minutes. Fluff with a fork, then stir in the margarine, turmeric, and salt. Cover and set aside.

2. For the vegetable stew, heat the oil in a large saucepan or soup pot. Add the onions and sauté over medium heat until translucent. Stir in cabbage and sauté until both it and the onion are lightly golden.

3. Add the remaining stew ingredients. Bring to a simmer, then cover and reduce the heat to medium-low. Cook, stirring occasionally, for 15 to 20 minutes. Add water as needed to produce a moist, but not soupy, consistency. The vegetables should be just tender, but still firm.

4. To serve, arrange the couscous on the outer edge of a large serving platter and make a well in the center. Pour the vegetable mixture in the center, then sprinkle with the garnishes. Let each guest place a mound of couscous on his or her dinner plate and top it with the vegetable mixture.

### VARIATION:

To make this dish more festive, top with sliced or slivered toasted almonds.

# Vegan Cholent

**SOY-FREE**

**NUT-FREE**

**8 TO 10 SERVINGS**

*Cholent is a Jewish classic that can be considered an early predecessor to slow-cooker recipes. In its original form, it's put in the oven before the Sabbath and cooked at a very low temperature for about 12 hours so that it can be eaten for the Sabbath midday or late-afternoon meal. It's not so much used as holiday fare per se, but I thought it would be fun to include it here as a main dish option. With seitan standing in for the beef used in the original, it's a warming, hearty dish.*

⅔ cup pearl barley

2 tablespoons olive oil or other healthy vegetable oil

1 large onion, finely chopped

3 cloves garlic, minced

1½ to 2 pounds seitan, cut into bite-size pieces

1 large sweet potato, peeled and diced, or two medium white potatoes, peeled and diced

3 to 4 medium carrots, peeled and sliced

1 pound ripe, juicy tomatoes, diced, or one 14- to 16-ounce can diced tomatoes

½ cup dry red wine

1 15- to 16-ounce can small red beans

1 tablespoon sweet paprika, Spanish paprika, or cayenne pepper to taste

⅓ cup minced fresh parsley

Salt and freshly ground pepper to taste

1. Combine the barley in a saucepan with 1⅓ cups water. Bring to a gentle boil, then lower the heat, cover, and simmer until the water is absorbed, about 35 minutes. This will not cook the barley completely, but give it a head start as it is added to the stew.

2. Heat the oil in a large soup pot. Add the onion and sauté over medium-low heat until translucent. Add the garlic and seitan. Continue to sauté over medium heat, stirring frequently, until the seitan begins to brown lightly.

3. Add the barley, sweet or white potatoes, carrots, tomatoes, wine, and 2 cups water. Bring to a gentle boil, then lower the heat, cover, and simmer gently for 20 minutes. Add the beans and paprika. Cook over the lowest heat possible, stirring occasionally, for 1½ hours, until the barley and vegetables are tender and the flavors well married.

4. Stir in the parsley and season with salt and pepper. Cook over very low heat for 15 minutes longer, then serve.

## SLOW-COOKER CHOLENT

Robin Robertson, the author of *Fresh from the Vegetarian Slow Cooker* (and close to a billion other wonderful vegetarian and vegan cookbooks), kindly provided the following instructions for making cholent in a slow cooker—a modern segue for an age-old recipe:

1. In a skillet, sauté the onion, garlic, and seitan as directed in the second paragraph of the recipe instructions, then set aside. (Hint: some newer slow cookers allow you to go from stovetop to slow cooker, in which case the skillet is unnecessary.)

2. Proceed by combining all the ingredients, except the parsley, in a 6- to 7-quart slow cooker (including about 2½ cups of water—you'll need less water than the stovetop method).

3. Cover and slow cook on low for 6 to 8 hours or until the vegetables are tender. Gently stir about halfway through, if possible, to make sure the harder vegetables (carrots, etc.) are submerged in the cooking liquid. During the last hour of cooking, add the parsley and check the seasonings. If a bit more moistness is needed, add ½ cup or so additional water. If the cholent is cooked before you're ready to eat, turn your slow cooker to the "keep warm" setting.

# Moroccan-Flavored Tofu with Apricots and Olives

**Can be made GLUTEN-FREE by replacing flour with a gluten-free flour or potato starch**

**Can be made NUT-FREE by omitting almonds**

## 8 OR MORE SERVINGS

*Bursting with an offbeat combination of flavors—salty, sweet, mellow, and tart—this recipe was inspired by a classic Moroccan recipe. Most of the original ingredients remain in this veganized recipe; the baked tofu stands in for the chicken customarily used in this dish.*

- 3 tablespoons olive oil or other healthy vegetable oil
- 3 8-ounce packages baked tofu
- 1 medium onion, quartered and thinly sliced
- 4 cloves garlic, minced
- 6 scallions, white and green parts separated, thinly sliced
- 3 tablespoons unbleached white flour
- 2 cups prepared vegetable broth
- 1 to 2 teaspoons grated fresh or jarred ginger, to taste
- 1 teaspoon ground cumin
- Pinch of cinnamon
- 2 tablespoons lemon juice
- 2 tablespoons agave nectar
- 1 cup small green pimiento olives
- ¾ cup sliced dried apricots
- Salt and freshly ground pepper to taste
- 3 to 4 cups hot cooked quinoa (from 1½ to 2 cups raw)
- ½ cup slivered almonds, toasted
- ¼ to ½ cup minced fresh parsley

1. Heat half the oil in a large skillet. Add the baked tofu and sauté over medium heat until lightly browned on most sides. Remove tofu to a plate and set aside.

2. Heat the remaining oil in the skillet. Add the onion and sauté over medium-low heat until translucent. Add the garlic and white parts of the scallion and continue to sauté until all are golden.

3. Stir in the green parts of the scallion, then sprinkle in the flour, stirring it in quickly. Add the broth and bring to a simmer, stirring constantly until the mixture thickens.

4. Stir in the ginger, cumin, and cinnamon, followed by the lemon juice and agave nectar. Stir in the tofu, olives, and apricots. Season gently with salt and pepper. Stir together; add more lemon juice and sweetener if you'd like a more pronounced sweet and tart balance.

5. To serve, spread the cooked quinoa on a large serving platter; make a well in the center by pushing the grain off to the perimeter of the platter, then pour the tofu mixture into the center. Sprinkle the almonds and parsley evenly over the top and serve.

# Sweet Potato Tzimmes

**GLUTEN-FREE**

**SOY-FREE**

Can be made **NUT-FREE** by omitting walnuts

**6 TO 8 SERVINGS**

*In Yiddish, "tzimmes" means a big fuss or commotion. Fortunately, this mélange of sweet vegetables and dried fruits is not much of a fuss to make, and is a signature holiday dish (see photo on page 104).*

2 tablespoon olive oil or other healthy vegetable oil

I large red onion, quartered and thinly sliced

3 large carrots, sliced

3 large sweet potatoes, cooked or microwaved, then peeled and sliced

I large pear, peeled, cored, and sliced

½ cup chopped dried prunes

¼ cup chopped dried apricots

⅔ cup orange juice, preferably fresh

1½ teaspoons cinnamon

2 teaspoons minced fresh or jarred ginger

I teaspoon salt

¼ teaspoon nutmeg (or ½ teaspoon freshly grated)

⅓ to ½ cup finely chopped walnuts for topping, optional

1. Preheat the oven to 350° F.

2. Heat the oil in a large skillet. Add the onion and sauté over medium heat until translucent. Add the carrots and continue to sauté until the onion is golden. Combine with the remaining ingredients except the walnuts in a mixing bowl and stir until thoroughly mixed. Don't worry if the potato slices break apart.

3. Oil a shallow 2-quart baking dish. Pour in the sweet potato mixture and pat in evenly. Sprinkle the optional walnuts over the top. Bake for 45 minutes, or until the top begins to turn slightly crusty. Serve hot.

# Sweet Noodle Kugel

**Can be made GLUTEN-FREE by using gluten-free noodles**
**NUT-FREE**

## 8 SERVINGS

*This take on the classic Jewish comfort food is made dairy-free, but it's just as luscious as the original.*

8 to 10 ounces ribbon-style noodles (see Note)

8 ounces soft tofu

1 8-ounce container vegan sour cream

¼ cup agave nectar or maple syrup

⅔ cup dark or golden raisins

1 medium apple or pear, peeled, cored, and cut into small, thin slices

¼ cup Earth Balance or other non-hydrogenated margarine, melted

⅔ cup natural granulated sugar

2 teaspoons vanilla extract

1 teaspoon cinnamon

1. Preheat the oven to 350° F.

2. Cook the noodles according to package directions, then drain.

3. Meanwhile, cut the tofu into 3 or 4 slices, then blot well between layers of paper towel or a clean tea towel. Transfer to a large mixing bowl and mash until finely crumbled. Stir in the sour cream and agave nectar.

4. Stir in the cooked noodles and all the remaining ingredients. Transfer the mixture to an oiled, shallow, round or rectangular 2-quart casserole dish.

5. Bake for 35 to 40 minutes, or until the top begins to turn golden. Let stand 15 minutes before serving. This is also good served at room temperature.

**NOTE:** Kugel is traditionally made with egg noodles, but you can substitute them with quinoa ribbon noodles or rombi (a short, flat pasta shape).

# Turkish Eggplant Stew

**8 SERVINGS**

*Some years ago, while researching an article on Sephardic-style Jewish holiday fare, I gleaned many delicious ideas, including this one, from Uziel Sason, a friend who grew up in Turkey. Eggplant is always abundant in the Mediterranean, so it's not unusual to find it on almost any holiday table.*

2 medium eggplants (about 1½ to 2 pounds)

1 tablespoon olive oil or other healthy vegetable oil

1 medium onion, chopped

3 to 4 cloves garlic, minced

4 ripe, juicy tomatoes, diced

Juice of ½ to 1 lemon, or to taste

2 teaspoons natural granulated sugar

¼ to ½ cup chopped fresh parsley, to taste

Salt and freshly ground pepper to taste

1. Preheat the oven to 425° F.

2. Prick the eggplants in several places with a fork; place on a foil-lined baking sheet. Bake until softened and collapsed, about 45 to 55 minutes. Cool, slice open, and scoop the pulp from the skin. Discard the skin and chop the pulp into bite-size chunks.

3. Heat the oil in a large saucepan. Add the onion and sauté over medium-low heat until translucent. Add the garlic and continue to sauté until the onion is golden.

4. Add the eggplant, tomatoes, lemon juice, and sugar. Cook over low heat for 20 minutes, or until the tomatoes have softened into a sauce and the flavors have melded.

5. Stir in the parsley, then season with salt and pepper. Increase the lemon juice and sugar if you'd like a more pronounced sweet/sour flavor. Simmer for 5 minutes longer, then serve warm or at room temperature.

# Summer Squash Provençal

Can be made **GLUTEN-FREE** by using gluten-free specialty bread to make crumbs
**SOY-FREE**
**NUT-FREE**

**4 SERVINGS**

*Here's a great way to use late summer's bumper crop of tomatoes. Seasoned with the characteristic herbs of Provence, plus a touch of pungent black olives, this recipe can easily be doubled if you have a surplus of tomatoes.*

2 pounds mixed summer squashes (zucchini, yellow summer squash, and pattypan), sliced ¼ inch thick

4 medium firm, ripe tomatoes, sliced ¼ inch thick

Salt and freshly ground pepper to taste

2 large slices whole-grain bread

8 to 10 pitted cured black olives

¼ cup parsley leaves

¼ cup basil leaves

1 tablespoon fresh oregano, minced, or ½ teaspoon dried

1 teaspoon fresh thyme leaves or ¼ teaspoon dried

2 tablespoons extra-virgin olive oil

1. Preheat the oven to 375° F.

2. Arrange the squash and tomato slices in overlapping rows or circles in a lightly oiled round or rectangular shallow 2-quart baking dish. Sprinkle with salt and pepper.

3. Process the bread in a food processor until it is reduced to coarse crumbs. Add the olives and herbs. Drizzle in the olive oil while pulsing on and off, until the mixture resembles fine crumbs. Sprinkle the crumbs over the vegetables evenly.

4. Cover with foil and bake for 10 minutes, then bake uncovered for 15 minutes longer, or until the squash and tomatoes are tender but not overdone, and the crumbs are golden and crisp. Serve at once.

# Just-as-Sweet-as-Honey Cake

**SOY-FREE**

Can be made **NUT-FREE** by omitting almonds

**MAKES 2 LOAVES**

*Honey cake is a traditional dessert at Jewish celebrations, whether formal holidays or not, and is a fixture in the Ashkenazic Rosh Hashanah repertoire. In this recipe, dark agave nectar and maple syrup are combined to create a truly authentic flavor.*

2½ cups whole wheat pastry or spelt flour

1 tablespoon baking powder

2 teaspoons baking soda

1 tablespoon cinnamon

½ teaspoon ground ginger

½ teaspoon ground cloves or allspice

1 cup dark agave nectar or pure maple syrup, or half of each

1 cup applesauce

½ cup safflower oil

2 teaspoons vanilla extract

½ cup dark or golden raisins

¼ cup sliced almonds

1. Preheat the oven to 325° F.

2. Combine the first 6 (dry) ingredients in a mixing bowl. Make a well in the center of the dry ingredients and pour in the wet ingredients. Stir together until the wet and dry ingredients are thoroughly combined, then stir in the raisins.

3. Cut two pieces of baking parchment to fit the bottoms of two loaf pans. Lightly oil the sides. Divide the batter between the two lightly oiled loaf pans. Sprinkle the almonds evenly over the tops of the loaves.

4. Bake for 40 to 50 minutes, or until a knife inserted in the center of a loaf tests clean. Take care not to overbake.

5. Allow the cakes to cool completely. Use a knife to go around the sides of the loaves to loosen, if needed, and carefully remove the loaves from the pans by tipping them into your hand, then set on a platter. Cut each loaf into 12 slices to serve.

# Apple-Pumpkin Delight

**GLUTEN-FREE**

**SOY-FREE**

**NUT-FREE**

**8 SERVINGS**

*Although this isn't a Jewish recipe, but rather an invention of photographer Susan Voisin, it's incredibly appropriate to the "flavor" of the Jewish New Year holiday, as apples are used in abundance and pumpkins are a favorite Sephardic ingredient. Together, they make a light and unusual dessert. This is delicious served on its own or with vanilla or butter pecan vegan ice cream.*

1½  pounds sugar pumpkin, cushaw, or any orange winter squash

2  pounds Granny Smith apples (about 3 or 4 large apples)

½  cup natural granulated sugar

1  teaspoon cinnamon

¼  teaspoon nutmeg

⅓  teaspoon ground cloves

2  teaspoons cornstarch

1. To make the pumpkin easier to peel and cut, partially prebake it according to the directions on page 22. When cool enough to handle, peel the pumpkin and slice it into thin pieces about 1 x 2 inches (about ⅛ inch thick; the size matters less than the thickness). Peel the apples and slice a little thicker than the pumpkin.

2. Preheat the oven to 400° F.

3. Combine the sugar, cinnamon, nutmeg, cloves, and cornstarch in a small bowl. Oil a 2-quart casserole dish. Arrange half the pumpkin slices in the dish, and sprinkle with about ¼ of the sugar mixture; arrange half the apple slices over the pumpkin and sprinkle with another ¼ of the sugar mixture. Repeat the layers.

4. Cover with foil and bake for 30 minutes. Remove the foil and bake for 15 minutes longer, or until a knife inserted in the center goes through easily. Serve warm or at room temperature in individual dessert cups.

# Apple and Pear Strudel

**SOY-FREE**

Can be made **NUT-FREE** by omitting walnuts

**16 SERVINGS**

*This strudel is my kind of dessert—it's incredibly easy to make and yields a most impressive result. Check the label to be sure the frozen puff pastry you use is vegan.*

- 2 sheets frozen vegan puff pastry
- 2 medium-large apples, peeled and finely diced (about ¼-inch dice)
- 2 large ripe Bosc pears, peeled and finely diced
- ½ cup raisins
- ¼ finely chopped walnuts, optional
- ¼ cup natural granulated sugar
- 1 to 2 teaspoons cinnamon, to taste
- 2 teaspoons lemon juice

1. Allow the puff pastry to thaw for 45 minutes to an hour. Then, immediately turn the pastry sheets out onto a parchment-lined baking sheet.

2. Preheat the oven to 375° F.

3. Combine the remaining ingredients in a large mixing bowl and stir together well to distribute the cinnamon and sugar.

4. Divide the apple and pear mixture evenly between the two sheets of puff pastry. Spread evenly to the edges, leaving a 1-inch strip at the end farthest from you. Roll up, jelly roll–style, starting with the side closest to you. Finish with the seam side down. Make 6 shallow slashes crosswise at even intervals, to delineate 8 slices, on each roll.

5. Bake for 25 to 30 minutes, or until golden and puffed. Remove the rolls from the oven and transfer them from the baking sheet to a cooler surface—such as a tea towel spread on your counter—by grabbing two ends of the parchment.

6. Allow to cool completely or until just warm, then cut each strudel into 8 slices, using a sharp knife. Transfer to a serving platter and watch this dessert disappear.

# Rugelach

**MAKES ABOUT 40**

*These classic Jewish cream cheese cookies are easy to veganize with, you guessed it, vegan cream cheese. Some recipes call for long triangles of dough to be cut and rolled individually, resulting in pretty, crescent-type cookies. The easier way (which I'll always take, thank you very much), presented here, is how my mother-in-law made them. They're baked jelly roll–style, then cut into cookie-size sections while still warm. You can make an entire batch with either the first or second filling option (see below), or halve each filling and make both kinds. These freeze well.*

2 cups whole wheat pastry flour

¼ teaspoon salt

1 cup Earth Balance or other non-hydrogenated margarine

1 8-ounce container vegan cream cheese

**CHOCOLATE AND WALNUT FILLING**

1 cup walnuts

⅔ cup natural granulated sugar

½ cup dairy-free chocolate chips

2 teaspoons cinnamon

**APRICOT JAM AND WALNUT FILLING**

½ cup finely chopped walnuts

1 cup all-fruit apricot preserves, or as needed

1. Combine the flour and salt in a food processor. Add the Earth Balance and cream cheese, spooning them into the work bowl in heaping tablespoonsful so that you're not adding them in large clumps. Pulse on and off until the Earth Balance and cream cheese are evenly distributed into the flour.

2. Remove the mixture from the food processor and transfer to a lightly floured cutting board. Divide into four equal parts, shape into balls, then flatten until ½ inch thick. Wrap the disks in plastic wrap and refrigerate for a minimum of 2 hours or overnight.

3. When ready to bake, preheat the oven to 350° F. Line two baking sheets with baking parchment paper.

4. For the chocolate and walnut filling, place all the ingredients in the food processor and pulse on and off until the walnuts and chocolate chips are very finely chopped.

For the apricot jam and walnut filling, place the ingredients in the food processor and pulse on and off until the walnuts are very finely chopped.

5. Roll out one section of dough at a time on a well-floured cutting board, shaping more or less into a rectangle as you go. Spread the entire surface with ¼ of the filling of choice. Roll up, jelly roll–style. Repeat with the remaining dough.

6. Arrange on baking sheets with seam side down. Bake for 20 minutes, or until golden; make sure not to overbake, or they'll be more difficult to cut. Remove and allow to cool until just warm; cut each roll into approximately ¾-inch sections crosswise. Once the cookies are completely cooled, store in an airtight container.

# HANUKKAH MENU

Traditional Latkes, Vegan-Style

✿

Baba Ghanouj

✿

Hummus

✿

Tabbouleh

✿

Creamy Dilled Cucumbers

✿

Rugelach (page 157)

OR

Hanukkah chocolates

OR

Fresh fruit
(a platter of pineapple, mango,
and oranges makes a nice finale)

# Traditional Latkes, Vegan-Style

**Can be made GLUTEN-FREE by using both options for quinoa flakes**
**Can be made SOY-FREE by omitting sour cream option**
**NUT-FREE**

## MAKES ABOUT 3 DOZEN

*If you don't divulge the vegan secret to these latkes, no one will ever know. Everyone who has them swears they taste like the latkes they've always known and loved. The secret is that the grated potato is held together with oatmeal or quinoa flakes rather than eggs, and either option works splendidly. Use quinoa flakes for gluten-free latkes.*

¾ cup quick-cooking oats (oatmeal) or quinoa flakes

6 large potatoes, preferably russet, peeled and finely grated

1 medium carrot, grated (optional, but highly recommended)

1 medium onion, finely grated

½ cup matzo meal or quinoa flakes

Salt and freshly ground pepper to taste

Light vegetable oil for frying

Applesauce

Vegan sour cream (homemade, see page 96, or store-bought), optional

**1.** In a heatproof bowl, combine the oats with 1½ cups boiling water. Stir and set aside while preparing the other ingredients.

**2.** Combine the grated potato, optional carrot, onion, and matzo meal in a mixing bowl. Stir in the oatmeal, then season with salt and pepper.

**3.** Heat just enough oil to coat the bottom of a large, nonstick skillet or griddle. Drop enough potato batter to form 2½- to 3-inch pancakes. Fry on both sides over medium-high heat until golden brown and crisp.

**4.** Drain briefly on paper towels and place in a covered dish to keep warm until serving. Serve warm with applesauce, vegan sour cream, or both.

### VARIATIONS:

**SWEET POTATO LATKES:** Substitute one large peeled and diced sweet potato for two of the russet potatoes. You may need to increase the amount of oats slightly so they stick together.

**ZUCCHINI LATKES:** Substitute one medium zucchini for one of the russet potatoes. Add a few minced scallions or a bit of chopped fresh dill and parsley.

**LAZY LATKES:** If you're pressed for time and don't want to peel, cut, and grate potatoes, use two thawed 16-ounce bags of frozen, organic hash brown potatoes, which are basically plain, grated potatoes, and I promise not to tell anyone.

# Baba Ghanouj

**GLUTEN-FREE**

**SOY-FREE**

**NUT-FREE (if seeds are safe for you)**

**8 OR MORE SERVINGS**

*An eggplant lover's delight, this classic puree of roasted eggplant and tahini is delicious scooped up on wedges of pita bread.*

2 medium eggplants, about 2 pounds total

1 tablespoon olive oil or other healthy vegetable oil

1 large onion, chopped

3 to 4 cloves garlic, minced

¼ cup tahini (sesame paste)

Juice of 1 lemon, or more to taste

½ teaspoon ground cumin

Salt and freshly ground pepper to taste

1. Preheat the oven to 425° F. Arrange the whole eggplants on a foil-lined baking sheet. Bake about 30 to 40 minutes, until the skin is charred and the eggplants have collapsed, turning the eggplants with tongs once or twice during that time.

2. Remove from the oven and allow the eggplants to cool. When cool enough to handle, slip off the skins and stems.

3. Heat the oil in a skillet. Add the onion and sauté over medium heat until translucent. Add the garlic and continue to sauté until the onion is golden brown.

4. Combine the eggplant, the onion and garlic mixture, and the remaining ingredients in a food processor. Process until the mixture is a slightly chunky puree. Transfer to a serving bowl and serve at room temperature.

# Hummus

**GLUTEN-FREE**

**SOY-FREE**

**NUT-FREE (if seeds are safe for you)**

## 8 OR MORE SERVINGS

*Like the previous recipe, this classic dip should be scooped up on wedges of pita bread. Now that there are entire sections in supermarkets devoted to hummus, is there any point to making it at home? I think so. It has a fresher, livelier flavor, it makes a good quantity inexpensively, and you can vary it in a number of ways.*

- 1  20-ounce can chickpeas, drained and rinsed
- ⅓  cup tahini (sesame paste)
- 1  to 2 cloves garlic, crushed, optional

   Juice of 1 lemon

- 1  teaspoon ground cumin

   Salt and freshly ground pepper to taste

   Paprika for garnish

1. Combine all the ingredients except the paprika in a food processor. Add ⅓ cup water and process until smoothly pureed. Transfer to a serving bowl. Sprinkle with paprika. Serve at room temperature.

**VARIATIONS:**

Add a modest amount of any of the following for some fun and flavorful variations:

- •Wilted spinach
- •Fresh dill
- •Fresh parsley
- •Roasted red bell pepper
- •Artichoke hearts
- •Toasted pine nuts

# Tabbouleh

Can be made **GLUTEN-FREE** by using quinoa

**SOY-FREE**

**NUT-FREE**

## 8 OR MORE SERVINGS

*Once considered exotic, the classic bulgur, tomato, and parsley salad is nearly as well known as its frequent companion, hummus. A nice way to update this recipe is to make it with quinoa. Bulgur is nifty, but quinoa is even more nutritious, arguably tastier, and gluten-free, as well.*

1 cup medium-grind bulgur or quinoa, or a combination of both

3 medium-firm, ripe tomatoes (see Note)

½ to ¾ cup minced fresh parsley

3 to 4 scallions, minced

¼ cup minced fresh mint leaves

3 tablespoons extra-virgin olive oil

Juice of 1 to 1½ lemons, to taste

Salt and freshly ground pepper to taste

1. Combine the bulgur in a saucepan with 2 cups water. Bring to a slow boil, then lower the heat, cover, and simmer gently for 15 minutes, or until the water is absorbed. If you'd like a softer grain, add ½ cup of additional water and cook until absorbed. Fluff with a fork and let cool to room temperature. These instructions are the same for cooking quinoa.

2. Add all the remaining ingredients and let stand for 30 minutes to an hour. Serve at room temperature.

**NOTE:** Since this menu is for a time of year that's far from being tomato season, tomatoes-on-the-vine work well in this recipe.

# Creamy Dilled Cucumbers

**GLUTEN-FREE**

Can be made **SOY-FREE** by using coconut yogurt option

**NUT-FREE (if coconut is safe for you)**

**8 OR MORE SERVINGS**

*This refreshing Middle Eastern–inspired salad rounds out the selection of cold dishes.*

1 English (hothouse) cucumber, thinly sliced

1 6-ounce container plain coconut yogurt or ¾ cup vegan sour cream (homemade, see page 96, or store-bought)

¼ cup minced fresh dill

1 to 2 tablespoons lemon juice, to taste

Salt and freshly ground pepper to taste

1. Combine all the ingredients in a serving bowl and stir together well. If time allows, refrigerate for 30 minutes to an hour to chill before serving.

# CHAPTER FOUR

# EASTER

*As the earth reawakens, lively menus feature
spring flavors and fresh produce*

aster and Passover share two common ideas: Each holiday

heralds the arrival of spring, though from different symbolic

perspectives. Both holidays, however, connect us to our cultural

roots. Whether you're strongly connected to the religious roots

of these spring holidays or not, you can enjoy and cherish them with family and friends nonetheless.

Easter (celebrated on the Sunday following the full moon after the vernal equinox) is a holiday for both reflection and rejoicing. The parades, hunts for colorfully decorated eggs, festooned bonnets, and the Easter Bunny itself evolved from pagan customs; even the holiday's name may have been taken from Eostre, the Anglo-Saxon goddess of spring. Traditionally, ham or lamb is the centerpiece of Easter dinner, but, as you might expect, they are absent from the vegan table. Instead, the fresh produce of early spring is emphasized in these recipes and menus—light leafy greens, asparagus, lots of carrots, and bright, citrusy flavors.

**Beet and Carrot Salad, see page 181**

# AN EASTER MENU
# TO CELEBRATE SPRING

Potage Cressonier (Creole Potato and Watercress Soup)

Roasted Seitan, Peppers, and Portabellas

OR

Lemony Asparagus Risotto

Spring Greens with Citrus Dressing

Roasted Baby Carrots

Dessert (pages 188–197)

# Potage Cressonier
# (Creole Potato and Watercress Soup)

**GLUTEN-FREE**

**Can be made SOY-FREE by using coconut creamer**

**NUT-FREE (if you're not allergic to coconut)**

**6 SERVINGS**

*Inspired by a simple Creole recipe, this soup abounds with fresh parsley and peppery watercress, both Vitamin C–packed symbols of spring.*

2 tablespoons olive oil or other healthy vegetable oil

1 large onion, chopped

2 cloves garlic, minced

6 large peeled, diced white or yellow potatoes

1 32-ounce carton vegetable broth

1 cup soy or coconut creamer

1 cup rice milk, or as needed

1 large bunch watercress leaves (it's fine to include some stems)

1 cup minced fresh parsley

Salt and freshly ground black pepper

1. Heat the oil in a soup pot. Add the onion and sauté over medium heat until translucent. Add the garlic and continue to sauté until the onion is golden. Add the potatoes and broth. Bring to a gentle boil, then lower the heat, cover, and simmer until the potatoes are just tender, about 15 minutes.

2. Transfer about half the solid mixture to a food processor with a little of the liquid. Process until smoothly pureed and stir the mixture back into the soup pot. Or, simply insert an immersion blender into the soup pot and puree half the solid ingredients.

3. Stir in the creamer and rice milk and return to a simmer. Add the watercress and parsley and season with salt and pepper. Simmer for just 2 to 3 minutes longer—you want the greens to remain bright green—then remove from the heat and serve at once.

# Roasted Seitan, Peppers, and Portabellas

**NUT-FREE**

**8 SERVINGS**

*When you're preparing a multi-course meal, it's so nice when the entree can be made at the last minute with little hands-on time (and still be a crowd-pleaser). All of this is true for this hearty dish. If anyone in your family or a guest eats gluten-free, seitan is obviously not the choice for them. Go with the alternative main dish—the risotto that follows—or, if you're feeding a crowd, make both dishes. In that case, use the 375° oven temperature as for the risotto, and bake this dish 10 minutes or so longer than directed below.*

2 pounds seitan, cut into bite-size chunks (see Note)

1 red bell pepper, cut into wide strips

1 yellow bell pepper, cut into wide strips

2 medium-small zucchinis, sliced ½ inch thick

8 to 10 ounces portabella mushrooms, stemmed and sliced

¼ cup olive oil or other healthy oil

½ cup good-quality teriyaki marinade

3 to 4 scallions, thinly sliced

Freshly ground pepper to taste

Dried hot red pepper flakes to taste, optional

¼ cup minced fresh parsley

1. Preheat the oven to 400° F.

2. In a large mixing bowl, combine the seitan, bell peppers, zucchinis, mushrooms, olive oil, and teriyaki marinade. Stir together. Transfer to a roasting pan.

3. Roast in the oven for 15 minutes, stirring occasionally. Stir in the scallions, then roast for 5 to 10 minutes longer, or until the seitan and vegetables are lightly charred in spots.

4. Transfer the mixture to a serving dish. Season to taste with pepper and optional dried hot red pepper flakes. Sprinkle with parsley and keep covered until serving.

**NOTE:** See if you can find some really fresh seitan that's made in your local area. Check your natural foods store. The vacuum-sealed national brands are good, but fresh seitan is even better.

# Lemony Asparagus Risotto

**GLUTEN-FREE**

Can be made **SOY-FREE** by using soy-free vegan cheese

**NUT-FREE**

## 8 SERVINGS

*Oven baking is an almost effortless way to make risotto, as opposed to the traditional stovetop method, which requires continuous stirring. This way, you simply throw the basic ingredients into a casserole dish and stir them every 15 minutes, over the course of an hour, so you're free to work on other parts of the meal at the same time.*

- 2 cups Arborio rice
- 1 32-ounce carton vegetable broth
- 1 tablespoon extra-virgin olive oil
- 3 to 4 cloves garlic, finely minced
- 10 to 12 ounces fresh slender asparagus
- 2 good handfuls of baby spinach or baby arugula leaves
- ¼ cup minced fresh parsley
- Juice of 1 lemon
- 1 tablespoon organic lemon zest (optional, but highly recommended)
- Salt and freshly ground pepper to taste
- Grated vegan mozzarella cheese for topping, optional (Daiya is particularly good with this)

1. Preheat the oven to 375° F.

2. Combine the rice with the broth, 2 cups of water, the oil, and garlic in a deep 2½-quart casserole dish. Cover and bake for 1 hour, stirring every 15 minutes. Stir in 1 cup of additional water when you stir for the second time, then add 1 more cup of water when you stir for the third time.

3. Just after the third stirring, trim about an inch from the bottoms of the asparagus spears, and cut them into 1-inch lengths. Place in a skillet or saucepan with a small amount of water and steam, covered, for 2 to 3 minutes over medium heat, until bright green and tender-crisp. Add the spinach; cover and steam just until it's wilted.

4. After an hour, the rice should have a tender and creamy texture. Remove from the oven and stir in the asparagus and spinach mixture, followed by the remaining ingredients. Let stand for 5 to 10 minutes, then serve. Pass around grated cheese for topping, if desired.

# Spring Greens with Citrus Dressing

**GLUTEN-FREE**

**SOY-FREE**

**NUT-FREE**

**8 SERVINGS**

*This delightful salad benefits from a double dose of orange flavor and the surprising anise lilt of fennel.*

**DRESSING**

Juice of 1 orange (about ¼ cup)

¼ cup extra-virgin olive oil

2 tablespoons lemon juice, or more, to taste

1 teaspoon prepared yellow mustard

**SPRING GREENS**

1 small fennel bulb

12 or so baby carrots

2 to 3 ounces mixed baby greens, or as much as desired

1 bunch watercress leaves

Handful of green sprouts, such as pea shoots

3 to 4 small oranges such as clementines, peeled and sectioned

2 to 3 tablespoons toasted sunflower or pumpkin seeds, or as desired

1. Combine the dressing ingredients in a small bowl and whisk together.

2. Trim the tough stalks away from the fennel, reserving some of the feathery leaves for garnishing the salad. Trim the bottom of the bulb, halve lengthwise, then slice thinly.

3. If the baby carrots are thick, quarter them lengthwise, and if thin, halve them lengthwise. Combine the carrots and fennel in a serving bowl with the remaining ingredients and toss together.

4. Just before serving, add dressing as needed to moisten the salad (you'll use most or all of it, depending on how much of the greens you use) and toss together. Sprinkle some of the reserved fennel leaves over the top and serve.

# Roasted Baby Carrots

**GLUTEN-FREE**
**SOY-FREE**
**NUT-FREE**

**8 SERVINGS**

*This simple carrot side dish goes equally well with Roasted Seitan, Peppers, and Portabellas and Lemony Asparagus Risotto. It can be baked at the same time as either recipe, but will take slightly longer if you bake it at the same time as the risotto (which calls for a lower oven temperature).*

2   16-ounce bags baby carrots

2   tablespoons extra-virgin olive oil

3   tablespoons maple syrup

2   tablespoons lemon juice

¼   teaspoon cinnamon

      Pinch of salt

¼   cup minced fresh parsley

1. Preheat the oven to 375° F.

2. Combine all the ingredients except the parsley in a mixing bowl and stir together. Arrange in a foil- or parchment-lined nonstick roasting pan.

3. Bake for 25 to 35 minutes, stirring every 10 minutes or so, until the carrots are nicely glazed and lightly browned. Transfer to a covered serving dish, toss with the parsley, and serve.

## KINDER, HEALTHIER EASTER BASKETS

It's not too much of a stretch to create a healthier, dairy-free version of the traditional Easter basket. Simply replace too-sugary candy and milk chocolate with naturally sweetened gummy candies, which you can find in abundance in any natural foods store, and vegan chocolate Easter bunnies (page 187). For adults, trail mix or granola, tea, hot cocoa mix, and homemade muffins (page 189) make a nice mix for the holiday. Classic Carrot Cupcakes (page 191) or other healthy baked goods, small books and toys, and sticker books are also welcome additions to kids' Easter baskets.

# A GREEK-INSPIRED MENU

Lemony Spinach and Chickpea Soup

*

Fresh Pita or Other Flat Bread

*

Lentil and Tomato Salad

*

Magnificent Moussaka

OR

Spring Vegetable Tart

*

Citrus Rice

*

Dessert (pages 188–197)

# Lemony Spinach and Chickpea Soup

**GLUTEN-FREE**

**SOY-FREE**

**NUT-FREE**

## 8 OR MORE SERVINGS

*Vegans might not be able to eat avgolemono soup, the Greek Easter classic (because it relies heavily on egg), but the plethora of delicious ingredients in this sprightly soup more than makes up for it. Serve with fresh pita or other flat bread if desired.*

2 tablespoons extra-virgin olive oil

1 medium onion, finely chopped

3 to 4 cloves garlic, minced

1 32-ounce carton vegetable broth

1 16-ounce can chickpeas, drained and rinsed

2 medium carrots, coarsely grated or finely diced

1 medium zucchini, diced

1 bay leaf

2 teaspoons curry powder, more or less to taste

¼ teaspoon dried thyme

Juice of 1 lemon, more or less to taste

10 to 12 ounces baby spinach, rinsed

¼ cup minced fresh dill, more or less to taste

2 scallions, minced

Salt and freshly ground pepper to taste

1. Heat the oil in a soup pot. Add the onion and sauté over medium-low heat until translucent. Add the garlic and sauté until the onion is golden.

2. Add the broth, chickpeas, carrots, zucchini, bay leaf, curry, thyme, lemon juice, plus 2 cups water. Bring to a gentle boil, then lower the heat, cover, and simmer for 15 to 20 minutes, or until the carrots are tender. This part can be done ahead of time. If time allows, let the soup stand off the heat for a few hours.

3. Just before serving, return the soup to a simmer and stir in the spinach, dill, and scallions. Season with salt and pepper. Add more water if the soup seems too dense, and adjust all the seasonings, including the lemon juice.

# Lentil and Tomato Salad

GLUTEN-FREE

SOY-FREE

NUT-FREE

**6 TO 8 SERVINGS**

*This substantial salad can be made even heartier with the suggested Variations.*

1 cup raw lentils, sorted, rinsed, and cooked until done, but still firm, or two 15-ounce cans, drained and rinsed

2 cups small cherry or grape tomatoes, left whole, or halved if preferred (see Note)

3 scallions, green parts only, thinly sliced

¼ cup minced fresh dill, more or less to taste

½ cup minced fresh parsley, more or less to taste

¼ cup extra-virgin olive oil

Juice of 1 large lemon, or more, to taste

Salt and freshly ground pepper to taste

2 to 3 ounces mixed baby greens

**GARNISHES**

Cured black olives, such as Kalamata

Stuffed grape leaves, optional

Lemon wedges

Extra minced parsley

1. Combine the cooked lentils with the remaining ingredients except the greens. Toss gently but thoroughly.

2. Line a serving plate with the greens. Mound the lentil salad over them. Garnish with olives, optional grape leaves, and lemon wedges (for a more intense lemony flavor squeeze the juice over the greens). Sprinkle extra parsley over the top. Serve at room temperature.

**NOTE:** For added color, use a combination of red and yellow tomatoes.

**VARIATIONS:** For a more substantial salad, add one 16-ounce can chickpeas, drained and rinsed, or sprinkle crumbled tofu "feta" (see page 282) over the top.

# Magnificent Moussaka

**Can be made GLUTEN-FREE by using gluten-free breadcrumbs**
**NUT-FREE**

## 6 TO 8 SERVINGS

*Moussaka, a hearty, layered Greek casserole, is a heavenly dish—although I do put it in the category of "a project." The recipe isn't particularly complicated, but the number of steps involved is on the upper end of my personal limit. So even though preparing moussaka may be more involved than the usual fare, I still think it's worth it, evidenced by the fact that I like to make it occasionally, even when it isn't a special occasion.*

2 medium eggplants, about 1 pound each

2 tablespoons extra-virgin olive oil

1 cup finely chopped onion

3 to 4 cloves garlic, minced

1 28-ounce jar marinara sauce

1 teaspoon dried oregano

1 teaspoon dried thyme

Freshly ground pepper to taste

Olive oil or other healthy vegetable oil, as needed

½ cup garbanzo flour

1 teaspoon seasoning blend (such as Spike or Mrs. Dash)

### CUSTARD TOPPING

1 16-ounce tub silken tofu

2 tablespoons tahini

½ teaspoon salt

2 tablespoons nutritional yeast, optional

1 cup fine whole-grain breadcrumbs (see page 30)

1 cup grated mozzarella-style vegan cheese

**1.** Trim the eggplants and slice them ½ inch thick. If you don't care for the skin, you can peel it; otherwise, leave it on.

**2.** Heat the oil in a wide skillet. Add the onion and sauté over medium heat until translucent. Add the garlic and sauté until the onion starts to brown lightly. Transfer to a mixing bowl and stir in the marinara sauce, oregano, thyme, and pepper.

**3.** Combine the garbanzo flour, seasoning blend, and ½ cup water in a shallow mixing bowl and whisk until smooth.

**4.** Heat just enough oil to coat the same skillet used earlier. Dip each slice of eggplant into the garbanzo flour batter, allowing for a thin, even coat on each side. Arrange in batches in the skillet and cook on each side until golden brown. Remove to a plate lined with paper towels. Repeat until all the eggplant slices are battered and cooked.

**5.** Preheat the oven to 350° F.

**6.** Combine the tofu, tahini, salt, and optional nutritional yeast in a food processor. Process until completely smooth.

**7.** Oil a wide round or square 2-quart casserole dish. Layer the casserole as follows: half the breadcrumbs, half the marinara sauce, half the eggplant slices in one or two overlapping layers, the remaining sauce, then the remaining crumbs.

**8.** Spread the custard over the top, evenly and gently, using a flexible spatula, and finish with the grated cheese. Bake for 30 to 35 minutes, or until the top is lightly browned in spots. Let stand 10 minutes, then cut into wedges or squares to serve.

# Spring Vegetable Tart

NUT-FREE

*Puff pastry isn't the healthiest item in the world—let's just say that its ingredients are edible but not all that natural—but for special occasions, it transforms simple ingredients into something fun and festive. Check the ingredients list to be certain the brand you buy is vegan. This recipe makes two delicious, rectangular tarts that are easy on the cook and gorgeous to behold (see page vi).*

- 2 sheets frozen puff pastry
- 2 tablespoons olive oil or other healthy vegetable oil
- 1 medium-large red onion, quartered and thinly sliced
- 4 cloves garlic, minced
- 1 medium red bell pepper, cut into thin strips
- 16 slender asparagus spears, bottoms trimmed, cut into 2-inch sections
- 4 ounces baby bella or cremini mushrooms, cleaned, stemmed, and sliced
- 4 to 5 ounces baby spinach
- ⅓ cup very thinly sliced sun-dried tomatoes (oil-cured or not, as preferred)
- 2 teaspoons Italian seasoning blend, or to taste (or a combination of dried oregano, thyme, and basil)
- Salt and freshly ground pepper to taste
- 4 ounces grated nondairy mozzarella-style cheese

1. Thaw the puff pastry sheets for 45 minutes to an hour before using. Then immediately unfold carefully and arrange on two parchment-lined baking sheets.

2. Preheat the oven to 400° F.

3. Heat the oil in a large skillet or stir-fry pan. Add the onion and sauté over medium heat until translucent. Add the garlic and continue to sauté until the onion is golden.

4. Add the bell pepper, asparagus, and mushrooms to the skillet. Cover and cook for 2 to 3 minutes, lifting the lid to stir occasionally, just until the asparagus turns tender-crisp.

5. Add the spinach and dried tomatoes. Cover and cook just until the spinach wilts down, 1 minute or less. Remove from the heat and season to taste with the seasoning blend, salt, and pepper.

6. Sprinkle the grated cheese over the surface of the puff pastry. Distribute the vegetable mixture evenly over the surface of the pastry, then create a little lip by folding all four edges over just about a half inch.

7. Bake for 15 minutes, or until puffed and golden. Allow to stand for 5 minutes. Cut each into 6 sections, then serve.

**VARIATIONS:** This puff pastry recipe is eminently flexible in terms of fillings. Try broccolini or broccoli rabe in place of the asparagus. Substitute baby arugula for the baby spinach, or use half of each. If you use kale, give it a bit more time to wilt down. Or you can go really wild and substitute ramps, fiddleheads, dandelion greens, radishes and their greens—the possibilities are endless.

# Citrus Rice

**GLUTEN-FREE**

**SOY-FREE**

**Can be made NUT-FREE by eliminating optional almonds**

**8 SERVINGS**

*You'll enjoy this zesty side dish, especially if you have a microplane handy for zesting the fruit. Citrus Rice goes well with either Spring Vegetable Tart or Magnificent Moussaka. The bites of juicy orange are delightfully refreshing.*

- 1 tablespoon extra-virgin olive oil
- 1 medium onion, finely chopped
- 1⅓ cups long-grain brown rice
- 2 cups prepared vegetable broth
- ½ cup fresh orange juice (from about 2 medium oranges)
- Juice of ½ to 1 lemon, to taste
- 1 tablespoon orange zest (optional, but highly recommended)
- 1 tablespoon organic lemon zest (optional, but highly recommended)
- ½ teaspoon dried thyme
- Salt and freshly ground pepper to taste
- ¼ cup minced fresh parsley
- 3 small seedless oranges, such as clementines, peeled and sectioned
- ⅓ cup toasted slivered almonds, optional

1. Heat the oil in a large saucepan. Add the onion and sauté over medium heat until golden. Add the rice, broth, orange juice, lemon juice, optional zests, and thyme. Bring to a gentle boil, then cover and simmer until the water is absorbed, about 30 minutes.

2. If the rice isn't as tender as you'd like it, add another ½ cup broth or water and simmer until absorbed. Season to taste with salt and pepper.

3. Stir in the parsley and orange sections. Transfer to a covered serving dish, sprinkle the top with the optional almonds, and serve at once.

# A COLORFUL MEAL
# OF GLOBAL FLAVORS

Beet and Carrot Salad

Citrus-Roasted Tofu

Double Sesame–Roasted Asparagus and Cauliflower

Hungarian-Style Potatoes Paprikash
OR
Lemon, Garlic, and Rosemary–Roasted Potatoes

Dessert (pages 188–197)

# Beet and Carrot Salad

**GLUTEN-FREE**

**SOY-FREE**

Can be made **NUT-FREE** by omitting walnuts

**6 TO 8 SERVINGS**

*This classic combo, made even classier with chopped walnuts and parsley, brightens the holiday meal (see photo on page 164).*

4 medium beets (see Note)

6 medium carrots, peeled and cut into chunks

2 celery stalks, peeled and diced

2 shallots, minced, optional

¼ cup finely chopped walnuts

¼ cup minced fresh parsley

Several mint leaves, sliced, as desired to taste

Juice of ½ to 1 lemon, to taste

1 tablespoon agave nectar

Pinch of salt

Freshly ground pepper to taste

1. Cook or microwave the beets until about half done—you should be able to pierce them, but with a bit of resistance. When cool enough to handle, cut into chunks.

2. Grate the beets and carrots using the grating blade of a food processor.

3. Combine with the remaining ingredients in a serving bowl and stir together. Serve at once or cover and store in the refrigerator until serving.

**NOTE:** You can leave the beets raw, if you'd like; simply peel and cut into chunks before grating. I think that partially cooking them brings out more of their sweet flavor.

# Citrus-Roasted Tofu

**GLUTEN-FREE**

Can be made **NUT-FREE** by omitting almonds

**6 TO 8 SERVINGS**

*Tofu fans will love the light, citrusy flavors that permeate this elegant dish.*

2   14- to 16-ounce tubs extra-firm tofu

**ORANGE MARINADE**

Juice of 1 orange

Juice of 1 lemon

2   tablespoons reduced-sodium soy sauce

½   cup orange marmalade

1   tablespoons olive oil or other healthy vegetable oil

1   tablespoon yellow mustard

½   teaspoon dried tarragon

Several grindings of black pepper

1   tablespoon olive oil or other healthy vegetable oil

8   to 10 baby carrots, quartered lengthwise

1   to 2 cloves garlic, minced, optional

⅓   cup slivered almonds

¼   teaspoon curry powder

¼   cup minced fresh parsley

**1.** Preheat the oven to 425° F.

**2.** Cut each block of tofu into 8 slices (about ½ inch thick) crosswise. Blot well between several layers of paper towel or a clean tea towel.

**3.** Combine the ingredients for the marinade in a small mixing bowl and whisk together.

**4.** Arrange the tofu in a single layer on a parchment-lined roasting pan. Spoon the marinade generously over the surface of the tofu. Roast for 15 minutes, or until the tofu begins to turn golden.

**5.** Carefully flip the tofu with a spatula, and spoon more marinade over the surface (you will likely have a bit left over). Roast for 15 minutes longer, or until the tofu is firm and golden.

**6.** Meanwhile, heat the oil in a small skillet. Add the carrots, garlic, and almonds, and sauté over medium heat, stirring frequently, until both are golden. Stir in the curry powder and remove from the heat.

**7.** When the tofu is done, transfer to a rectangular or oval serving platter or two, depending on their size, with the slices slightly overlapping one another. Sprinkle the carrot-almond mixture evenly over the surface, topped by the parsley. Serve at once, passing around the additional marinade.

# Double Sesame–Roasted Asparagus and Cauliflower

**GLUTEN-FREE**

**SOY-FREE**

**NUT-FREE (if seeds are safe for you)**

## 8 SERVINGS

*Sometimes simple can be sublime, as in the case of this very basic side dish. Roasting brings out the flavors of these two companionable vegetables with little embellishment.*

12 ounces slender asparagus

1 small head cauliflower, cut into very small florets

1½ tablespoons olive oil or other healthy vegetable oil

1½ tablespoon dark sesame oil

1 tablespoon lemon juice

1 to 2 tablespoons sesame seeds, to taste

Salt and freshly ground pepper to taste

**1.** Preheat the oven or toaster oven to 425° F.

**2.** Trim any woody bottoms from the asparagus, and peel the bottom halves of the spears if needed. Combine the asparagus with the cauliflower in a foil- or parchment-lined baking pan.

**3.** Combine the oils and lemon juice in a small bowl and whisk together. Drizzle over the vegetables and mix together.

**4.** Roast for 15 to 20 minutes, stirring occasionally, until just tender and golden. Remove from the oven and season with salt and pepper. Transfer the vegetables to a serving plate. Sprinkle with sesame seeds and serve at once. Don't worry if the dish cools; it's just as good warm or at room temperature.

# Hungarian-Style Potatoes Paprikash

**GLUTEN-FREE**

**SOY-FREE**

**NUT-FREE**

**8 OR MORE SERVINGS**

*From the potato-loving Slavic cuisine, here's a simple potato dish to fall in love with.*

8 medium-large Yukon Gold or red-skinned potatoes

2 tablespoons olive oil or other healthy vegetable oil

1 large onion, finely chopped

3 to 4 cloves garlic, minced

2 medium green bell peppers, cut into narrow strips

4 medium firm, ripe tomatoes, diced

1 tablespoon sweet paprika

½ teaspoon caraway seeds, optional

Salt and freshly ground pepper to taste

1. Cook, bake, or microwave the potatoes until about half done. A knife should pierce one, with a bit of resistance.

2. When cool enough to handle, peel the potatoes and cut into large dice.

3. Heat the oil in a large skillet. Add the onion and sauté over medium-low heat until translucent. Add the garlic and bell peppers and continue to sauté until all are golden.

4. Add the potatoes, tomatoes, paprika, optional caraway seeds, and ½ cup water. Raise the heat and cook until the liquid comes to a simmer, then cook over low heat for 8 to 10 minutes, or until the potatoes are done and the liquid thickens into a sauce. Season with salt and pepper and serve.

# Lemon, Garlic, and Rosemary–Roasted Potatoes

**GLUTEN-FREE**

**SOY-FREE**

**NUT-FREE**

## 8 OR MORE SERVINGS

*Roasted potatoes, flavored with rosemary, were a traditional dish of the old Roman Easter. Here is a contemporary interpretation of this dish.*

10 to 12 medium-small Yukon Gold potatoes, unpeeled

3 tablespoon extra-virgin olive oil

Juice of 1 lemon

1 to 2 teaspoons organic lemon zest, optional

4 to 6 cloves garlic, thinly sliced

Leaves from 2 to 3 sprigs rosemary, to taste

Salt and freshly ground pepper to taste

1. Preheat the oven to 425° F.

2. Scrub the potatoes well and cut away any black spots. Cut them into quarters lengthwise.

3. Combine the potatoes in a mixing bowl with the olive oil, lemon juice, and optional lemon zest and toss together.

4. Transfer potato mixture into a roasting pan. Roast for 20 minutes, stirring after 10 minutes, then add the garlic and rosemary. Roast for 5 to 10 minutes longer, or until the potatoes are golden and crisp.

5. Transfer to a serving dish, season with salt and pepper, and serve.

# CHOCOLATE WITH COMPASSION

Chocolates—especially chocolate bunnies—are an intrinsic part of what makes Easter great fun. And to sweeten the deal, it's now known that chocolate—especially the dark variety—has some health benefits as well. Eating chocolate not only gives immediate pleasure to the palate, but boosts serotonin and endorphins (the body's feel-good and falling-in-love hormones). Other studies have claimed that chocolate is good for the heart and boasts cancer-fighting antioxidants. But let's face it; chocolate lovers love it because it's so very delectable, not because it may help fight disease sometime down the road.

Chocolate does have its dark side, though, and here I'm not referring to the semisweet or bittersweet varieties. Some major chocolate corporations don't source their chocolate carefully. What this means is that their cocoa comes from areas, particularly in West Africa, where human trafficking and child labor—and even child slave labor—are prevalent. Google the words "chocolate" and "slavery" together and, unfortunately, you'll get an eyeful.

Many if not most organic chocolate companies are Fair Trade, ensuring that those who grow, import, and distribute the products adhere to practices that do not force cocoa growers to accept substandard wages and working conditions. Green and Black's, Newman's Own, and Rapunzel are among those companies that distribute Fair Trade chocolates.

If you don't want your children (as well as the children of all ages in your circle) to miss out on chocolate Easter bunnies, there's good news. The Easter Bunny may be mythical, but organic, vegan Fair Trade chocolate Easter bunnies really do exist. Make sure you leave yourself some extra time if placing orders online, which is where you'll most easily find these types of chocolate treats.

# DESSERTS AND TREATS

Basic Vegan Muffins with Fruity Variations

❧

Classic Carrot Cupcakes

❧

Chocolate-Orange Cake

❧

Strawberry Snack Cake

❧

Lemon Coconut Bars

❧

Early Spring Fruit Bowl

# Basic Vegan Muffins
# with Fruity Variations

**Can be made SOY-FREE by using applesauce or coconut yogurt**

**Can be made NUT-FREE by omitting nuts from the variations**

**MAKES ONE DOZEN**

*These fruit-filled muffins are just the thing for breakfast, especially if you're anticipating a big Easter dinner. And why not fill your baskets with some delicious muffins instead of the usual candy and snacks? This basic muffin recipe— one I've been using for years—is my favorite. The beauty of it is that it can be varied in myriad ways. Suggestions follow, but feel free to vary them any way you'd like.*

2  cups whole wheat pastry flour

2  teaspoons baking powder

1  teaspoon baking soda

⅓  cup natural granulated sugar

1  cup vanilla nondairy yogurt (soy or coconut), or applesauce

2  tablespoons safflower oil

2  teaspoons vanilla extract

⅓  cup rice milk

1. Preheat the oven to 350° F.

2. Combine the first 4 (dry) ingredients in a mixing bowl and stir together.

3. Make a well in the center of the flour mixture and pour in the yogurt, oil, vanilla, and enough rice milk to make a smooth, stiff batter. Stir together until thoroughly combined.

4. Stir in the additional ingredients of your choice (options follow), then divide the batter among 12 foil-lined muffin tins.

5. Bake for 20 to 25 minutes, or until the tops of the muffins are golden and a knife inserted into the center of one tests clean. When cool enough to handle, transfer the muffins to a plate or rack to cool. Serve warm or at room temperature.

**FRUITY VARIATIONS:**

**APPLE MUFFINS:** Peel and dice 2 medium-size sweet apples to stir into the batter. Add ½ cup raisins or dried cranberries and/ or ¼ cup finely chopped walnuts—and at least 1 teaspoon of cinnamon, of course!

**BANANA–CHOCOLATE CHIP MUFFINS:** Add 1 large chopped banana, ¾ to 1 cup semisweet chocolate chips or mini-chips, and ¼ cup chopped nuts if you like, as well as a pinch of nutmeg.

*(Continued on next page)*

**LEMON-BERRY MUFFINS:** Easter time is a bit too early for fresh berries, though in some warmer areas, strawberries might be making their appearance. Add 1 cup fresh or frozen berries (small wild frozen blueberries work particularly well in muffins), or 1 cup very sweet chopped fresh strawberries, or the equivalent of drained, frozen strawberries. I like berry muffins that are nice and lemony. If you do, too, substitute lemon juice for the rice milk in the master recipe and add 1 tablespoon or more of lemon zest (make sure to use organic lemon for its zest).

**PEAR AND DRIED FRUIT MUFFINS:** Add 1 peeled and finely diced ripe pear and ½ cup dried fruit—golden or dark raisins, or chopped dried apricots or mango. Add a teaspoon or two of grated fresh or jarred ginger to the batter, or a tablespoon or two of minced crystallized ginger.

**PIÑA COLADA MUFFINS:** Add ¾ cup finely chopped fresh or canned (well-drained) pineapple. Use coconut yogurt rather than soy yogurt or applesauce. If you'd like to get really fancy, add ¼ cup grated coconut and/or ¼ cup finely chopped macadamia nuts.

# Classic Carrot Cupcakes

**NUT-FREE**

**Can be made SOY-FREE without cream cheese frosting option**

**MAKES 1 DOZEN CUPCAKES WITH FROSTING**

*Carrot cupcakes are a classic Easter treat, and how nice that they're so easily veganized. These beauties are just packed with carrot goodness.*

2 cups whole wheat pastry or spelt flour

1½ teaspoons baking powder

1 teaspoon baking soda

2 teaspoons cinnamon

½ teaspoon allspice

½ cup maple syrup

¾ cup applesauce

¼ cup safflower oil

2 teaspoons vanilla extract

¼ cup plain or vanilla nondairy milk, as needed

2 cups firmly packed grated carrot

½ cup dark or golden raisins, optional

### CREAM CHEESE FROSTING, OPTIONAL

⅔ cup vegan cream cheese

⅓ cup powdered sugar

⅓ cup finely chopped walnuts, optional

1. Preheat the oven to 350° F.

2. Combine the first 5 ingredients in a large mixing bowl and stir together.

3. Make a well in the center of the flour mixture and add the syrup, applesauce, oil, and vanilla. Stir until well combined, then add enough nondairy milk to make a smooth and slightly stiff batter.

4. Stir in the grated carrots and optional raisins. Divide among 12 foil-lined muffin tins. Bake for 25 minutes, or until a small knife inserted in the center of a muffin comes out clean. Set the muffins on a rack or on plates to cool.

5. To make the optional frosting, combine the ingredients in a food processor fitted with the metal blade. Process until creamy and smooth. Use a flexible cake spatula to remove from the container. Spread on the cupcakes once they've cooled to room temperature, then sprinkle with the optional walnuts.

**VARIATION:** If you want to make these extra adorable, sauté 12 small, slender baby carrots in a bit of non-hydrogenated margarine and agave nectar or maple syrup until tender-crisp. Arrange one carrot atop the cream cheese frosting on each cupcake, and add a tiny sprig of dill at the top of each.

# Chocolate-Orange Cake

**Can be made SOY-FREE by using coconut yogurt**
**NUT-FREE (if you're not allergic to coconut)**

## 16 SERVINGS

*This gorgeous Bundt cake is a bit fancier than those I usually make, so I was very happy that Susan Voisin contributed this exquisite recipe. This cake's WOW! factor is multiplied by the fact that it's nearly fat-free.*

1½  cups unbleached flour

1½  cups whole wheat flour
(preferably white whole wheat)

1½  cups natural granulated sugar

2  teaspoons baking soda

1  teaspoon salt

½  cup dry unsweetened cocoa
powder

1  teaspoon cinnamon

¾  cup nondairy yogurt (soy
or coconut)

1  teaspoon vanilla

2  tablespoons balsamic vinegar

½  cup fresh orange juice

2  tablespoons grated orange peel

### CHOCOLATE ICING

½  cup powdered sugar

1  tablespoon dry unsweetened
cocoa powder

2  teaspoons orange juice

¼  teaspoon vanilla extract

Extra orange juice as needed

### ORANGE ICING

½  cup powdered sugar

1  teaspoon orange juice

¼  teaspoon vanilla extract

Extra orange juice as needed

1. Spray a Bundt cake pan with nonstick spray and dust it lightly with unsweetened cocoa. Preheat oven to 350° F.

2. Combine the flours, sugar, baking soda, salt, cocoa, and cinnamon in a large mixing bowl. Add the yogurt, vanilla, balsamic vinegar, orange juice, and 1½ cups water. Beat by hand or with a mixer on low speed just until well combined, about 1 to 2 minutes. Stir in the grated orange peel, and pour into the prepared pan.

3. Bake for about 30 to 40 minutes, until a toothpick inserted in the middle comes out clean. Cool in the pan for 10 minutes and then invert it onto a serving platter and cool completely.

4. When the cake is cool, make the icings. For each icing, mix the ingredients in separate small bowls. One half teaspoon at a time, stir in enough extra orange juice to make a drizzling consistency. Drizzle the chocolate icing over the cake, wait a few minutes for it to set, and then drizzle the orange icing.

# Strawberry Snack Cake

Can be made **SOY-FREE** by using non-soy yogurt and nondairy milk

Can be made **NUT-FREE** by avoiding almond milk

**MAKES 9 SQUARES**

*On the East Coast, fresh strawberries start to make their appearance in April (although, admittedly, most are shipped from sunny California). They are used to great advantage in this easy, tasty little cake contributed by Susan Voisin.*

1¾  cups cake flour

¾  cup natural granulated sugar

1  teaspoon baking soda

¼  teaspoon baking powder

½  teaspoon salt

⅓  cup nondairy yogurt (soy or coconut)

½  teaspoon vanilla extract

½  cup vanilla nondairy milk

2  tablespoons lemon juice

**STRAWBERRY TOPPING**

1  pound strawberries, stemmed and sliced

2  tablespoons cornstarch

½  cup natural granulated sugar

1. Combine the flour, sugar, baking soda, baking powder, and salt in a mixing bowl. Add the yogurt, vanilla, nondairy milk, lemon juice, and ½ cup water. Mix until just blended–don't overmix. Pour into an oiled 8 x 8–inch pan and bake at 350° F until a knife inserted into the center tests clean, about 30 minutes. Remove and allow to cool completely.

2. Combine the strawberries, cornstarch, sugar, and ¼ cup water in a saucepan. Cook over medium-high heat until sauce boils and thickens. Spread over top of cake. May be served warm or chilled.

# Lemon Coconut Bars

**GLUTEN-FREE (oats are generally considered gluten-free, but to be on the safe side, use quinoa flakes)**

**NUT-FREE (if coconut is safe for you)**

### MAKES ABOUT 24 BARS

*A selection of Easter treats wouldn't be complete without something lemony. And this one is not only lemony but gluten-free and really easy—an unbeatable combination.*

1½ cup quinoa flakes or quick-cooking (not instant) oats

½ cup natural granulated sugar

1 cup unsweetened coconut flakes

½ cup Earth Balance or other non-hydrogenated margarine

1 cup rice milk

1 cup coconut or soy creamer

½ cup lemon juice

½ cup natural granulated sugar

⅓ cup cornstarch

Coconut flakes for topping

Powdered sugar for topping, optional

**1.** Preheat the oven to 350° F.

**2.** Combine the quinoa flakes, sugar, coconut flakes, and margarine in a food processor. Pulse on and off until the Earth Balance is completely integrated into the dry mixture.

**3.** Line a 9 x 13–inch baking pan with baking parchment long enough to go up the sides of the pan. Once the dessert is cooled, you'll be grabbing these ends to lift everything out of the pan.

**4.** Press the mixture evenly into the parchment-lined pan using the back of a spatula. Bake for 15 to 17 minutes, or until the sides begin to turn golden.

**5.** Pour ½ cup of the rice milk into a small bowl. Pour the rest into a medium saucepan, along with the creamer, lemon juice, and sugar. Bring the mixture to a simmer.

**6.** Combine the reserved rice milk with the cornstarch and whisk until completely dissolved. Once the mixture in the saucepan comes to a simmer, turn the heat to low and pour the dissolved cornstarch in, whisking constantly. Cook just until the mixture is thickened, whisking continuously and vigorously to avoid lumps—this takes almost no time at all.

**7.** Pour the lemon mixture over the baked crust in the pan. Sprinkle with extra grated coconut and the optional powdered sugar. Allow it to cool to room temperature, then refrigerate for at least 2 hours to firm up.

**8.** When ready to serve, grab the sides of the parchment and lift the entire thing out of the pan. Place on a cutting board. Use a sharp knife to cut into bars, cutting into 4 sections lengthwise and 6 sections crosswise to make 24 bars. If you'd like, you can cut smaller sections.

# Early Spring Fruit Bowl

**GLUTEN-FREE**

**Can be made SOY-FREE by using coconut yogurt option**

**NUT-FREE (if coconut is safe for you, otherwise choose soy yogurt or omit yogurt altogether)**

**8 TO 10 SERVINGS**

*The lush fruits of summer may be a couple of months off, but there are plenty of ways to make a lovely fruit salad any time of year. An easy fruit salad served with some fine vegan chocolates is a wonderful way to end a meal if you're not inclined to bake.*

2  Bosc pears, quartered, cored, and diced

2  Granny Smith apples, cored and diced

2  small oranges, sectioned and seeded

1  to 2 cups green or red seedless grapes

1  to 2 cups fresh or unsweetened canned pineapple chunks

½  cup sliced dried apricots or other dried fruit (dates, mission figs, etc.)

1  6-ounce container nondairy yogurt (soy or coconut), optional

1. Combine all the ingredients in a serving bowl. Serve chilled or at room temperature.

# CHAPTER FIVE

# INDEPENDENCE DAY AND SUMMER ENTERTAINING

*The ultimate vegan grilling guide, plus lots of cool summer dishes for easy entertaining*

When William Shakespeare wrote, "Summer's lease hath all too short a date," he spoke for nearly everyone. Who among us doesn't have the sense that this season seems to disappear in a flash? It's not so much about the climate—summer heat is something many of us can do without—but the sense of greater ease, less hurry, and long, sunny days is what makes the season so appealing. Summertime often brings more opportunities than other seasons to take the time to visit friends and family. And for those of us who are fruit and veggie worshippers, what better time to enjoy a plant-based diet, when the widest array of splendid produce is in season?

Although summer cooking and entertaining are about so much more than grilling, this chapter focuses on outdoor food preparation because it's an area where vegans and vegetarians can

**Fresh Corn and Tomatillo Salsa, see page 229**

sometimes feel left out, especially at Fourth of July gatherings. This has changed quite a lot in the last decade or so, as even omnivores have discovered how amazing grilled vegetables can taste. Still, developing our own favorites on our own grills is a necessity for vegans and vegetarians, since eating foods prepared on the same grill with meat isn't an option. Unique culinary fireworks can be created with alternative protein foods and produce; this chapter will serve as a resource.

In addition to an extensive grilling guide and a good number of recipes for grilled foods, you'll also find a selection of cool dishes for nearly effortless entertaining. These are great summertime recipes for company anytime and for warm-weather parties and potlucks.

## THE VEGAN GRILL: A BASIC GUIDE TO GRILLING
## PLANT-BASED PROTEINS AND VEGETABLES

I'm going to admit up front that I'm not a grilling expert. But that's actually very good news for all of you who aren't pros either. Why? Because if I can grill, anyone can. When I first developed some basic grilling guidelines for *Vegetarian Celebrations*, many more years back than I care to admit, I had a somewhat basic charcoal unit. For a few years, it served me in good stead. I took a hiatus from grilling when it came time to retire this particular barbecue. When I wanted to revisit outdoor grilling I found myself less willing to stand over hot flaming charcoals—and even less excited about puttering around with a gas unit.

So, I purchased a compact yet roomy (and very reasonably priced) electric grill. Okay, I know that true grill aficionados might not feel that this is "real" grilling, but it does the job of quick outdoor high-heat cooking (with those nifty grill marks). It's a perfect choice for the grill-shy, for anyone with a small porch or patio, and for apartment dwellers. This kind of grill doesn't send overpowering fumes wafting into your neighbors' domain—and anything that makes summer food preparation easier and more fun also makes it more inclusionary.

In general, grilling is more art than science. You need to experiment at first to become familiar with the equipment you're using, whether it's a fancy gas-powered unit, a classic charcoal or electric grill, or a simple barbecue pit in the ground. Each unit (not counting the homemade pit) comes with enough information to get you started on the basic techniques. Since grilling is an area that many vegans and vegetarians have traditionally avoided, this chapter will present straightforward recipes and tips. Once you've tried some of these, chances are you'll want to experiment with your own ideas and combinations.

Since cut vegetables and protein foods are more likely to fall through the grates of anything but an electric grill, you would do well to look into purchasing a grill basket or grill pan for ease and convenience.

## GRILLING PROTEIN FOODS: TOFU, TEMPEH, AND SEITAN

These plant-based proteins have a porous texture that quickly soaks up tasty marinades. All three need only a short time to brown once on the grill, and are versatile and adaptable, yielding numerous easy ways to prepare them. Some notes of particular interest about this protein triumvirate:

TOFU: Because of its consistency, tofu needs to be handled tenderly on the grill. For regular tofu, choose extra-firm, and press it well before marinating. If you'll be using tofu for kebabs, cut it into ¾-inch-thick slices. For any other purpose, cut it into ½-inch-thick slices. Arrange the slices on several layers of paper towels or a clean, absorbent tea towel. Cover with another layer of paper towels or another tea towel, then with a cutting board. Place a weight, such as a heavy skillet, on the board for 20 to 30 minutes. Tofu to be used for kebabs may then be diced. If you're using it for other recipes, prepare the tofu as directed.

Baked tofu works well on the grill. You don't need to press it beforehand, as it's much firmer and drier than the tub variety. Just slice it ½ inch thick, or into large cubes for kebabs. Because of its firmness, baked tofu works very well on skewers.

⬤ TO GRILL: Cut blocks of regular tofu into ½-inch-thick slices crosswise to make rectangular slabs. Press as directed above. Pour enough Sweet and Savory Grilling Sauce (page 224), Teriyaki Marinade (page 225), or Hoisin Marinade (page 225) to coat the bottom of a shallow dish. Arrange the tofu slabs in it, then spoon some additional marinade over the slices. Marinate for 30 minutes to 1 hour.

Cut baked tofu into rectangular, ½-inch-thick slabs and brush both sides with enough marinade to lightly coat.

Prepare the grill. Grill the tofu slices on each side until nicely browned. The time will vary depending on the type of grill being used, but figure on about 5 to 7 minutes per side. Arrange the grilled tofu slices on a serving platter and top with additional marinade, or pass the marinade around with the tofu. Each tub of regular tofu will serve 3 to 4; each 8-ounce package of baked tofu will serve 2 to 3.

**TEMPEH:** There are two kinds of vegans in this world: those who love tempeh, and those who want nothing to do with it. If you like tempeh, you'll love it grilled. If you don't, grilling it probably won't change your mind. Tempeh is a practically ready-to-eat food and needs no preparation other than cutting and marinating. Generally, tempeh should be cut into ½-inch-thick slices crosswise. You can try cutting it into squarish shapes for kebabs, but it can sometimes crumble apart when skewered, so it's not ideal for that use. I don't find that marinating tempeh before grilling makes much difference, so you can skip this step.

**TO GRILL:** You can cut tempeh one of two ways for the grill. Cut each 8- to 10-ounce package into ½-inch-thick slices crosswise. Combine in a mixing bowl with enough marinade to lightly coat it. Or, cut each package of tempeh in half crosswise, then cut each slab in half through the thickness to get 4 thinner, rectangular slabs. Brush both sides with enough marinade to lightly coat.

Prepare the grill. Grill slices in a grill basket if you're using anything other than an electric grill, turning them several times until nicely charred, about 10 minutes. Or grill the slabs on each side until nicely charred, about 5 minutes per side.

**SEITAN:** Before marinating seitan (cooked wheat gluten), it should be drained well and blotted briefly with paper towels. Grilling is a great boon to seitan; its meaty texture allows it to crisp up nicely on the outside while remaining tender and moist on the inside. I've found that marinating seitan before grilling doesn't make a whole lot of difference in terms of flavor and texture.

**TO GRILL:** Seitan comes in rather irregular-shaped pieces, so you don't get nice squares as you do with tofu and tempeh, but no matter; it may not be pretty, but grilled seitan is fantastic. Cut the seitan into large bite-size chunks. Combine them in a mixing bowl with enough Teriyaki Marinade (page 225), Hoisin Marinade (page 225), or (my favorite) Sweet and Savory Grilling Sauce (page 224) to coat. No matter which marinade you choose, you may want to cut back on the soy sauce in the recipes, since seitan is already a bit salty to begin with.

Prepare the grill. Put seitan in a grill basket if you're using anything other than an electric grill, turning it several times until the seitan is nicely charred, about 10 minutes total, or until the outside is dark brown and crisp.

**TWO FINAL NOTES:**

○ Don't send any of these proteins to the grill over-saturated with marinade—they'll char more quickly, without making a big mess, if you give them a light coating. Once off the grill, they are nice when served with extra marinade to pass around.

○ I highly recommend allowing regular tofu to marinate for 30 minutes to an hour before grilling, since it absorbs flavors beautifully; however, marinating baked tofu, tempeh, and seitan doesn't make a great deal of difference to their flavors and textures, so it isn't necessary.

## IDEAS FOR VEGGIE KEBAB COMBOS

Here is a trio of compatible combinations for skewered veggies. Let these suggestions inspire your own ideas, using the marinade of your choice on pages 224–226. My favorite marinade for just about every veggie kebab combo is Teriyaki Marinade (page 225).

○ Parboiled or microwaved baby onions, tomato chunks or cherry tomatoes, green bell peppers, firm-cooked or microwaved potato or sweet potato chunks.

○ Yellow summer squash, broccoli florets (lightly steam first), mushrooms, and tofu or seitan.

○ Zucchini, eggplant, cherry tomatoes, green or red bell peppers.

# VEGETABLE KEBABS

Colorful kebabs are a festive way to serve grilled vegetables and are quick and easy to prepare. Exact quantities of vegetables and specific recipes are unnecessary and, in fact, detract from the fun of improvising. Just keep these general guidelines in mind:

**use** flat-bladed skewers rather than rounded ones because they hold the vegetables better and keep them from rotating as you turn them on the grill.

**consult** the Guide to Grilling Vegetables (pages 206–210) for general information on grilling specific kinds of vegetables.

**use** from 3 to 5 different vegetables, with a variety of colors.

**prepare** 2 skewers of vegetables per serving.

**cut** vegetables into bite-size pieces, not larger than approximately 1-inch chunks, but better larger than too small.

**combine** vegetables that have the same cooking times. Otherwise, a skewer containing, for instance, cherry tomatoes and baby onions or onion chunks, will result in the tomatoes becoming overcooked before the onions have lost their raw taste. To work around this, harder vegetables can be steamed or microwaved and combined with softer vegetables.

**add** tofu or seitan, both of which are compatible with any combination of vegetables, to make main-dish kebabs. (Tempeh is a bit trickier to skewer.)

**choose** one of the marinades on pages 224–226, according to the flavors that are most compatible with the rest of the meal you are serving. Turn vegetables carefully on the grill, and cook until they are charred to your liking. Most kebabs on most grills should be done in about 10 to 12 minutes total time.

**assemble** the kebabs on the skewers, then baste them with the marinade of choice with a basting brush.

The great flavors of fresh summer vegetables become even more extraordinary when exposed to the high heat of a grill. A slight sweetness emerges, which, combined with slight charring, results in sensational flavors. In this list of good-to-grill vegetables I give approximate cooking times, since they are highly variable depending on the kind of grill you use, the cut or thickness of the vegetables, and even the kind of marinade you use. Whatever your choice, be sure to monitor the process carefully.

Depending on the theme of your meal, you may choose any of the marinades on pages 224–226. Olive Oil–Lemon Marinade (page 226) is the most neutral and all-purpose of the marinades. If you prefer the flavor of the vegetables alone, you can just brush or toss them with olive oil. Teriyaki Marinade (page 225) gives vegetables a delicious Asian spin and, if you use a gentle hand, isn't overpowering. Hoisin Marinade (page 225) is a bit more assertive than teriyaki, but is wonderful on veggies that can stand up to it, like eggplant and green beans. I don't recommend Sweet and Savory Grilling Sauce (page 224) for most individually grilled vegetables, since it tends to overpower their flavors. It is good, though, used with vegetable kebabs that are combined with tofu or seitan.

**BELL PEPPERS:** Cut peppers into large chunks. Brush on both sides with marinade of your choice (pages 224–226) or simply with olive oil. Grill on both sides until nicely charred, about 6 to 8 minutes total. Once cool enough to handle, they can be cut into smaller pieces, depending on their use.

Bell peppers are also a standard ingredient in vegetable kebabs; simply cut into 1- to 1½-inch squares and skewer through the center.

**BOK CHOY:** Baby bok choy is a perfect veggie for the grill. If your little bok choys are really small, simply toss them with Teriyaki Marinade (page 225) or Olive Oil–Lemon Marinade (page 226) and put them whole on the grill. Turn several times until nicely charred, about 8 to 10 minutes total. If the baby bok choy you're using is of the plumper variety, cut each in half lengthwise through the thickest part and grill each side for about 4 minutes, or until nicely charred.

**BROCCOLI:** Cut broccoli crowns into large florets, about 3 inches long, including the stem. Steam the broccoli until bright green and just barely crisp-tender. Rinse under cool water. Toss with Olive Oil–Lemon Marinade (page 226) or Teriyaki Marinade (page 225). Grill, turning frequently, for about 6 to 8 minutes total, or until charred to your liking. Broccolini is good on the grill, too, as is broccoli rabe. Cut these into long spears and follow the directions as for broccoli.

**CABBAGE:** When seared on the grill, the humble cabbage becomes quite a delicacy. Red cabbage lends itself particularly well to grilling, but if green cabbage is what you have on hand, that works well, too. Use a small head of cabbage. Cut it into quarters through the stem end, leaving it intact so the leaves stay together. Brush the open sides with olive oil or Olive Oil–Lemon Marinade (page 226). Grill on each open side for 4 to 5 minutes, or until nicely charred.

**CARROTS:** Carrots are often overlooked when it comes to grilling, but they are a treat. Peel and cut them into 4- or 5-inch lengths, then cut them in half lengthwise. Brush the carrots on both sides with a marinade of your choice (pages 224–226). Roll the carrots around on the grill until they're lightly charred, about 7 to 10 minutes total.

**CORN:** Peel and husk as many ears of corn as needed and soak them in cold water for an hour or so. Wrap each ear of corn individually in aluminum foil. Grill them for 20 to 30 minutes, turning the cobs every few minutes, or until they're light charred (you'll have to open the foil using oven mitts to peek occasionally). Alternatively, the corn can be microwaved until barely done, then set on the grill and turned a few times until lightly browned on all sides.

**EGGPLANT AND JAPANESE EGGPLANT:** Summer is the time to use the season's smaller eggplants, which have fewer seeds and are less bitter. White, red-and-white, and the standard dark purple varieties all come in more compact form in the summer. Cut eggplants into ½-inch-thick slices. Brush on both sides with the marinade of your choice (pages 224–226). Grill on both sides until tender and nicely browned, about 5 to 7 minutes on each side.

Japanese eggplants may simply be stemmed and cut in half lengthwise. Brush both sides with marinade. Grill on both sides until tender and the fleshy parts are lightly browned, about 6 to 8 minutes total. No matter the variety of eggplant, my favorite marinade for it is Hoisin Marinade (page 225), but they're also good with Teriyaki Marinade (page 225). If you'd like a more neutral flavor, Olive Oil–Lemon Marinade (page 226) is the way to go.

**GREEN BEANS:** These are such a treat, especially when barbecue season dovetails with the availability of seasonal, local green beans. Toss raw green beans with marinade. My favorite for green beans is Teriyaki Marinade (page 225), but Olive Oil–Lemon Marinade (page 226) works well, too. Grill the beans, gently rolling them with tongs to expose all sides to the coals for about 7 to 10 minutes total, or until charred to your liking. If you're using anything other than an electric grill, you will probably want to put the green beans in a grill basket.

**MUSHROOMS:** Mushrooms are delicious grilled individually or used in kebabs. Choose larger mushrooms, wipe them clean, and trim away the stems. Toss the mushrooms with marinade (pages 224–226). If you're using anything other than an electric grill, you might want to place smaller mushrooms in a grill basket; portabella mushrooms, however, can go right on the grill. Grill for 5 or 6 minutes total, or until charred to your liking, turning frequently. Brush the mushrooms with additional marinade if need be, since they tend to dry out quickly.

**ONIONS:** Different types and sizes of onions call for different treatments on the grill. Peel and cut large onions into ½-inch-thick slices. Brush both sides with Olive Oil–Lemon Marinade (page 226). Grill the onion slices on both sides until tender and charred to your liking, about 10 minutes total. Red and sweet Vidalia onions are particularly delicious prepared this way.

For kebabs, parboil or microwave tiny onions until about half done (or until a skewer can pierce them, but with a bit of resistance).

**POTATOES:** Potatoes, whether large or small, should be precooked or microwaved until they're about half done. If time allows, let potatoes cool before cutting and grilling them; this helps them hold their shape. Cut large potatoes in thick slices and brush both sides or toss them with olive oil, Olive Oil–Lemon Marinade (page 226), or Sweet and Savory Marinade (page 224). Grill on both sides until nicely browned, about 7 to 10 minutes total.

Cut tiny new potatoes in half and toss them with enough Olive Oil–Lemon Marinade to coat lightly. Place them in a grill basket and grill until nicely browned, tossing the potatoes every couple of minutes or so, about 8 minutes total.

**RADICCHIO:** Cut a head of radicchio into quarters, leaving the stem end intact. Brush the radicchio with Olive Oil–Lemon Marinade (page 226). Grill on each cut side, for 4 to 5 minutes, or until lightly charred.

**SCALLIONS:** Whole grilled scallions are quite tasty, but must be watched carefully and removed from the grill before the green parts get too charred. Brush the scallions with Olive Oil–Lemon Marinade (page 226) or Teriyaki Marinade (page 225) and set them on the grill for about 3 to 5 minutes total, or until they begin to brown.

**SUMMER SQUASHES:** Summer squashes are excellent candidates for the grill, since their not-too-hard, not-too-soft raw texture yields great results. Tiny zucchini or yellow summer squash can be cut in half lengthwise. Regular-size squashes can be cut into long diagonal slices. Cut delicately flavored pattypan squashes crosswise into ¼-inch-thick slices. Toss them (or slices of any other kind of summer squash, for that matter) with Olive Oil–Lemon Marinade (page 226) or Teriyaki Marinade (page 225) and grill both sides until charred to your liking, about 7 to 10 minutes total.

**SWEET POTATOES:** Although they're not a particularly summery vegetable, sweet potatoes are so good on the grill. Microwave them in their skins until they're about half done. When the sweet potatoes are cool enough to handle, cut them into ¾-inch-thick slices. Letting them cool before cutting and grilling helps ensure that they'll hold their shape. Combine the slices in a bowl with the marinade of your choice; I think sweet potatoes are particularly delicious with Hoisin Marinade (page 225). Grill the slices on both sides until they're nicely browned, about 7 to 10 minutes total.

**TOMATOES:** Tomatoes tend to get soft very quickly on the grill, and they're tricky to turn, but the results are tasty and worth the effort. For really good summer tomatoes, I like to stick with the simple taste of Olive Oil–Lemon Marinade (page 226).

Slice large, firm tomatoes at least ½ inch thick or cut plum tomatoes in half lengthwise and brush lightly with marinade. Grill the slices on both sides until the edges brown, about 4 to 6 minutes total. Red or yellow cherry or grape tomatoes are excellent for kebabs, and don't require any special preparation before grilling. I don't recommend setting them right on the grill on their own, however. No matter what kind of grill you use, you'll want to use a grill basket for tomatoes.

# GRILLED DISHES

Grilled Eggplant Teriyaki

❧

Grilled Eggplant Curry

❧

Grilled Pepperonata with Vegan Sausage

❧

Grilled Ratatouille

❧

Grilled Golden Potatoes with Parsley-Cucumber Sauce

❧

Triple-Protein Mixed Grill with Sweet Potatoes

❧

Grilled Pizzas with Tapenade and Chard

❧

Grilled Summer Squash with Chickpeas and Artichokes

❧

Grilled Tempeh with Green Beans and Pineapple

❧

Grilled Pineapple

❧

Spicy Grilled Green Beans with Walnuts

# Grilled Eggplant Teriyaki

**GLUTEN-FREE (make sure the soy sauce used in making the marinades is gluten-free)**

**NUT-FREE (if seeds are safe for you, otherwise omit sesame seeds)**

**6 SERVINGS**

*Eggplant and grills are just made for one another. Here's a simple way to prepare Japanese eggplant.*

6 Japanese eggplants (1½ to 2 pounds total)

Teriyaki Marinade (page 225) or Hoisin Marinade (page 225), as needed

2 scallions, green parts only, thinly sliced

½ red bell pepper, finely diced

1 tablespoon sesame seeds

1. Slice the eggplants in half lengthwise.

2. Prepare the grill. Brush the eggplant slices generously on the open sides with the marinade of your choice. Grill flesh-side down for 5 minutes, or until nicely browned, then flip and grill on the other side for 3 to 4 minutes, until tender.

3. Arrange the eggplants on a serving dish. Spoon a little extra marinade over each one, then sprinkle evenly with the scallions, red pepper, and sesame seeds. Serve warm or at room temperature.

# Grilled Eggplant Curry

**GLUTEN-FREE (make sure to use a gluten-free grain)**
**SOY-FREE**
**NUT-FREE**

**6 SERVINGS**

*This vegetable dish was inspired by Baingan Bharata, which appears frequently on Indian restaurant menus. Once the eggplant has been grilled and is cool enough to handle, this dish is made quickly and easily. I've added chickpeas to make it a main dish. Serve over hot cooked grains. Use the smaller, sweeter eggplants available during the summer for this dish—white, striped, and Japanese are all good choices.*

3 or 4 small summer eggplants (1½ to 2 pounds total)

Extra-virgin olive oil for basting eggplants

1 tablespoon extra-virgin olive oil

1 medium onion, finely chopped

2 cloves garlic, minced

1 small fresh, hot chili pepper, seeded and minced, optional

1 pound ripe, juicy tomatoes, diced

1 16-ounce can chickpeas, drained and rinsed

2 teaspoons curry powder or garam masala, or to taste

1 teaspoon ground cumin

Salt and freshly ground pepper to taste

Chopped fresh cilantro to taste

Hot cooked grain of your choice (brown Basmati rice, couscous, quinoa, or other), optional

1. Prepare the grill.

2. Cut eggplants into ½-inch-thick slices. Brush some olive oil on both sides of each slice. Grill the eggplant on both sides until tender and nicely browned, about 5 to 7 minutes on each side. Transfer to a plate to cool. When cool enough to handle, cut each eggplant slice into strips.

3. Heat the oil in a large skillet. Add the onion and sauté over medium-low heat until translucent, then add the garlic and optional chili pepper, and sauté until the onion is golden.

4. Add the eggplant, tomatoes, chickpeas, curry, and cumin. Cook over medium-low heat, covered, for 10 minutes, or until the tomatoes have softened. Season to taste with salt and pepper and remove from heat. Stir in the chopped cilantro and serve either as is or over hot cooked grains.

# Grilled Pepperonata
# with Vegan Sausage

**NUT-FREE**

**6 OR MORE SERVINGS**

*This vegan rendition of an Italian classic (sausage and peppers) is absolutely wonderful made on the grill.*

Olive Oil–Lemon Marinade
(page 226)

4 bell peppers, various colors, cut into large bite-size chunks

½ medium red onion, cut into ¼-inch-thick slices, rings separated

1 14-ounce package Tofurky or Field Roast Sausage, cut into ¾-inch slices

2 medium-size ripe tomatoes, diced

½ cup pitted black brine-cured olives (such as Kalamata)

¼ to ½ cup sliced basil leaves, to taste

1. Prepare the grill.

2. Combine the marinade in a large mixing bowl with the peppers, onion, and sausage. Stir together.

3. When ready to grill, lift the sausage, peppers, and onions from the bowl with a large slotted spoon and arrange in a more or less single layer on the grill. If using other than an electric grill, you may want to use a grill pan or basket, as the chunks of sausage are relatively small.

4. Cook on the grill for 5 to 7 minutes, then turn with tongs and cook for 5 to 7 minutes longer, or until the vegetables and sausage are lightly charred.

5. Transfer the sausage and vegetables to a large serving bowl or roomy platter. Add the tomatoes, olives, and basil and toss lightly. Drizzle with just enough extra marinade to moisten. Serve at once.

# Grilled Ratatouille

**GLUTEN-FREE (make sure to use a gluten-free grain)**
**SOY-FREE**
**NUT-FREE**

**6 TO 8 SERVINGS**

*Grilling transforms this classic French stew into an appetizing warm salad.*

2 to 3 small summer eggplants, about 1 pound total (see introduction to Grilled Eggplant Curry on page 213)

2 medium onions

1 medium zucchini or 2 small zucchinis, about ½ pound total, cut in half lengthwise

1 large green or red bell pepper, cut into large chunks

Olive Oil–Lemon Marinade (page 226), as needed

1 large, ripe tomato, diced

¼ cup chopped black olives

8 to 10 fresh basil leaves, sliced, or more, to taste

2 tablespoons chopped fresh parsley, or more, to taste

1 to 2 tablespoons extra-virgin olive oil, to taste

2 tablespoons red wine vinegar

Salt and freshly ground pepper to taste

1. Cut the eggplant into ½-inch-thick slices.

2. Peel the onions and cut in half. Steam or microwave until just tender.

3. Prepare the grill. Brush the vegetables lightly with Olive Oil–Lemon Marinade. Grill the eggplant on both sides until nicely browned and quite tender, about 15 minutes total. Grill the onions, zucchini, and bell pepper, turning after a few minutes, until marked with brown on both sides, about 10 to 15 minutes total.

4. When all the vegetables are cool enough to handle, chop them into fairly large chunks and combine in a serving bowl. Stir in the tomato, olives, herbs, olive oil, and vinegar, and toss well. Season to taste with salt and pepper. Serve warm or at room temperature.

# Grilled Golden Potatoes
# with Parsley-Cucumber Sauce

**GLUTEN-FREE (make sure to use a gluten-free grain)**

**SOY-FREE**

**NUT-FREE**

**6 TO 8 SERVINGS**

*A lively cucumber sauce is a refreshing contrast to the deep, smoky flavors of grilled foods.*

12 medium golden potatoes, scrubbed

Extra-virgin olive oil, as needed

**SAUCE**

1 cup firmly packed fresh parsley

2 tablespoons minced fresh dill, or more to taste, optional

¼ cup extra-virgin olive oil

2 tablespoons white wine vinegar or apple cider vinegar

1 cup peeled, seeded, and chopped cucumber

2 scallions, coarsely chopped

½ cup pitted brine-cured black olives, halved

Salt and freshly ground pepper to taste

1. Cook or microwave the potatoes until barely tender. Let them cool to room temperature, then cut into quarters. Place potatoes in a mixing bowl; drizzle in a little olive oil and toss gently to coat.

2. Prepare the grill.

3. Grill the potatoes for a total of 8 to 10 minutes, turning once or twice, until nicely charred. Transfer to a serving container.

4. Combine the sauce ingredients in a food processor. Pulse on and off until the mixture is a coarse puree, drizzling in 1 to 2 tablespoons of water to loosen the consistency.

5. Pour the sauce over the potatoes and stir together. Stir in the olives and season with salt and pepper. Serve warm or at room temperature.

# Triple-Protein Mixed Grill
# with Sweet Potatoes

**NUT-FREE**

**6 TO 8 SERVINGS**

*Here's a good dish to make when you're catering to hearty appetites. I particularly like it with Hoisin Marinade (page 225), which does something special for the sweet potatoes.*

2 large sweet potatoes

1 14- to 16-ounce tub extra-firm tofu

1 10- to 12-ounce package baked tofu (any variety, but smoked is nice), cut into thick slices

1 14-ounce package vegan sausage links, sliced about ¾ inch thick, or 16 ounces seitan, cut into bite-size chunks

1 medium red or orange bell pepper, cut into large chunks

Hoisin Marinade (page 225) or Sweet and Savory Marinade (page 224)

Minced fresh parsley for garnish, optional

Minced scallion for garnish, optional

1. Cook, bake, or microwave the sweet potatoes ahead of time, just until they can be pierced through but are still quite firm. When cool enough to handle, peel and cut into thick slices.

2. Prepare the grill.

3. Depending on the shape of the sweet potatoes, cut smaller slices into half-circles, and larger slices into quarters.

4. Cut the extra-firm tofu into 6 slabs crosswise. Blot thoroughly between layers of paper towel or a clean tea towel. Cut into large chunks.

5. Combine the sweet potatoes with the two kinds of tofu and the sausage in a large mixing bowl. Add the bell pepper, then stir in just enough marinade to coat everything evenly.

6. Cook on the grill for 3 to 4 minutes, then gently turn two or three times, continuing to cook for 3 minutes or so after every turn, until there are grill marks on most sides of the proteins and vegetables.

7. Transfer to a serving platter. Toss with enough additional marinade to moisten. Top with fresh parsley and/or scallion, if you'd like, then serve at once.

# Grilled Pizzas with Tapenade and Chard

**Can be made GLUTEN-FREE by using specialty gluten-free crusts**
**SOY-FREE**

## 8 SERVINGS

*This makes a great midsummer appetizer, or a nice companion to other grilled vegetables or protein foods.*

1 recipe Olive and Dried Tomato Tapenade (page 279)

1 tablespoon extra-virgin olive oil

3 to 4 cloves garlic, minced

1 good-size bunch chard or other greens of your choice stemmed, washed, and chopped

Lemon juice, to taste

Salt and freshly ground pepper to taste

2 12-inch or 4 small (8-inch) pizza crusts or flat breads such as panini or pitas

1. Make the recipe for tapenade and set aside.

2. Heat the oil in a medium skillet. Add the garlic and sauté until golden. Add the chard, in batches if needed. Cover and cook until wilted and just tender, adding just enough water to keep the bottom of the skillet moist.

3. When done to your liking, remove from the heat, and if need be, transfer to a colander to squeeze out excess liquid. Transfer back to the skillet; season with lemon juice, salt, and pepper.

4. Divide the tapenade among the pizzas (or flat breads) and spread evenly. Top evenly with chard.

5. Prepare the grill. Spray the grill with cooking oil spray. Grill the pizzas (or flat breads) until the bottoms are lightly charred. Don't overcook!

6. To serve, if using large crusts, cut each into 8 wedges; if using small crusts, cut each into quarters. Serve at room temperature.

**VARIATIONS:** Add a layer of eggplant or mushrooms. Use one long Japanese eggplant, sliced ¼ inch thick, or 6 ounces mushrooms, stemmed and sliced. Toss with olive oil and grill in a grill basket until lightly charred. Scatter here and there over the greens on the pizzas.

# Grilled Summer Squash
# with Chickpeas and Artichokes

**GLUTEN-FREE (make sure to use a gluten-free grain)**

**SOY-FREE**

**NUT-FREE**

**6 SERVINGS**

*This lively medley makes a substantial salad served with one of your favorite grilled proteins (see pages 200–203).*

2 medium yellow summer squashes, cut in long diagonal slices, about ¼ inch thick

1 medium zucchini, cut to match yellow squashes

Olive Oil–Lemon Marinade (page 226), as needed

1 15- to 16-ounce can chickpeas, drained and rinsed

1 12-ounce jar marinated artichoke hearts, chopped, with liquid

¼ cup oil-packed sun-dried tomatoes, thinly sliced

1 to 2 tablespoons balsamic or white wine vinegar, to taste

¼ cup minced fresh parsley

2 to 3 scallions, green parts only, thinly sliced

1 tablespoon fresh oregano leaves, or 1 teaspoon dried

Salt and freshly ground pepper to taste

Mixed baby greens

1. Prepare the grill.

2. Combine the squashes in a mixing bowl with enough marinade to moisten. Grill the vegetables for a total of 6 to 8 minutes, or until nicely charred on both sides. If using anything other than an electric grill, you may want to use a grilling basket.

3. Transfer the vegetables to a mixing bowl. Stir in the chickpeas, artichoke hearts and liquid, dried tomatoes, vinegar, parsley, scallions, and oregano. Toss together.

4. Season with salt and pepper. Line a serving platter with greens and mound the salad over them. Serve at room temperature.

# Grilled Tempeh with Green Beans and Pineapple

**GLUTEN-FREE (make sure the soy sauce used in the marinade is gluten-free)**

**NUT-FREE**

**6 TO 8 SERVINGS**

*Grilled pineapple makes a heavenly foil for the assertive flavor of the hoisin-marinated tempeh and vegetables in this recipe.*

1 recipe Grilled Pineapple (page 221)

2 10-ounce packages tempeh, any variety

1 recipe Hoisin Marinade (page 225)

10 to 12 ounces fresh green beans, trimmed

2 medium red bell peppers, cut into ½-inch strips

1. Prepare the grill.

2. Grill the pineapple according to the recipe. When done, arrange the grilled pineapple slices around the perimeter of a large serving platter, leaving an opening in the center.

3. Slice the tempeh into ½-inch strips crosswise. Combine in a mixing bowl with enough marinade to coat. Spread the tempeh in a single layer on the grill. If using anything other than an electric grill, use a grill basket. Grill for 10 minutes total, flipping the tempeh occasionally with tongs until nicely charred here and there. Arrange in half of the open circle surrounded by pineapple.

4. Combine the green beans and bell peppers in the mixing bowl; add enough marinade to coat, and toss gently. Spread in a single layer on the grill; likewise, if using anything other than an electric grill, use a grill basket. Grill for 8 to 10 minutes total, flipping them occasionally with tongs until nicely charred here and there. Arrange in the other half of the open circle surrounded by pineapple.

5. Serve warm or at room temperature. Pass around additional marinade for individual servings.

# Grilled Pineapple

**GLUTEN-FREE**

**SOY-FREE**

**NUT-FREE**

**8 OR MORE SERVINGS**

*Grilled pineapple is amazing—try it even if you're not using it in a recipe (such as Grilled Tempeh with Green Beans and Pineapple). It goes well with just about anything!*

1  medium, fresh pineapple

3  tablespoons agave nectar

1  tablespoon lime or lemon juice

¼  teaspoon cinnamon

**1.** Trim the leafy crown from the pineapple and discard.

**2.** Standing the pineapple firmly upright, slice off the tough skin, using downward motions with a sharp knife.

**3.** Cut the pineapple flesh away from the tough core, then cut into ½-inch slices, a bit larger than bite-size.

**4.** In a large mixing bowl, toss the pineapple with agave nectar and lime juice. Sprinkle in the cinnamon and toss again.

**5.** Prepare the grill. Place the pineapple pieces on the grill in a single layer. Grill for 3 to 4 minutes on each side, just until you get some nice grill marks. Don't overcook, as the pineapple may dry out.

# Spicy Grilled Green Beans with Walnuts

**GLUTEN-FREE (make sure that the soy sauce used in the marinade is gluten-free)**

**8 OR MORE SERVINGS**

*Crunchy grilled green beans are so appealing flavored with a rich, nutty coating of walnuts and sesame oil. This makes a nice side dish, but it's also good as an appetizer.*

1½ pounds green beans, trimmed

Teriyaki Marinade (page 225)

1 tablespoon dark sesame oil

5 to 6 cloves garlic, minced

½ cup finely chopped walnuts

1 to 2 fresh hot green chilies, seeded and minced, to taste, or dried hot red pepper flakes to taste

1. Prepare the grill.

2. Combine the green beans with enough marinade to coat lightly and evenly. Grill, gently rolling green beans with tongs to expose all sides for 7 to 10 minutes total, or until charred to your liking. If you are using anything other than an electric grill, you will probably want to put the green beans in a grill basket.

3. Transfer the green beans to a mixing bowl.

4. Heat the sesame oil in a small skillet. Add the garlic and sauté over low heat for a minute or so, then add the walnuts. Continue to sauté, stirring frequently, until the garlic is golden. Transfer to the mixing bowl; add chilies to taste. Toss well to combine with the green beans.

5. Add more marinade to moisten, if desired. Transfer to a serving platter and serve at room temperature.

# MARINADES, RELISHES, SALSAS, AND SAUCES

Sweet and Savory Grilling Sauce

Teriyaki Marinade

Hoisin Marinade

Olive Oil–Lemon Marinade

Triple Tomato Relish

Salsa Fresca with Variations

Fresh Corn and Tomatillo Salsa

# Sweet and Savory Grilling Sauce

**GLUTEN-FREE (make sure the soy sauce is gluten-free)**
**NUT-FREE**

**MAKES ABOUT 2 CUPS**

*This easy, no-cook sauce falls into the realm of sweet and pungent tomato-based sauces generically known as "barbecue sauce." It takes minutes to prepare, and I prefer it to the store-bought kind.*

1½ cups tomato sauce

3 tablespoons agave nectar
or maple syrup

1 tablespoon molasses

1 tablespoon extra-virgin olive oil

2 tablespoons reduced-sodium soy
sauce, or to taste

1 teaspoon paprika

1 teaspoon smoked paprika,
optional

1 teaspoon chili powder, or more,
to taste

1 teaspoon dried oregano

1. Combine all the ingredients in a mixing bowl and whisk together. Cover and let stand for at least an hour to allow the flavors to meld.

# Teriyaki Marinade

**GLUTEN-FREE (make sure the soy sauce is gluten-free)**
**NUT-FREE**

**MAKES ABOUT ¾ CUP**

*This flavorful marinade gives an Asian twist to grilled vegetables and protein foods.*

- ⅓ cup reduced-sodium soy sauce
- 2 tablespoons olive oil or other healthy vegetable oil
- 1 tablespoon dark sesame oil
- 3 tablespoons agave nectar
- 3 tablespoons rice vinegar or white wine vinegar
- 1 to 2 cloves garlic, minced, optional
- 1 to 2 teaspoons grated fresh or jarred ginger

1. Combine all the ingredients in a small bowl and whisk together. If brushing on foods, swirl the marinade often to keep it from separating.

# Hoisin Marinade

**GLUTEN-FREE (make sure the soy sauce is gluten-free)**
**NUT-FREE**

**MAKES ABOUT 1 CUP**

*Look for hoisin sauce, a sweet and pungent condiment, in the Asian foods section of your supermarket. This recipe is a bit more assertive than Teriyaki Marinade and is delicious with all proteins and vegetables.*

- ½ cup hoisin sauce
- ⅓ cup fruit juice (preferably orange, mango, or pineapple)
- 2 tablespoons olive oil or other healthy vegetable oil
- 2 tablespoons lemon or lime juice
- 1 to 2 tablespoons reduced-sodium soy sauce, to taste
- 1 to 2 teaspoons minced fresh or jarred ginger, to taste

1. Combine the ingredients in a small bowl and whisk together.

# Olive Oil–Lemon Marinade

**GLUTEN-FREE**
**SOY-FREE**
**NUT-FREE**

**MAKES ABOUT ¼ CUP**

*This basic marinade is excellent for grilling vegetables. The bite of lemon balances the fruity taste of the olive oil.*

½ cup extra-virgin olive oil

¼ cup lemon juice

½ teaspoon fresh oregano leaves, or a generous pinch of dried oregano

½ teaspoon fresh thyme or lemon thyme leaves, or a generous pinch of dried thyme

Freshly ground pepper to taste

1. Combine all the ingredients in a small bowl and whisk together. When brushing on vegetables, swirl the marinade around often to keep the oil and lemon mixture from separating.

# Triple Tomato Relish

**GLUTEN-FREE**

**SOY-FREE**

**NUT-FREE**

**MAKES 3 CUPS**

*This pretty, raw relish makes a tasty topping for grilled vegetables and proteins. One idea: Arrange slabs of grilled tofu on a platter and top with a strip of this relish down the center. Send the remaining relish around the table for additional topping.*

¾ cup yellow cherry or grape tomatoes, halved

¾ cup red cherry or grape tomatoes, halved

1 cup finely diced ripe tomato, any good summer variety

½ cup fresh herb combo of your choice (whole oregano leaves, whole thyme leaves, minced fresh dill, minced fresh parsley, or sliced basil leaves)

2 tablespoons extra-virgin olive oil

2 tablespoons red wine vinegar

Pinch of natural granulated sugar

Salt and freshly ground pepper to taste

1. Combine all the ingredients in a serving bowl and toss together. Serve at once.

# Salsa Fresca with Variations

**GLUTEN-FREE**

**SOY-FREE**

**NUT-FREE**

**MAKES ABOUT 2 CUPS**

*When tomatoes are at their best, it's well worth making salsa at home, rather than buying it in jars. This makes a delicious appetizer to serve with tortilla chips.*

2 cups diced ripe tomatoes

1 or 2 scallions, chopped

1 or 2 jalapeño peppers, seeded and coarsely chopped, to taste

¼ cup chopped fresh cilantro or parsley

Juice of ½ lemon or lime, or more to taste

1 teaspoon ground cumin

½ teaspoon salt

1. Combine the ingredients in a food processor. Pulse on and off until the mixture is a coarse puree. Store in an airtight container, refrigerated, until needed. Transfer to a shallow serving bowl to serve.

**VARIATIONS:**

**CHIPOTLE:** Substitute fresh jalapeño peppers with 1 or 2 canned chipotle chilies in adobo (during processing).

**FRESH CORN:** Add the kernels from 1 lightly cooked or grilled ear of corn, after processing.

**PEACH, NECTARINE, MANGO, OR APRICOT:** Add from ½ to 1 cup pitted and coarsely chopped fruit (during processing).

**BELL PEPPER:** Add a finely diced raw, grilled, or jarred roasted bell pepper after processing.

**CUCUMBER-DILL:** Add a garden-fresh Kirby or ½ medium cucumber and ¼ cup minced fresh dill after processing.

**SUN-DRIED TOMATO:** Add ¼ cup or more sliced dried tomatoes after processing.

**FRESH PEACH OR NECTARINE:** Add two finely diced ripe peaches or nectarines after processing.

**GARLIC AND/OR ONION:** If you know your guests will be able to tolerate raw onion or garlic, add a small quantity of either or both while processing. But don't serve it to me, since I'm one who can't tolerate the allium family in the raw!

# Fresh Corn and
# Tomatillo Salsa

**SOY-FREE**

**NUT-FREE**

**MAKES ABOUT 2 CUPS**

*Here's a delicious salsa that highlights summer corn and tomatillos, both of which come to market at about the same time. It's especially good served as an appetizer with tortilla chips, and you can use leftovers as a topping for vegan quesadillas and burritos (see photo on page 198).*

2 medium ears fresh corn, lightly cooked or grilled (page 207)

6 to 8 tomatillos, husked and quartered

½ medium red bell pepper, diced

¼ to ½ cup fresh cilantro, to taste

1 to 2 small fresh hot chili peppers, such as jalapeño or serrano, seeded and chopped

¼ medium red onion, coarsely chopped, or 2 scallions, sliced

1 teaspoon ground cumin

Juice of ½ to 1 lime or lemon

Salt to taste

1. When the corn is cool enough to handle, stand each ear on its flat end. Using a downward motion of a sharp knife, cut the kernels off.

2. Combine all the ingredients in a food processor. Pulse on and off until the mixture is coarsely and evenly chopped. Don't puree!

3. Transfer to a serving bowl. Serve at once or cover and refrigerate until needed.

# COOL DISHES FOR
# SUMMER ENTERTAINING

Cold Sesame Noodles

Cold Teriyaki Noodles with Asian Vegetables

Israeli Couscous Summer Pilaf

Pasta and Red Quinoa Salad

Southwestern Potato Salad with Avocado, Corn, and Peppers

Midsummer Garden Potato Salad

Baked Tofu and White Bean Salad

Corn Fritters with Cilantro Sauce

🌿

Asian-Flavored Tofu and Cucumber Platter

🌿

Piquant Summer Rice and Corn Salad

🌿

Tomato and Bread Salad with Chickpeas

🌿

Summer Tomato Salad with Peaches and Pecans

🌿

Vegan Caprese

🌿

Mixed Greens with Avocado and Blueberries

# Cold Sesame Noodles

**10 TO 12 SERVINGS**

*Here's my rendition of a vegan classic—noodles richly enveloped in a luscious peanut butter and tahini sauce. Double yum!*

1 tablespoon dark sesame oil

1 medium onion, chopped

1 to 2 cloves garlic, minced

½ cup smooth natural peanut butter

⅓ cup sesame tahini

2 tablespoons lemon or lime juice

2 to 3 tablespoons reduced-sodium soy sauce, to taste

1 to 2 teaspoons chili powder, to taste

2 tablespoons agave nectar or other sweetener

Pinch of cayenne pepper, or to taste

16 ounces Chinese wheat noodles, soba, or linguine

1 medium red bell pepper, cut into narrow 2-inch strips

3 to 4 scallions, thinly sliced

2 tablespoons sesame seeds

1. Heat the oil in a small skillet. Add the onion and sauté over medium-low heat until translucent. Add the garlic and continue to sauté until the onion is golden. Transfer to a food processor with the peanut butter, tahini, lemon juice, soy sauce, chili powder, agave nectar, cayenne, and ¾ cup water. Process until completely smooth.

2. Cook the noodles according to package directions until *al dente*. Drain and rinse the noodles under cold running water until they're cool.

3. Combine the noodles in a serving bowl with the sauce and half the bell pepper and scallions. Toss well. Taste and adjust any of the seasonings from the sauce: lemon juice, soy sauce, chili powder, sweetener, and cayenne; toss well again. Scatter the remaining bell pepper strips and scallion over the top, followed by the sesame seeds, and serve.

# Cold Teriyaki Noodles with Asian Vegetables

**NUT-FREE (if seeds are safe for you; otherwise omit sesame seeds)**

**10 OR MORE SERVINGS**

*If you like tempeh and colorful Asian-style noodle dishes, look no further. But even if you don't like tempeh, you can still make this dish using thinly sliced baked tofu.*

| | |
|---|---|
| 8 to 10 ounces Asian noodles, any long variety (udon, soba, or somen) | |
| 1½ tablespoons olive oil or other healthy vegetable oil | |
| 1 tablespoon reduced-sodium soy sauce | |
| 1 10-ounce package tempeh or one 8-ounce package baked tofu, cut crosswise into ¼-inch-thick strips | |
| ¾ cup cleaned, sliced mushrooms (shiitake, cremini, or baby bella) | |
| 1 heaping cup snow peas, trimmed and cut in half lengthwise | |
| 1 cup baby carrots, halved lengthwise | |
| 1 15-ounce can baby corn, drained | |
| 4 large stalks bok choy, with leaves, or 1 or 2 whole baby bok choy, thinly sliced | |
| 2 to 3 scallions, thinly sliced | |
| ¼ cup minced fresh cilantro | |
| ¼ cup bottled teriyaki sauce | |
| 2 tablespoons dark sesame oil | |
| 1 tablespoon lime juice, rice vinegar, or white wine vinegar, or to taste | |
| Pinch of dried hot red pepper flakes, or to taste | |
| Freshly ground pepper to taste | |
| Sesame seeds for garnish, optional | |

1. Cook the noodles according to package directions until *al dente*. Drain and rinse the noodles under cold running water until cool.

2. Heat the oil and soy sauce in a medium skillet. Add the tempeh or tofu and sauté over medium-high heat until nicely browned on most sides.

3. Add the mushrooms to the skillet with just a small amount of water. Cover and cook until wilted, about 2 minutes. Add the snow peas; cover and cook for 30 to 45 seconds, just until they turn bright green.

4. Combine the tempeh mixture with the cooked noodles in a large serving bowl. Add the remaining ingredients (except the optional garnish) and toss together. Taste and adjust flavors to your liking. Garnish with sesame seeds if desired. Serve at room temperature.

# Israeli Couscous Summer Pilaf

Can be made **GLUTEN-FREE** by replacing couscous with quinoa (use 1 cup raw quinoa)

**SOY-FREE**

Can be made **NUT-FREE** by omitting nuts

**8 TO 10 SERVINGS**

*Israeli couscous is one fun little pasta. It's round and quick cooking, and has a very pleasant mouth feel. Look for it in bulk in natural foods stores, or in the Middle Eastern section of the international aisle in well-stocked supermarkets. Combined with herbs, raw veggies, and lush stone fruit, it makes for a light and refreshing foil to grilled foods or well-seasoned plant-based protein dishes. It also makes for a lovely dish to share when you're invited to a summer potluck. Make sure to use a firm, flavorful cucumber with a minimum of seeds.*

1½ cups Israeli couscous

1 heaping cup cucumber, quartered and thinly sliced

1 large stalk celery, diced

2 scallions, minced

¼ cup minced fresh dill

10 to 12 basil leaves, thinly sliced, or more, to taste

4 medium-firm, ripe apricots or 3 medium-firm, ripe nectarines, pitted and diced

1 heaping cup halved cherry or grape tomatoes (red or yellow, or a combination)

1 medium-firm, ripe avocado, peeled and diced

3 tablespoons extra-virgin olive oil (or less if you'd like a lower-fat dish)

2 to 3 tablespoons lemon juice, or more, to taste

Salt and freshly ground pepper to taste

Mixed baby greens, as needed

¼ cup toasted pine nuts or ⅓ cup toasted slivered almonds

1. Bring 5 cups of water to a boil in a medium saucepan. Add the Israeli couscous and cook at a rapid simmer for about 8 minutes, or until *al dente*. Drain and rinse with cool water until the couscous is at room temperature.

2. In a mixing bowl, combine the couscous with the remaining ingredients except the last two. Toss well to combine.

3. Line a large serving platter with some greens. Mound the salad over them, letting some of the greens show along the edge. Sprinkle the top with the toasted nuts. Serve at once or cover loosely with plastic wrap and refrigerate until needed.

# Pasta and Red Quinoa Salad

**Can be made GLUTEN-FREE by using gluten-free pasta**

**Can be made SOY-FREE by replacing vegan mayonnaise with a soy-free salad dressing**

**NUT-FREE**

## 8 OR MORE SERVINGS

*Is this a pasta salad or a cool pilaf? It's a bit of both. The combination of pasta with quinoa makes for a sturdy and hearty cold dish with a great variety of flavors and textures.*

1 cup quinoa (red or regular, or a combination)

2 cups small pasta (tiny shells, ditalini, or other)

8 baby carrots, quartered lengthwise

1 red or yellow bell pepper, cut into approximately ½-inch dice

2 to 3 tablespoons minced fresh dill

¼ cup minced fresh parsley

2 scallions, green parts only, thinly sliced

3 tablespoons olive oil

¼ cup red wine vinegar

¼ cup vegan mayonnaise

Salt and freshly ground pepper to taste

1 cup halved cherry tomatoes

⅓ cup chopped green pimiento olives

1. Combine the quinoa with 3 cups water in a medium saucepan. Bring to a rapid simmer, then cover and simmer gently until the water is absorbed, about 15 to 20 minutes. If the quinoa is not quite done, add ½ cup water and continue to cook until absorbed. Allow to stand off the heat, uncovered, until at room temperature.

2. Cook the pasta according to package directions until *al dente*, then drain.

3. Combine the cooled quinoa with the cooked pasta in a large serving bowl. Add the remaining ingredients except the last two. Toss gently but thoroughly.

4. If time allows, cover the salad and refrigerate for 1 to 2 hours before serving. Just before serving, stir in the cherry tomatoes and olives.

# Southwestern Potato Salad with Avocado, Corn, and Peppers

**GLUTEN-FREE**

**SOY-FREE**

**NUT-FREE**

**8 SERVINGS**

*An offbeat potato salad, this one sparkles with lively, surprising flavors.*

4 medium red-skinned or golden potatoes

1 large sweet potato

2 medium ears fresh corn, lightly cooked

3 small bell peppers, one each of various colors (red, yellow, orange, green, or purple), cut into narrow, 2-inch strips

2 medium-firm, ripe avocados, pitted, peeled, and diced

Juice of 1 lime, or more, to taste

2 medium-firm, ripe tomatoes, finely diced

2 tablespoons extra-virgin olive oil

¼ cup minced fresh cilantro

1 cup salsa, homemade (page 228) or store-bought (see Note)

1 small, fresh hot chili (such as jalapeño or serrano), optional

1 to 2 scallions, thinly sliced

1 teaspoon ground cumin

Salt and freshly ground black pepper, to taste

1. Cook, bake, or microwave the potatoes and sweet potato ahead of time until done but still nice and firm.

2. Meanwhile, combine the corn and bell peppers in a large serving bowl. Toss the avocado with the lime juice. Combine the potatoes and avocado in a large serving bowl along with the remaining ingredients. Toss gently but thoroughly and serve.

**VARIATION:** For an even heartier salad, add 1½ to 2 cups cooked or canned pinto or kidney beans.

**NOTE:** Any of the variations of Salsa Fresca (see page 228) will work with this. Or, if using store-bought salsa, try an interesting variety like peach-mango or chipotle.

# Midsummer Garden Potato Salad

**GLUTEN-FREE**

Can be made **SOY-FREE** by eliminating vegan mayonnaise and increasing the quantities of olive oil and lemon juice

**NUT-FREE** (if seeds are safe for you; otherwise eliminate seeds)

## 8 SERVINGS

*Here's another delicious rendition of potato salad, filled with garden-fresh flavors.*

- 5 medium golden potatoes
- 1 14- to 16-ounce can small red beans, drained and rinsed
- 1 medium, yellow summer squash, diced
- 2 medium, juicy tomatoes, diced
- 2 medium carrots, thinly sliced
- ½ cup basil leaves, sliced
- ¼ cup minced fresh parsley
- 2 scallions, green parts only, thinly sliced
- ½ cup brine-cured black olives, such as Kalamata, halved if you prefer

  Mixed baby greens

  Toasted pumpkin seeds or sunflower seeds, for topping, optional

### DRESSING

- ¼ cup vegan mayonnaise
- 3 tablespoons extra-virgin olive oil
- 2 tablespoons yellow mustard
- 2 to 3 tablespoons white wine vinegar

  Salt and freshly ground pepper to taste

1. Cook, bake, or microwave the potatoes ahead of time until done but still nice and firm. When cool enough to handle, peel and dice them.

2. Combine the potatoes with the remaining salad ingredients in a mixing bowl.

3. In a small bowl, combine the dressing ingredients and whisk together. Pour over the potato mixture and toss together. Season with salt and pepper.

4. Line a serving platter with greens and mound the potato salad over them, leaving a border of greens showing around the edges. Sprinkle with the optional seeds and serve.

# Baked Tofu and White Bean Salad

**GLUTEN-FREE (make sure baked tofu is prepared with gluten-free soy sauce)**

**NUT-FREE**

**8 SERVINGS**

*This hearty salad, which is so easy to throw together, recalls both a classic Italian tuna and white bean salad, as well as the French Salade Niçoise.*

1 6- to 8-ounce package baked tofu, any variety, cut into ¼-inch dice

1 15- to 16-ounce can great northern or cannellini beans, drained and rinsed

½ cup chopped pitted black olives, such as Kalamata

2 large celery stalks, diced

1 cup halved cherry or grape tomatoes

¼ cup chopped fresh parsley, or more, to taste

⅓ cup sliced basil leaves, optional

2 tablespoons extra-virgin olive oil

Juice of 1 lemon

Salt and freshly ground pepper to taste

Mixed baby greens or baby arugula, as needed

1. Combine all the ingredients except the greens and toss together.

2. Arrange a layer of greens on a serving platter and mound the salad over it. Serve at once, or cover and refrigerate until needed.

# Corn Fritters
# with Cilantro Sauce

Can be made **GLUTEN-FREE** by replacing unbleached white flour with

a gluten-free flour or equivalent amount of additional cornmeal

**SOY-FREE**

**NUT-FREE**

**MAKES ABOUT 24**

*At the height of fresh corn season, these simple fritters can be served as a tasty side dish or as an appetizer. They're good warm or at room temperature.*

## CILANTRO SAUCE

½ cup tomatillo salsa

½ cup cilantro leaves

Juice of ½ lime, or more to taste

¼ teaspoon salt

## CORN FRITTERS

5 medium ears fresh, uncooked corn

½ cup unbleached white flour

½ cup cornmeal

2 scallions, chopped

1 cup rice milk

1 teaspoon ground cumin

Salt and freshly ground pepper to taste

1 small fresh hot chili pepper, seeded and minced, optional

Oil for frying

1. Place the salsa, cilantro, lime juice, and salt in a food processor. Pulse on and off until the cilantro leaves are finely minced. Transfer the sauce to a small serving bowl.

2. Break each ear of corn in half; stand it on the flat end, and scrape the kernels off with a sharp knife. Combine the corn kernels with the remaining ingredients, except the oil, in a food processor. Pulse on and off until the corn is finely minced but not pureed.

3. Heat enough oil to coat a large skillet or griddle. When really hot, ladle the batter onto the skillet to form 2½- to 3-inch rounds (this will be somewhat less than ¼ cup each). Cook over medium heat until golden brown on each side. Transfer each batch to a paper towel–lined plate. Repeat until all the batter is used up.

4. To serve, place the sauce in the center of a platter and surround with the fritters. Place a small spoon in the sauce so that everyone can spread a bit on the fritters.

# Asian-Flavored Tofu
# and Cucumber Platter

**GLUTEN-FREE (make sure teriyaki sauce and hoisin sauce are gluten-free)**

**Can be made NUT-FREE by eliminating optional peanuts or cashews**

## 8 OR MORE SERVINGS

*Here's a summer platter that's substantial, yet quite refreshing. It's one of my favorites. I love the interplay of the sautéed tofu triangles and crunchy cucumbers and sprouts.*

### SAUCE

- 3 tablespoons teriyaki or hoisin sauce
- 2 tablespoons lime juice
- 2 tablespoons dark sesame oil
- 1 tablespoon agave nectar or maple syrup

    Pinch of dried hot red pepper flakes, or to taste

### TOFU

- 1 16-ounce tub tofu, drained
- 1 tablespoon olive oil or other healthy vegetable oil
- 8 ounces fresh mung bean sprouts
- 2 medium Kirby cucumbers, or 1 medium narrow cucumber, or half a hothouse cucumber, thinly sliced
- ½ medium red bell pepper, cut into short, very thin strips
- ½ cup minced fresh cilantro
- 4 scallions, thinly sliced

    Mixed baby greens, baby spinach, or arugula, or a combination

- ¼ cup finely chopped peanuts or cashews, optional

1. Combine the teriyaki, lime juice, sesame oil, agave, and red pepper flakes in a small bowl and stir together. Set aside.

2. Cut the tofu into 8 slabs crosswise. Blot well on paper towels or on a tea towel. Cut each slab into 2 squares, and each square into 2 triangles. Heat the olive oil in a wide skillet. Add the tofu and sauté over medium-high heat until golden and crisp on both sides. Transfer to a mixing bowl.

3. Place the bean sprouts in the skillet with a small amount of water. Steam for 2 minutes over medium heat, just until wilted. Transfer to a colander and rinse under cold running water until cool.

4. Combine the sprouts with the tofu in the mixing bowl and add the cucumbers, bell pepper, half the cilantro, and half the scallions. Pour in the sauce and toss gently until everything is evenly coated.

5. Line a serving platter with greens. Mound the tofu mixture over the greens and sprinkle with the nuts, followed by the remaining cilantro and scallions. Serve at once or cover and refrigerate until needed, up to several hours.

# Piquant Summer Rice and Corn Salad

**GLUTEN-FREE**

**SOY-FREE**

**NUT-FREE (if seeds are safe for you; otherwise eliminate seeds)**

## 10 OR MORE SERVINGS

*This is a good, sturdy buffet dish, filled with sunny flavors. The optional lemon or lime zest adds a nice touch, so do make the extra effort if you own a microplane grater.*

1½ cups raw long-grain brown or basmati rice, rinsed

2 to 3 tablespoons extra-virgin olive oil

2 cups cooked fresh corn kernels (from about 3 medium ears)

1 12-ounce jar marinated artichoke hearts, chopped, liquid reserved

2 to 3 scallions, thinly sliced

⅔ cup pitted cured black olives, such as Kalamata

2 cups halved cherry or grape tomatoes (try a combination of red and yellow)

1 small zucchini or yellow summer squash, quartered and thinly sliced

½ cup minced fresh parsley

Juice of 1 lemon or lime

1 to 2 tablespoons organic lemon or lime zest, optional

1 tablespoon agave nectar

Salt and freshly ground pepper to taste

½ cup toasted pumpkin seeds or pepitas, or ⅓ cup toasted sunflower seeds

1. Combine the rice with 3½ cups of water in a saucepan and bring to a gentle boil. Cover and simmer until the water is absorbed, about 35 minutes. If the rice needs more cooking, stir in ½ cup of additional water and cook until it's absorbed. Transfer the rice to a serving bowl. Stir in about half the oil and let the rice cool to room temperature.

2. Add all but the last ingredient to the serving bowl and stir gently to combine with the rice. If time allows, let the salad stand at room temperature for an hour or so before serving. Just before serving, stir in the pumpkin seeds.

# Tomato and Bread Salad with Chickpeas

**SOY-FREE**

**NUT-FREE**

**8 OR MORE SERVINGS**

*The addition of chickpeas to this panzanella-style salad makes it more substantial. For best results, use the most flavorful summer tomatoes you can find.*

2 cups soft whole-grain bread, preferably from an Italian or French loaf, cut into 1-inch cubes

2 to 2½ pounds flavorful ripe tomatoes, diced

¼ to ½ cup chopped fresh basil, or more to taste

¼ cup minced fresh dill, optional (but highly recommended)

½ cup pitted brine-cured black olives, cut in half

1 small cucumber, quartered lengthwise, seeds trimmed, and diced, or 2 small Kirby cucumbers, sliced

1 15- to 16-ounce can chickpeas, drained and rinsed

¼ cup extra-virgin olive oil

3 tablespoons red or white wine vinegar

1 teaspoon prepared yellow or Dijon mustard

Salt and freshly ground pepper to taste

1. Heat a wide nonstick skillet. Spray with cooking oil spray. Add the bread cubes and toast in the skillet for 10 to 15 minutes, stirring frequently, until golden and crisp.

2. In a large serving bowl, combine the bread cubes with the tomatoes, basil, dill, olives, cucumber, and chickpeas.

3. Combine the olive oil, vinegar, and mustard in a small bowl and whisk together. Pour over the salad and toss together. Season with salt and pepper and serve at once.

# Summer Tomato Salad with Peaches and Pecans

**GLUTEN-FREE**

**SOY-FREE**

**6 TO 8 SERVINGS**

*Use ripe tomatoes and peaches from the garden or farmers' market—not the kind that come with stickers on them! Fresh local tomatoes and peaches seem to reach their peak of flavor at the same time and are a compatible duo. Pecans add a surprising twist to this easy summer salad.*

1½ pounds mixed tomatoes (try a variety of heirloom, yellow, and red cherry or grape tomatoes)

4 medium, lush, ripe peaches, pitted and diced

1 Kirby cucumber, quartered and sliced, optional

½ cup toasted pecan halves (substitute walnuts if you prefer)

¼ to ½ cup basil or mint leaves, to taste, or a combination of the two

2 tablespoons extra-virgin olive oil

1 tablespoon balsamic vinegar, or more, to taste

Pinch of salt

1. Combine all the ingredients in a serving bowl and stir together. Serve at once.

# Vegan Caprese

## 4 TO 6 SERVINGS

*This is one of my favorite summer dishes, and though it barely qualifies as a recipe, it's impressive enough to be greeted with delight every time.*

8 to 10 ounces of good vegan cheese (my favorite for this recipe is Vegan Gourmet mozzarella)

4 medium-size lush, ripe tomatoes

A handful of basil leaves

Good, fruity olive oil

1. Slice the cheese so that it's about 2 inches square by about ¼ inch thick.

2. Cut the tomatoes about ¼ inch thick as well. Arrange them in overlapping rows on an attractive serving platter.

3. Sprinkle with sliced basil leaves, then drizzle lightly with olive oil. If you'd like, finish with a grind of black pepper, though this is optional.

4. This is a dish to make just before you serve it. You don't want to refrigerate it, since the tomatoes will get mushy and the basil will turn brown. Each serving consists of 3 to 4 slices each of cheese and tomatoes.

# Mixed Greens with Avocado and Blueberries

**GLUTEN-FREE**

**SOY-FREE**

**NUT-FREE**

## 8 SERVINGS

*This gorgeous salad is a snap to make and adds a splash of color (and lots of antioxidants) to a summer meal.*

2 to 3 ounces mixed baby greens

2 good handfuls baby spinach or baby arugula

1 cup fresh blueberries

1 medium red bell pepper, cut into short, narrow strips

1 medium yellow bell pepper, cut into short, narrow strips

⅓ cup chopped and lightly toasted walnuts

2 medium firm, ripe avocados, peeled and diced

2 tablespoons olive oil or other healthy vegetable oil, as desired

2 tablespoons lemon juice, or more, to taste

1. Combine all the ingredients in a serving bowl and toss together. Cover and set aside until ready to serve, or serve at once.

# SOUPS

Watermelon and Peach Gazpacho

Fresh Tomato Soup with Crunchy Vegetable Garnish

Chilled Potato-Corn Chowder

Cold Avocado and Green Pea Soup

# Watermelon and Peach Gazpacho

**GLUTEN-FREE**

**SOY-FREE**

**NUT-FREE**

**6 SERVINGS**

*Adding summer fruit to a classic tomato gazpacho works surprisingly well. The sweet and piquant flavors play off of one another in this palate-pleaser.*

### THE BASE

2 cups coarsely chopped ripe tomatoes

2 cup coarsely chopped pitted watermelon

½ medium red bell pepper

⅔ large cucumber, peeled and cut into chunks

2 scallions, green parts only, cut into several pieces

Handful of cilantro or parsley sprigs

### TO FINISH THE SOUP

⅓ large cucumber, peeled, seeded, and finely diced

1 cup halved cherry or grape tomatoes (red and/or yellow)

½ medium red bell pepper, diced

½ cup finely chopped peeled carrot or baby carrots

2 cups finely diced pitted watermelon

2 medium, ripe peaches

Juice of ½ to 1 lemon or lime, to taste

1 small, fresh hot chili, seeded and minced, or dried hot red pepper flakes to taste

Salt and freshly ground pepper to taste

1. Place the first six ingredients (the base) in a food processor. Puree until fairly smooth.

2. Transfer the puree to a serving dish. Add the remaining ingredients and stir together. Cover and refrigerate for at least an hour before serving.

**VARIATION:** Nectarines are a fine substitution for peaches in this soup.

# Fresh Tomato Soup
# with Crunchy Vegetable Garnish

**GLUTEN-FREE (omitting optional croutons)**
**SOY-FREE**
**NUT-FREE**

## 8 SERVINGS

*Made with late summer's incomparably flavorful tomatoes, this soup is the epitome of tomato heaven. It's a great way to use any tomatoes that have gotten a bit overripe.*

2 tablespoons extra-virgin olive oil

1 large onion, chopped

3 cloves garlic, minced

2 large celery stalks, diced

2 cups prepared vegetable broth, or as needed

2 pounds ripe, flavorful tomatoes, coarsely chopped (try a combination of red and yellow tomatoes)

¼ cup chopped fresh basil

2 tablespoons chopped fresh dill

2 tablespoons lemon juice

Salt and freshly ground pepper to taste

1 pint (2 cups) yellow and/or red cherry or grape tomatoes, halved

### CRUNCHY VEGETABLE GARNISH

2 ears corn, cooked until just done, kernels scraped off cob

½ cup crisp cucumber, seeded and finely diced

⅓ cup finely diced radish, turnip, or carrot

Croutons, optional

1. Heat the oil in a medium skillet. Add the onions, garlic, and celery and sauté over medium heat, stirring frequently, until all are soft and golden.

2. Combine the onion mixture with ½ cup of the broth in a food processor and puree until smooth. Transfer to a soup tureen or similar serving dish.

3. Place the tomatoes in the food processor and pulse on and off until finely chopped, but not pureed. Transfer to the tureen.

4. Stir in the basil and dill, and if the soup is too dense, add a little additional broth. The soup should have a slightly thick consistency. Season with lemon juice, salt, and lots of pepper.

5. Combine all the ingredients for the vegetable garnish, except the croutons, in a small bowl. Ladle the soup into individual bowls and divide the garnish over the top of each, followed by a few croutons, if you'd like.

# Chilled Potato-Corn Chowder

**GLUTEN-FREE**
**NUT-FREE**

## 8 SERVINGS

*Here's a refreshing take on classic chowder. Potatoes and fresh corn are right at home in a creamy base, and fresh herbs tie all the flavors together.*

6 medium red-skinned or golden potatoes

4 medium ears fresh corn, broken in half, and cooked or grilled (see grilling instructions on page 207)

1½ tablespoons olive oil or other healthy vegetable oil

2 scallions, white and green parts separated, minced

1 medium carrot, peeled and finely diced

1 large celery stalk, finely diced

1 16-ounce tub firm silken tofu

4 ounces vegan cream cheese

Juice of 1 lemon, or more, to taste

2 teaspoons all-purpose seasoning blend (see sidebar on page 31)

1 teaspoon ground cumin

1 32-ounce carton vegetable broth

½ cup minced, mixed fresh herbs of your choice (use any combination of basil, dill, parsley, cilantro, and oregano)

Salt and freshly ground pepper to taste

1. Cook or microwave the potatoes in their skins until done. When cool enough to handle, peel and dice them and place in a soup tureen or similar serving container. Mash a small portion of the potatoes with a potato masher.

2. When the cooked or grilled corn is cool enough to handle, stand each half on its flat end and scrape the kernels off with a sharp knife. Place in the serving container.

3. Heat the oil in a small skillet. Add the white parts of the scallions and the carrot. Sauté over medium heat for a minute or two. Add the celery and green parts of the scallions and continue to sauté for another minute or so, just until the vegetables soften a bit.

4. Combine the tofu, cream cheese, lemon juice, seasoning blend, cumin, and 1 cup of the broth in a food processor. Process until the mixture is smoothly pureed, then transfer to the soup tureen or serving bowl.

5. Combine with the potato and corn mixture, then stir in the sautéed vegetables.

6. Add enough additional broth to give the soup a slightly thick consistency. Stir in the herbs and season with salt and pepper. Cover the bowl and chill for at least 2 hours before serving.

# Cold Avocado and Green Pea Soup

**GLUTEN-FREE**

**SOY-FREE**

**NUT-FREE**

## 6 TO 8 SERVINGS

*Chilled soups are one of my favorite ways to feel refreshed in the summer heat. What makes any cold soup even better for me is if it needs no cooking at all, like this one. And it adds a gorgeous burst of green to the table, as well.*

3 ripe avocados (two can be very ripe, one needs to be firm enough to dice)

1 16-ounce bag plus 1 cup frozen peas, completely thawed

2 scallions, green parts only, minced

¼ cup parsley leaves

Juice of ½ to 1 lime or lemon, to taste

1 teaspoon curry powder

3 cups rice milk, or as needed

Salt and freshly ground pepper to taste

### OPTIONAL GARNISHES

Lightly cooked fresh corn kernels

Short, narrow strips of corn tortillas, pan-toasted until crisp

1. Peel and pit the two riper avocados; cut them into large chunks, and place in a food processor or blender.

2. Add the 16-ounce bag of peas to the food processor or blender (setting aside the additional cup of peas), followed by the scallions, parsley, lime juice, curry powder, and 1½ cups of the rice milk. Process until velvety smooth. Transfer to a soup tureen or similar serving bowl.

3. Peel and finely dice the remaining avocado and add it to the soup along with the remaining peas. Add enough additional rice milk to give the soup a slightly thick consistency.

4. Season with salt and pepper. If time permits, cover and allow the soup to chill in the refrigerator for an hour or two before serving. Pass around optional garnishes for topping individual servings.

# FRUITY DESSERTS

Fresh Berry Sauce

Unbaked Peach and Berry Crumble

Summer Fruit Platter with Pineapple Yogurt

# Fresh Berry Sauce

**GLUTEN-FREE**
**SOY-FREE**
**NUT-FREE**

**6 TO 8 SERVINGS**

*Use this luscious sauce on nondairy ice cream or nondairy yogurt. Try combining ripe sliced peaches or nectarines with nondairy yogurt; top individual servings with this sauce. It's also wonderful on pancakes.*

2 cups fresh berries (use blueberries alone or in combination with blackberries or raspberries)

½ cup berry, pomegranate, or apple juice

2 teaspoons cornstarch or arrowroot

1 to 2 tablespoons agave nectar or maple syrup

1. Combine the berries in a medium-size saucepan with juice. Bring to a simmer, cover, and cook gently until all the berries have burst, about 6 to 8 minutes.

2. In a small bowl or glass, combine the cornstarch with just enough water to dissolve it smoothly. Stir slowly into the berry mixture and simmer until thickened, about 1 minute.

3. Add agave nectar to taste and remove from the heat. Serve warm (not hot) or room temperature.

# Unbaked Peach and Berry Crumble

**Can be made GLUTEN-FREE by using quinoa flakes instead of oats**

## 6 TO 8 SERVINGS

*When you want a lovely summer dessert but don't feel like fussing (or baking) here's just the thing. I particularly like this with raspberries.*

½ cup quick-cooking oats or quinoa flakes

⅓ cup finely chopped walnut or pecan halves

2 tablespoons natural granulated sugar

Pinch of cinnamon

2 tablespoons Earth Balance or other non-hydrogenated margarine, divided

6 to 8 medium juicy peaches or nectarines, unpeeled

2 tablespoons maple syrup

Pinch of cinnamon

1 cup raspberries or blueberries, or half of each

½ teaspoon cinnamon

Frozen nondairy ice cream for topping, optional (see Note)

1. Combine the first 4 ingredients for the crumble topping in a small bowl. Heat 1 tablespoon of margarine in a medium skillet. Add the crumble topping. Stir quickly to coat with the margarine and toast the mixture over medium heat for 3 to 5 minutes. Transfer back to the bowl and set aside.

2. Cut each peach in half lengthwise. Twist gently to separate the halves, then remove the pit. Cut each peach into thin slices.

3. Heat the remaining margarine in the same skillet. Add the peaches, syrup, and cinnamon. Sauté, stirring frequently, until the peaches have softened but still hold their shape, about 5 to 7 minutes.

4. Transfer the peaches to a shallow serving bowl and scatter the berries over them, followed by the crumble topping.

5. Cover and refrigerate until needed or serve at once. This is good served cold or warm. Top each serving with a scoop of the optional nondairy ice cream.

**NOTE:** This is great with basic vanilla. Using butter pecan, mango, or one of the coconut-based varieties is nice if you want to go for a little extra flair.

**GLUTEN-FREE**

**Can be made SOY-FREE by using coconut yogurt**

**NUT-FREE (if coconut yogurt is safe for you; otherwise use the soy yogurt option)**

## 6 TO 8 SERVINGS

*For this presentation, the kind and amount of fruit matters less than the quality and arrangement of it. This almost qualifies as a "non-recipe," but including it here is a gentle reminder to include fruit-filled desserts in your midsummer entertaining plans. For the platter, use at least four kinds of fruit from the suggestions below.*

### PINEAPPLE YOGURT

1½ cups piña colada, vanilla, or lemon nondairy yogurt (soy or coconut)

1 8-ounce can crushed pineapple, well drained

1 to 2 teaspoons grated fresh or jarred ginger, or to taste

### FRUIT PLATTER

Melon wedges, as desired (use a combination of red and yellow watermelon, cantaloupe, and honeydew)

Fresh pineapple chunks

2 or 3 peaches or nectarines, pitted and sliced

4 or so plums or pluots, pitted and quartered

1 cup or so blueberries or blackberries

1 cup or so strawberries, hulled

½ cup toasted slivered or sliced almonds

1. Combine all the ingredients for the pineapple yogurt in a small serving bowl and stir until well blended. Place in the center of a large serving platter.

2. Arrange the fruit artfully on the platter around the bowl of yogurt. Let guests help themselves to fruit on individual small plates, with a dollop of the yogurt spooned over each serving, followed by the optional toasted nuts.

# SUMMER FRUIT DESSERT IDEAS: DECLARING FREEDOM FROM RECIPES

Even with the air conditioner running, I'm not fond of baking during the summer. I simply have no desire to turn on the oven, so cookies, cakes, and pie can all wait until the nip of autumn is in the air. Summer is the time to take full advantage of fruit, when there's the most variety. A beautiful fruit platter or fruit salad filled with melons, berries, and stone fruit (Summer Fruit Platter with Pineapple Yogurt, opposite) has no equal as a finish to a summer meal. Accompany these kinds of fruity presentations, if desired, with one of the many fantastic frozen nondairy ice creams. These have proliferated over the last decade or so, and, in some venues, nondairy ice creams seem to be overtaking their dairy counterparts in terms of sheer variety. Here are a few more recipe-free ideas for summer entertaining.

*Red, white, and blue parfaits:* Hull and slice a pint of sweet, ripe strawberries. Wash and stem a pint of blueberries. Place ¼ cup of blueberries in each of 8 parfait cups or tumblers. Cover with ¼ to ½ cup vanilla or butter pecan nondairy ice cream; then top with ¼ cup strawberries.

*Fruit skewers:* For a fun change of pace from fruit salad, thread chunks of cantaloupe, honeydew, watermelon, whole small strawberries, and stone fruits onto bamboo skewers.

*Drunken strawberries:* Hull and slice a pint or two of strawberries and put in a bowl. Sprinkle in a teaspoon or two of natural granulated sugar to draw out their juices. Stir in ¼ cup or so of kirsch, amaretto, or other sweet liqueur. Let stand for about 30 minutes. Serve over nondairy ice cream—any flavor!

*Fruit duos and trios:* Sometimes, combining two or three beautiful, lush fruits can be just as appealing—and more dramatic—than a fruit salad. Try pairing offbeat varieties of common fruits with colorful partners. Look for yellow watermelon, greengage plums, and pluots (a plum/apricot hybrid), for example, and partner them with berries, apricots, honeydew, and black plums with deep red flesh—the possibilities are limited only by what's in season.

CHAPTER SIX

# BRUNCHES, APPETIZERS, AND POTLUCK DISHES

**I**n this last chapter you'll find an array of delectable recipes suitable for many occasions that call for cooking and sharing—casual brunches for company, for example. Also included is a selection of hot and cold appetizers as well as sturdy dishes that work well whether you serve them as components of informal at-home buffets or transport them to potlucks and other cooperatively prepared festivities. Finally, I'd like to leave you with a trio of additional tips for making at-home entertaining fun and stress-free:

○ Consider serving casual meals buffet-style. Guests like to serve themselves—whatever they like, in the amounts they like (and it's less work for the host). In addition, it's often awkward to pass hot and/ or heavy serving platters around the table. Once your guests have filled their plates and are ready to sit down to eat, make sure that any food that should stay warm is covered; a lot of the dishes in this chapter taste just as good warm or at room temperature as they do hot, so there's no need for 1950s-style chafing dishes (although they are rather nifty).

○ I like to have all the food ready ahead of time so I can sit and relax with my guests once they've arrived. Other cooks prefer to assemble a small crowd around them as they finish preparing the food. If you're one of the latter, more power to you, since you'll probably get lots of offers for

**A Big Pot of Really Good Chili, see page 294**

on-the-spot help. But if you don't want this kind of prep to go on for hours, at least have your veggies and other ingredients ready, so you can put the finishing touches on any of the dishes you're making in front of a live audience.

○ Above all, try to leave stress out of the equation when you're planning and making meals. Let go of perfection. Serve your vegan creations with pride, and your efforts will be appreciated by others.

## HEARTY BRUNCH FARE

"Brunch" is a tidy word that comes straight to the point—a meal that's a cross between breakfast and lunch. But as a concept, brunch is so much more than just that—it calls to mind leisurely eating, casual elegance, and celebrations large and small.

The concept of brunch used to evoke images of eggs Benedict with Hollandaise sauce, huge omelets, or bagels with cream cheese and lox, among other foods so heavy that you'd want to rush back to bed in a lethargic stupor. This need not be the case. Contemporary brunches can be designed around wholesome, natural ingredients and seasonal produce. The following menus for intimate brunches will leave you and your guests with the wonderful sense of having celebrated but not overindulged.

Use these stress-free menus to plan any fun and casual meal, whether you're entertaining overnight guests or celebrating New Year's Day.

# THREE BRUNCH MENUS

## SOUTHWEST BRUNCH

Baked Tofu-Tortilla Extravaganza

✿

Refried Beans

✿

Roasted Squashes and Peppers

✿

Grape tomatoes and black olives

✿

Platter of orange or grapefruit sections and sliced avocado

## SAVORY SKILLET BRUNCH

Multi-Veg Hash Browns

❧

Rosemary Potato and Sausage Skillet

OR

Spinach or Arugula Scrambled Tofu


## SOUTHERN COMFORT BRUNCH

Hoppin' John (Black-Eyed Peas and Rice)

❧

Simple Garlicky Greens

❧

Apple and Broccoli Coleslaw

# Baked Tofu-Tortilla Extravaganza

**GLUTEN-FREE**

Can be made **SOY-FREE** by using a soy-free nondairy cheese
and using cashew cream (see page 96) instead of soy-based sour cream

**NUT-FREE**

**6 TO 8 SERVINGS**

*This is a favorite go-to recipe for company brunch. I've been making it for years, and it never fails to please, especially if you start out with some grape tomatoes and black olives and finish with a platter of grapefruit sections and sliced avocado.*

- 1  16-ounce tub firm tofu
- 2  tablespoons extra-virgin olive oil
- 1  large onion, finely chopped
- 2  cloves garlic, minced
- 8  corn tortillas, cut into approximately 1-inch square pieces
- 1  14- to 16-ounce can crushed tomatoes
- 2  medium-firm, ripe tomatoes, diced
- 1  fresh, hot green chili pepper, seeded and minced, or one 4- to 8-ounce can mild green chilies, chopped
- 1  teaspoon ground cumin, or more, to taste
- 1  teaspoon chili powder, or more, to taste
- 1  teaspoon dried oregano

   Salt to taste

- 1  cup grated cheddar-style nondairy cheese

   Vegan sour cream (homemade, see page 96, or store-bought) for topping, optional

1. Preheat the oven to 400° F.

2. Cut the tofu into ½-inch-thick slices, and blot the slices gently between paper towels or a clean tea towel. Cut the slices into ½-inch dice.

3. Heat the oil in a large skillet. Sauté the onion over medium heat until translucent. Add the garlic and tofu dice and continue to sauté until all are golden.

4. Combine the tofu mixture with all the remaining ingredients except the last two and stir until thoroughly mixed. Pour into an oiled 2-quart casserole dish (round or oval is most attractive, but rectangular works as well) and pat in.

5. Sprinkle the cheese over the top. Bake for 25 minutes, or until the cheese is melted. Let stand for 5 minutes, then cut into squares or wedges to serve. Pass around sour cream for topping individual servings if desired.

# Refried Beans

**GLUTEN-FREE**
**Can be made SOY-FREE by using a soy-free nondairy cheese,**
**or eliminating nondairy cheese option**
**NUT-FREE**

### 6 TO 8 SERVINGS

*Frijoles Refritos are the perfect complement to the tortilla casserole in this menu. You can make this side dish mild or piquant, depending on what type of chilies you'd like to use. This is a good dish to make ahead of time.*

1½ tablespoons olive oil or other healthy vegetable oil

1 medium onion, minced

3 to 4 cloves garlic, minced

2 15- to 16-ounce cans pinto beans

1 fresh, hot chili pepper, seeded and minced, or one 4-ounce can mild green chilies, diced

Salt to taste

½ cup grated Jack- or cheddar-style nondairy cheese, optional

Minced fresh cilantro for garnish, optional

1. Heat the oil in a large skillet. Add the onion and sauté over medium heat until translucent. Add the garlic and continue to sauté until both are golden.

2. Add the pinto beans and sauté until warmed, about 5 minutes, stirring frequently.

3. Add ½ cup water, then mash the beans coarsely with a potato masher. Add chilies and continue to cook over low heat, adding small amounts of water, until the beans have the consistency of a very thick sauce, about 8 minutes.

4. Sprinkle in the optional cheese and cook until completely melted. Transfer to a serving bowl and sprinkle with a small amount of cilantro if desired.

# Roasted Squashes and Peppers

**GLUTEN-FREE**

**SOY-FREE**

**NUT-FREE**

### 8 OR MORE SERVINGS

*This colorful array of veggies, served as a warm salad, is a lovely foil for hearty casseroles and beans.*

2 medium zucchini, cut into thick slices

1 medium yellow summer squash, cut into thick slices

1 large red bell pepper, cut into long, wide strips

1 large yellow bell pepper, cut to match red pepper

2 tablespoons extra-virgin olive oil

2 tablespoons red wine vinegar or balsamic vinegar

½ teaspoon dried oregano

¼ teaspoon dried thyme

¼ cup sliced sun-dried tomatoes, oil-cured or not, as you prefer

Salt and freshly ground pepper to taste

Mixed baby greens as desired

1. Preheat the oven to 425° F.

2. Combine the squashes and bell peppers in a mixing bowl. Drizzle in the oil and vinegar, then sprinkle in the oregano and thyme and toss well.

3. Pour the vegetables into a foil- or parchment-lined roasting pan. Bake for 20 to 25 minutes, stirring every 5 to 10 minutes, or until they begin to brown.

4. Remove from the oven. Stir in the dried tomatoes and season with salt and pepper.

5. Line a serving platter with greens, and mound the roasted vegetables over them. Serve warm or at room temperature.

# Multi-Veg Hash Browns

**GLUTEN-FREE**
**SOY-FREE**
**NUT-FREE**

## 6 TO 8 SERVINGS

*This is an excellent companion for Spinach or Arugula Scrambled Tofu (see page 272). Here, traditional potato hash browns are given an interesting twist with the addition of companionable root vegetables.*

4 medium Yukon Gold or red-skinned potatoes

4 to 6 medium mixed root vegetables (choose 2 to 3 from among golden beets, sweet potato, turnips, parsnip daikon radish, etc.)

3 tablespoons extra-virgin olive oil

1 medium onion, finely chopped

¼ cup minced fresh parsley

1 teaspoon sweet paprika

Salt and freshly ground pepper to taste

1. To give the potatoes (including sweet potato, if using) a head start, cook, bake, or microwave them until you are just able to pierce them with a fork. When cool enough to handle, peel and dice them.

2. Peel and dice the other root vegetables you will be using, cutting them to a consistent size for even cooking.

3. Heat half the oil in a large skillet. Add the onion and sauté over medium heat until just starting to turn golden.

4. Add the diced potatoes and other root vegetables. Drizzle in the remaining oil; sauté over medium-high heat, stirring frequently, until the vegetables are evenly browned.

5. Remove from the heat; stir in the parsley and paprika, season with salt and pepper, and serve.

# Rosemary Potato and Sausage Skillet

**NUT-FREE**

**6 TO 8 SERVINGS**

*As an alternative to hash browns, this dish is quite robust—a good choice if your brunch crowd is extra-hungry. It also pairs beautifully with Spinach or Arugula Scrambled Tofu (see page 272).*

6 medium-large potatoes, red-skinned or Yukon Gold, well scrubbed

2 tablespoons extra-virgin olive oil

1 to 2 medium leeks, white parts only, chopped and rinsed well

2 Tofurky or Field Roast vegan sausage links, cut in half lengthwise, then into ½-inch slices

1 medium red bell pepper, cut into short, narrow strips

3 to 4 scallions, thinly sliced

Leaves from 2 sprigs fresh rosemary

1 teaspoon paprika

Salt and freshly ground pepper to taste

Dried hot red pepper flakes to taste, optional

1. Cook, bake, or microwave the potatoes ahead of time until they can be pierced with a fork but are still nice and firm. When cool enough to handle, cut in half lengthwise, then cut into ½-inch-thick half-circles.

2. Heat half the oil and 2 tablespoons of water in a large skillet. Add the leeks, cover, and sweat over medium heat for 3 minutes.

3. Add the remaining oil, then stir in the potatoes, sausage, and bell pepper. Turn the heat up to medium-high and sauté until the vegetables are golden, stirring frequently.

4. Stir in the scallions, rosemary, and paprika, and sauté for 2 to 3 minutes longer. Season with salt, pepper, and red pepper flakes, and serve.

# Spinach or Arugula Scrambled Tofu

**GLUTEN-FREE**

**NUT-FREE**

**6 TO 8 SERVINGS**

*Here's a colorful, tasty tofu scramble that's festive enough for a company brunch, but simple enough to make for a weekend meal for you and yours. To complete the meal, add a simple green salad, fresh greens, and a beautiful seasonal fruit platter*

- 2 16-ounce tubs firm or extra-firm tofu
- 2 tablespoons olive oil or other healthy vegetable oil
- 2 medium red bell peppers, cut into strips
- 1 teaspoon all-purpose seasoning blend (see sidebar on page 31)
- 1 to 2 teaspoons curry powder, to taste
- ¼ teaspoon turmeric
- 3 to 4 scallions, sliced
- 2 medium firm, ripe tomatoes, diced
- 6 to 8 ounces baby spinach or arugula leaves

  Salt and freshly ground pepper to taste

1. Cut the block of tofu into 6 equal slabs. Blot well between layers of paper towels. Cut the slabs into ½-inch dice.

2. Heat the oil in a wide skillet. Add the tofu and bell pepper and sauté over medium heat, stirring frequently, until the tofu is golden on most sides and the bell pepper has softened.

3. Sprinkle in the seasoning, curry powder, and turmeric, and stir until the tofu dice are more or less evenly coated with the spices.

4. Stir in the scallions and tomatoes and cook for 2 to 3 minutes, or until softened.

5. Add the spinach or arugula, cover, and cook until wilted. Stir the spinach into the tofu mixture. Remove from the heat, season with salt and pepper, and serve from the skillet.

# Hoppin' John
# (Black-Eyed Peas and Rice)

**NUT-FREE**

**6 SERVINGS**

*Black-eyed peas are considered a good-luck food in the Deep South and are traditionally eaten on New Year's Day. Sometimes, a few coins are mixed into the dish, and finding a coin in your helping brings good luck. Even if you pass, as I do, on the coins, cooking up a big batch of Hoppin' John seems like an appealing choice for New Year's Day. Green Chili Corn Bread or Muffins (page 11) are perfect complements to this hearty dish. Sliced oranges make a nice finish.*

1  cup raw brown rice, rinsed

3  tablespoons extra-virgin olive oil

1  14-ounce package Tofurky or one 13-ounce package Field Roast vegan sausages, cut into ½-inch slices

1  large onion, finely chopped

3 to 4  cloves garlic, minced

1  14- to 16-ounce can diced tomatoes, with liquid

2  teaspoons dried basil, or ¼ cup fresh basil

1  teaspoon dried thyme

1  15- to 16-ounce can black-eyed peas, drained and rinsed

Dried hot red pepper flakes, to taste

Salt and freshly ground pepper to taste

½  cup minced fresh parsley, plus more for topping

**1.** Combine the rice with 2½ cups water in a saucepan and bring to a boil. Lower the heat and simmer gently until the water is absorbed, about 30 minutes.

**2.** Meanwhile, heat 1 tablespoon of the oil in an extra-wide skillet. Add the sausage and sauté over medium heat, stirring frequently, until golden brown on most sides, about 5 to 7 minutes total. Remove to a plate and set aside.

**3.** Heat the remaining oil in the same skillet. Add the onion and sauté over medium heat until translucent. Add the garlic and continue to sauté until the onion is golden.

**4.** Add the tomatoes, dried basil (if using fresh basil, save for later), thyme, and black-eyed peas. Cook for 5 minutes over low heat, then stir in the sausage and cook for 5 minutes longer.

**5.** Once the rice is done, stir it into the mixture, then season with the red pepper flakes, salt, and lots of pepper. Stir together well and simmer over low heat for 10 to 15 minutes. Add a small amount of water to keep the mixture moist. Stir in the parsley and fresh basil if using, then pass around additional parsley for topping individual servings.

# Simple Garlicky Greens

**GLUTEN-FREE**
**SOY-FREE**
**NUT-FREE**

**6 SERVINGS**

*This is a very simple way to prepare chard, kale, or collard greens—a "mess o' greens," as they were once commonly referred to—but sometimes simple is best. This is definitely true when it comes to something as good as leafy greens.*

1 large bunch (1 to 1½ pounds) greens of your choice

1 tablespoon extra-virgin olive oil

3 to 4 cloves garlic, minced

Juice of ½ lemon

Salt and freshly ground pepper to taste

1. Remove stems and thick midribs from whatever type of greens you are using. It's important to wash them thoroughly, dousing a batch at a time in a large bowl to make sure that all sand and grit are removed.

2. If you'd like to use the midribs, slice them very thin. Otherwise, discard (or save for another use), then stack a few leaves and cut them into wide strips.

3. Heat the oil in a large soup pot or steep-sided stir-fry pan. Add the garlic and sauté over low heat for 2 to 3 minutes, until golden.

4. Add the greens to the pot. For chard and kale, add just enough water to keep the bottom of the pot moist. For collards, add 1 to 1½ cups water, as needed. Check frequently. Chard takes 3 to 5 minutes, kale about 5 minutes, and collards 10 to 15 minutes.

5. When done, drain and transfer to a colander. Press out some of the liquid, then transfer to a cutting board and chop further, if desired.

6. Transfer the greens to a serving dish, toss with the lemon juice. Season to taste with salt and pepper and serve at once.

# Apple and Broccoli Coleslaw

**GLUTEN-FREE**

**Can be made NUT-FREE by omitting optional walnuts**

**6 TO 8 SERVINGS**

*This simple slaw offers color, crunch, and a nice contrast to the hearty flavors of Hoppin' John and the garlicky greens in this menu.*

3 cups green cabbage, or a combination of green and red cabbage, coarsely shredded

1 large, crisp red apple, cored, cut into 8 wedges, and thinly sliced

2 large celery stalks, cut diagonally

1 cup very finely chopped broccoli florets

¼ cup finely chopped walnuts, optional

½ cup vegan mayonnaise, or as desired

2 tablespoons lemon juice

1. Combine all the ingredients in a serving bowl and toss together well. Cover and let stand for 15 minutes or so before serving.

# EASY APPETIZERS

Marinated Mushrooms, Asparagus, and Artichokes

Olive and Dried Tomato Tapenade

Spanish-Style Ajillo Asparagus with Mushrooms

Olive Bar Medley with Tofu "Feta"

Smoky Cheddar Cheez

Roasted Red Pepper and Sun-Dried Tomato Guacamole

Spinach and Cucumber Spread

White Bean and Sun-Dried Tomato Pâté

Green Pea, Parsley, and Pistachio Dip or Spread

Dilled Miso-Tahini Dip

Pan-Grilled Polenta

Bruschetta

# Marinated Mushrooms, Asparagus, and Artichokes

**GLUTEN-FREE (served with gluten-free accompaniments)**

**NUT-FREE**

### 6 TO 8 APPETIZER-SIZE SERVINGS

*This little appetizer salad is nice served in tandem with Olive and Dried Tomato Tapenade (page 279) and/or Smoky Cheddar Cheez (page 284) or Bruschetta (page 291), or serve with fresh sliced baguette as well.*

8 ounces small button mushrooms

8 ounces slender asparagus

1 10-ounce package frozen artichoke hearts, thawed and cut in half

1 small zucchini, quartered lengthwise and sliced

1 large half-sour dill pickle, chopped

2 tablespoons minced fresh dill, or more, to taste

2 tablespoons minced fresh parsley

⅓ cup vegan mayonnaise

Juice of ½ lemon

Salt and freshly ground pepper to taste

1. Wipe the mushrooms clean and trim the stem bottoms if they look dark or fibrous. If the mushrooms are larger than button size, cut them in half. Place in a skillet with just enough water to keep moist; cover and steam over moderate heat for 2 minutes, then drain and let cool.

2. Trim the bottoms of the asparagus, then cut the stalks into 1-inch pieces. Using the same skillet, add just enough water to keep the bottom moist, cover, and steam until the asparagus is bright green and crisp-tender. Drain and rinse with cool water.

3. Combine the mushrooms and asparagus in a serving dish. Add the artichoke hearts, zucchini, pickle, and herbs. In a small bowl, mix the mayonnaise and lemon juice until smoothly combined. Pour over the vegetables and toss well. Add salt and pepper to taste and toss again. This can be made ahead and refrigerated until needed.

# Olive and Dried Tomato Tapenade

**GLUTEN-FREE (served with gluten-free accompaniments)**
**SOY-FREE**

**MAKES I CUP**

*Really easy and very tasty, this is a good go-to appetizer when you have little time to spare—it's done in minutes. It's equally good with Bruschetta (page 291), Pan-Grilled Polenta (page 290), flat breads, or a fresh, sliced baguette.*

½ cup pitted brine-cured black or green olives

½ cup sun-dried tomatoes, oil-cured or not, as preferred

½ cup fresh parsley leaves

¼ cup walnut or pecan pieces

I tablespoon lemon juice, or to taste

1. Place all the ingredients in a food processor with ¼ cup water. Pulse on and off until everything is finely and evenly minced. If needed, add a small amount of additional water so that the mixture comes together.

2. Transfer to an attractive crock and serve with the desired accompaniments.

# Spanish-Style Ajillo Asparagus with Mushrooms

**GLUTEN-FREE (served with gluten-free accompaniments)**
**SOY-FREE**
**NUT-FREE**

**6 OR MORE SERVINGS**

*This is inspired by the garlicky Spanish tapas dish* champiñones al ajillo, *which relies on mushrooms alone. Adding asparagus makes it a more substantial dish, and it benefits nicely from the dry red wine and other seasonings. This garlicky dish is traditionally served with slices of warm, fresh bread. And since you've already opened a bottle of red wine, serve it with this appetizer as well.*

8 ounces asparagus

8 ounces mushrooms (cremini or baby bella combined with a smaller amount of shiitakes works nicely)

2 tablespoons extra-virgin olive oil

6 to 8 cloves garlic, minced (about 2 tablespoons)

¼ cup good, dry red wine or sherry

Juice of ½ lemon (about 2 tablespoons)

½ teaspoon paprika, preferably smoked Spanish paprika, or more, to taste

Dried hot red pepper flakes to taste, optional

Salt and freshly ground pepper to taste

¼ cup minced fresh parsley

1. Trim about an inch from the bottom of the asparagus stalks. Unless they are nice and slender, peel the bottom halves with a vegetable peeler.

2. Clean the mushrooms, then stem and quarter them.

3. Heat the oil in a medium skillet. Add the garlic and sauté over low heat until golden. Add the mushrooms and asparagus, and cook over high heat for about 2 minutes, stirring constantly.

4. Lower the heat to medium and add the wine, lemon juice, paprika, and dried pepper flakes. Cook for about 3 minutes longer, or just until the asparagus is tender-crisp and the mushrooms have softened.

5. Remove from the heat. Season with salt and pepper. Transfer to a serving platter, and sprinkle with the parsley. This is good served warm or at room temperature.

# Olive Bar Medley
# with Tofu "Feta"

**GLUTEN-FREE**
**NUT-FREE**

## 12 SERVINGS

*Small servings of this colorful and briny appetizer go a long way. Choose two or three different varieties of pitted olives from your supermarket's olive bar. You can also spice up the mix with any of the extra items suggested in the ingredient list, such as pickled peppers or garlic. If you'd like to pair this appetizer with some others, my suggestion would be to choose something mellow, like Green Pea, Parsley, and Pistachio Dip or Spread (page 288), a fresh sliced baguette, Bruschetta (page 291), or Pan-Grilled Polenta (page 290) for a gluten-free choice.*

8   ounces extra-firm tofu

3   tablespoons lemon juice

2   tablespoons extra-virgin olive oil

¼   teaspoon salt

¼   teaspoon oregano

1½  cups mixed, cured, pitted olives

2   celery stalks, thinly sliced
    on the diagonal

1   small red bell pepper, cut
    into narrow strips

½   to ¾ cup pepperoncini, cherry
    peppers, other small pickled
    peppers, or pickled garlic,
    or a combination

1. Slice the tofu into 4 slabs, crosswise. Blot between layers of paper towel or clean tea towels until you get out as much moisture as you can. Cut the slabs into ½-inch dice. Place in a serving dish, in a single layer. Toss with the lemon juice and oil; sprinkle with the salt and oregano. Let stand for 30 minutes.

2. Add the remaining ingredients to the serving dish and toss gently. This recipe can be made ahead of time and refrigerated until needed, or served at once. Let guests serve themselves, spooning portions onto individual small plates; serve with cocktail forks or toothpicks.

# Smoky Cheddar Cheez

**GLUTEN-FREE**

Can be made **SOY-FREE** by omitting vegan cream cheese and adding ¼ cup of additional cashews

**8 TO 10 SERVINGS**

*Like the Creamy Cracked-Pepper Cheez on page 79, this is the kind of treat I find completely addictive. You can make it as a spread in no time, or let it set up into slices. I like it both ways and hope that you will, too. Like the other spreads in this section, Smoky Cheddar Cheez is good with a sliced fresh baguette, whole-grain crackers, crisp breads, or Bruschetta (page 291). It's also quite nice served with chunks of red bell pepper and celery stalks cut into short pieces.*

1 cup raw cashews

½ cup baby carrots

1 cup rice milk

¼ cup agar flakes, optional

¼ cup vegan cream cheese

¼ cup nutritional yeast flakes

2 to 3 tablespoons lemon juice, to taste

1 teaspoon prepared yellow or Dijon mustard

2 teaspoons mesquite seasoning, or more, to taste

1 teaspoon sweet paprika

1 teaspoon salt

Pinch of turmeric

1. Combine the cashews, carrots, and rice milk in a small saucepan. Bring to a rapid simmer, then cover and simmer gently for 5 to 8 minutes, or until the carrots are tender-crisp. If you plan to make slices, stir in the agar flakes and continue to simmer for 5 minutes longer.

2. Transfer the mixture to a food processor along with the remaining ingredients and process until very smooth. Stop the machine and scrape down the sides of the work bowl with a rubber spatula from time to time. It takes a good few minutes to make this smooth (at least 3 minutes, depending on the speed of your processor).

3. If you skipped the agar and plan to serve this as a spread, transfer to an attractive crock. Allow to cool, then cover and let stand at room temperature until needed, or cover and chill.

4. If you used the agar, transfer the mixture to a lightly oiled loaf pan (or 2 mini-loaf pans). Pat in as smoothly as you can. Refrigerate for at least 2 hours.

5. Before serving, run a knife around the edges of the loaf pan(s). Turn upside down onto a serving platter. If you'd like, sprinkle a little extra mesquite seasoning over the top. Slice ¼ inch thick.

# Roasted Red Pepper and Sun-Dried Tomato Guacamole

**GLUTEN-FREE (served with gluten-free accompaniments)**

**SOY-FREE**

**NUT-FREE**

**MAKES ABOUT 2 CUPS**

*Guacamole and tortilla chips are always a welcome appetizer duo. The addition of dried tomatoes and roasted peppers lifts this recipe from the familiar to the fantastic. It's best to make this recipe just before serving to preserve the bright color of the avocado.*

2  medium, very ripe avocados, pitted, peeled, and mashed

Juice of ½ to 1 lemon, to taste

1  jarred, roasted red pepper, drained and finely chopped

¼  cup sun-dried tomatoes (oil-cured or not, as preferred), cut into strips

1  medium-firm, ripe tomato, finely diced

¼  cup finely chopped onion, or 1 to 2 scallions, minced

¼  cup minced fresh cilantro

1  jalapeño pepper, seeded and minced, or one 8-ounce can diced mild green chilies

1  teaspoon ground cumin

Salt and freshly ground pepper to taste

Good-quality tortilla chips

1. Combine the mashed avocados with the lemon juice in a mixing bowl and stir together. Add the remaining ingredients and stir again. Transfer to a shallow serving bowl or crock and serve with tortilla chips.

# Spinach and Cucumber Spread

**GLUTEN-FREE (served with gluten-free accompaniments)**

**NUT-FREE**

## MAKES ABOUT 2 CUPS

*One of my old favorites, this tasty spinach spread never loses its charm. Serve it with the usual suspects—whole-grain crackers, flat breads, Bruschetta (page 291), Pan-Grilled Polenta (page 290), or raw veggies. This wonderful spread is compatible with carrots, cauliflower, bell pepper, and celery.*

½ cup finely chopped, seeded cucumber

1 10-ounce package frozen spinach, thawed, moisture completely squeezed out

1 12.3-ounce package firm silken tofu

Juice of ½ lemon

1 scallion, minced

1 tablespoon minced fresh dill, or 1 teaspoon dried dill

1 teaspoon all-purpose seasoning blend (see sidebar on page 31), more or less to taste

¼ teaspoon dried basil

Freshly ground pepper to taste

1. Spread the chopped cucumber over two or three layers of paper towels. Cover with another two layers, then place a cutting board or some other weight on top. Let stand.

2. Place the spinach in the food processor and process until smoothly pureed. Add the remaining ingredients (except the cucumber) and process until the spinach is well incorporated with the tofu, but not completely pureed.

3. Transfer to a serving bowl and stir in the cucumber. Serve at once or cover and refrigerate until needed.

# White Bean and Sun-Dried Tomato Pâté

**GLUTEN-FREE (served with gluten-free accompaniments)**

**SOY-FREE**

**NUT-FREE**

**MAKES ABOUT 2 CUPS**

*Here's another old standby that never fails to please. It goes well with whole-grain crackers, flat breads, Bruschetta (page 291), and Pan-Grilled Polenta (page 290). For an extra-fancy presentation, hollow out a round loaf of bread to make a container for it. Make the sliceable version of Smoky Cheddar Cheez (page 284) and serve with crisp red grapes for a lovely array of appetizers.*

1 tablespoon olive oil or other healthy vegetable oil

1 large onion, chopped

2 cloves garlic, minced

1 15- to 16-ounce can cannellini or great northern beans, drained and rinsed

¼ cup oil-cured sun-dried tomatoes

Juice of ½ lemon

2 to 3 tablespoons chopped fresh parsley

¼ teaspoon dried thyme

Salt and freshly ground pepper to taste

**1.** Heat the oil in a skillet. Add the onion and sauté over moderate heat until translucent. Add the garlic and continue to sauté until the onion is just beginning to brown.

**2.** Combine the onion mixture with all the remaining ingredients except the salt and pepper in a food processor and process until completely smooth. Drizzle in 2 tablespoons of water or so to loosen the consistency. Stop and scrape down the sides of the work bowl as needed.

**3.** Season to taste with salt and pepper. Pat into an attractive shallow crock to serve, or into a bread "bowl" as suggested in the recipe introduction. Place on a large platter and surround with whole-grain crackers and crisp breads.

# Green Pea, Parsley, and Pistachio Dip or Spread

**GLUTEN-FREE (served with gluten-free accompaniments)**
**SOY-FREE**

**MAKES ABOUT 1 CUP**

*This festive dip is quite versatile. It's great with raw vegetables, especially baby carrots, red bell pepper, and Belgian endive leaves. It also makes an elegant appetizer served with Pan-Grilled Polenta (page 290).*

1 cup frozen green peas, thawed

½ cup very firmly packed parsley leaves

½ cup shelled toasted pistachios (see Note)

1 tablespoon extra-virgin olive oil

Juice of ½ lemon, or more, to taste

½ teaspoon salt, or to taste

Freshly ground pepper to taste

1. Steam the peas in a steamer basket or in a small saucepan with just enough water to keep moist, until bright green and just tender-crisp. Drain and rinse under cool water.

2. In a food processor, combine the peas with the parsley, pistachios, olive oil, lemon juice, salt, pepper, and ¼ cup water. Process until the mixture is an even, coarse puree, stopping occasionally to scrape down the sides of the work bowl. The mixture should have the consistency of pesto sauce.

3. If you'd like a looser consistency, drizzle in a little more water with the machine running. Taste, and if you'd like a more lemony flavor, add the juice of the other half lemon as well.

**NOTE:** Look for pre-shelled pistachios in well-stocked supermarkets and natural foods stores.

# Dilled Miso-Tahini Dip

**GLUTEN-FREE (served with gluten-free accompaniments; make sure the optional nutritional yeast is gluten-free)**

**NUT-FREE**

**MAKES ABOUT 1½ CUPS**

*Scoop up this delicious dip with raw vegetables, bagel chips, or wedges of pita bread.*

8 ounces soft or firm tofu

¼ cup tahini (sesame paste)

3 tablespoons mellow white miso

1 tablespoon fresh lemon juice

2 to 3 tablespoons chopped fresh dill

1 scallion, chopped

2 tablespoons nutritional yeast, optional

1. Cut the tofu into 3 or 4 slabs. Blot well between layers of paper towel or clean tea towel.

2. Combine all the ingredients in a food processor or blender. Process until smooth. Transfer to a serving bowl and serve at once, or cover and refrigerate until needed.

# Pan-Grilled Polenta

**GLUTEN-FREE**
**SOY-FREE**
**NUT-FREE**

**8 TO 10 SERVINGS**

*Pan-grilled polenta is a great alternative to bread or crackers for serving with almost any of the spreads in this section, especially if you eat gluten-free. It's particularly good with Olive and Dried Tomato Tapenade (page 279) or Green Pea, Parsley, and Pistachio Dip or Spread (page 288).*

2  18-ounce tubes polenta

Olive oil cooking spray

**1.** Cut the puckered ends off each tube of polenta, then cut into 12 slices each, about ½ inch thick.

**2.** Heat a wide, nonstick pan or griddle that has been generously sprayed with olive oil cooking spray. Arrange the polenta slices on the griddle. Cook both sides over medium-high heat until golden and crisp, about 8 minutes per side.

**3.** Transfer to a platter and serve with your choice of dip or spread.

**VARIATION:** Cut each round of polenta into 4 little wedges before pan-grilling. Serve on a platter with cocktail toothpicks.

# Bruschetta

**Can be made GLUTEN-FREE by using gluten-free specialty bread**

**SOY-FREE**

**NUT-FREE**

**8 TO 10 SERVINGS**

*These garlicky toasts are a handy accompaniment for many dips and spreads. You can also use them for dipping into hot soups.*

1   long fresh baguette or Italian bread (not too skinny, please!)

Olive oil cooking spray

1   large clove garlic, halved

1. Preheat the oven to 350° F.

2. Cut the bread into approximately ½- to ¾-inch-thick slices. Place them on a nonstick baking sheet. Spray the tops lightly with the cooking oil. Bake for 7 minutes, then turn them, spray lightly again, and continue to bake for 5 to 7 more minutes, until golden and crisp. Remove from the oven and cool completely.

3. When cool enough to handle, rub one side of each slice of toast with the open side of the garlic. To serve, place the toast in a (preferably cloth) napkin-lined bowl or basket.

# POTLUCK AND BUFFET DISHES

Plantain Fritters with Black Bean Dip

A Big Pot of Really Good Chili

Chipotle Black Bean and Corn Salad

Festive Five-Bean Salad

Bean-Thread Noodles and Asian Vegetables
in Creamy Cashew Sauce

Three-Part Harmony Composed Salad Platter

Rice Noodles with Watercress and Cilantro

Pasta Puttanesca (Pasta with Olive Sauce)

Pappardelle with Swiss Chard

# Plantain Fritters with Black Bean Dip

**GLUTEN-FREE**

**SOY-FREE**

**NUT-FREE**

## 8 OR MORE SERVINGS

*My younger son, Evan, brought this recipe home from an extended stay in Costa Rica, where he discovered that it's a favorite pub snack. I was going to put it in the appetizer section at first, but it's so plentiful and robust that it doesn't take much more to make a meal of it. A bountiful green salad would be a great companion if you want to make it at home for your family; for company, you might want to add a soup. As a potluck or buffet offering, it's unusual and quite appealing.*

### BLACK BEAN DIP

- 1 tablespoon extra-virgin olive oil
- 2 to 3 cloves garlic, minced
- 1 15- to 16-ounce can black beans, drained and rinsed
- 1 tablespoon lemon or lime juice, or more, to taste
- 1 teaspoon chili powder or jerk seasoning, or more, to taste

  Salt and freshly ground pepper to taste

### BATTER

- 1 cup garbanzo flour
- 1 tablespoon cornstarch
- 1 tablespoon extra-virgin olive oil

  Pinch of salt

### PLAINTAINS

- 4 ripe plantains, peeled and cut into long diagonal slices about ¼ inch thick

  Olive oil or other healthy vegetable oil for sautéing

  Chopped fresh cilantro and/or minced scallion, for garnish

**1.** Heat the oil in a medium saucepan. Add the garlic and sauté over low heat until golden.

**2.** Add the beans, lemon juice, chili powder, and ½ cup water. Bring to a simmer, then mash the beans coarsely with a potato masher, just enough to break them up a bit. Add a bit more water if needed; the mixture should have a flowing but not soupy consistency. Simmer gently for 3 to 4 minutes. Season with salt and pepper, then cover and remove from the heat.

**3.** Combine all the ingredients for the batter in a large mixing bowl with 1 cup water and whisk together. Add the plantain slices to the batter and stir until they're evenly coated.

**4.** Heat enough oil to coat the bottom of a large nonstick skillet. Scoop the plantain slices from the bowl with a fork, and carefully arrange in the hot skillet, a few at a time. Cook on both sides over medium-high heat until golden brown. Keep an eye on them, as they cook very quickly.

**5.** Remove cooked slices to a paper towel–lined plate and continue until the fritters are done, adding layers of paper towel as needed.

**6.** To serve, transfer the bean dip to a serving bowl (a ceramic crock is nice). Garnish with cilantro and/or scallions. Place the bowl in the center of a large platter and surround with the plantain fritters. Serve warm or at room temperature.

# A Big Pot of Really Good Chili

**GLUTEN-FREE**

**SOY-FREE**

**NUT-FREE**

## 12 OR MORE SERVINGS

*When you need a heaping helping of something fast, inexpensive, and filling, few things are better than a big pot of chili. Of course, bean chilies—without the* carne*—have become a vegetarian standard; this is the recipe I've been making for years. It's a great choice for casual winter parties and for Super Bowl Sunday (see photo on page 260).*

2   tablespoons extra-virgin olive oil

2   medium onions, finely chopped

4   to 6 cloves garlic, minced

1   medium green bell pepper, diced

1   medium red bell pepper, diced

3   28-ounce cans beans of your choice (try a combination of pinto, pink, and black beans), drained and rinsed

1   28-ounce can diced tomatoes, with liquid

1   16-ounce can tomato sauce

1   to 2 jalapeño or other hot peppers, seeded and minced, or one 8-ounce can mild or hot green chilies, chopped

1   tablespoon chili powder

1   tablespoon unsweetened cocoa powder

2   teaspoons dried oregano

2   teaspoons ground cumin

Salt and freshly ground pepper to taste

Chopped ripe tomatoes for garnish

Chopped cilantro or parsley for garnish

**1.** Heat the oil in a large soup pot. Add the onion and sauté over medium-low heat until translucent. Add the garlic and sauté until the onion is golden. Add the remaining ingredients except the last three. Bring to a simmer, then cover and simmer gently for 30 minutes, stirring occasionally, until the peppers are tender and the flavors have melded.

**2.** Season with salt and pepper, and adjust the other seasonings. If time allows, let the chili stand for up to several hours before serving. Heat through as needed. The chili should be nice and thick; if it has gotten too thick, stir in a cup of water. Serve in individual bowls, garnished with tomatoes and cilantro.

**VARIATIONS:**

- Add a cup or two of cooked corn kernels toward the end of cooking time.
- Add a medium or large, firm-cooked sweet potato, peeled and diced.
- Add a diced zucchini or yellow summer squash about halfway into the cooking time.
- Serve with grated nondairy cheddar cheese on the side for garnishing individual servings.
- Serve with vegan sour cream (homemade, see page 96, or store-bought).
- Put out extra "hot stuff" like minced fresh chili peppers, dried hot red pepper flakes, or hot sauce.

# Chipotle Black Bean and Corn Salad

**GLUTEN-FREE**

**SOY-FREE**

**NUT-FREE (if pumpkin seeds are safe for you)**

**10 TO 12 SERVINGS**

*Smoky, spicy chipotle chilies jazz up this classic potluck dish. Black bean and corn salad is a great summer dish when fresh corn is abundant, but it tastes just as good in winter if you use frozen kernels.*

2   15- to 16-ounce cans black beans

2   cups cooked fresh or frozen corn kernels

1   large red bell pepper, cut into short, narrow strips

1   large green bell pepper, cut into short, narrow strips

2   to 3 scallions, thinly sliced

1   or 2 canned chipotle chilies in adobo, finely chopped

¼   to ½ cup chopped fresh cilantro or parsley

2   tablespoons fresh oregano leaves, or 1 teaspoon dried

1   teaspoon ground cumin

Juice of 1 lime

2   tablespoons red or white wine vinegar

3   to 4 tablespoons extra-virgin olive oil

Salt and freshly ground pepper to taste

Toasted pumpkin seeds or pepitas for garnish

Round or triangular tortilla chips for garnish

1. Combine all the ingredients except the pumpkin seeds and tortilla chips in a serving bowl and toss together thoroughly.

2. This hearty salad can be made several hours ahead and refrigerated until needed. Before serving, give the mixture a good stirring; sprinkle toasted pumpkin seeds over the top and tuck tortilla chips around the edges for garnish.

# Festive Five-Bean Salad

**GLUTEN-FREE**

Can be made **SOY-FREE** by eliminating edamame

or replacing them with baby lima beans

**NUT-FREE**

## 10 OR MORE SERVINGS

*Why settle for the three beans called for in the eponymous salad, when you can use five? Edamame and arugula add flavor, color, and a contemporary twist to the classic salad—a good choice when you need a potluck or company dish that's fast, inexpensive, and goes a long way.*

### DRESSING

- ½ cup store-bought raspberry vinaigrette
- 2 tablespoons yellow or Dijon-style mustard
- 1 tablespoon all-purpose seasoning blend (see sidebar on page 31)

### SALAD

- 1 cup fresh or thawed frozen shelled edamame
- 2 cups fresh green beans, trimmed and cut into 1-inch lengths, or thawed frozen cut green beans
- 1 15- to 16-ounce can navy beans, drained and rinsed
- 1 15- to 16-ounce can small red or kidney beans, drained and rinsed
- 1 15- to 16-ounce can black beans, drained and rinsed
- 2 large celery stalks, diced
- 1 medium red bell pepper, diced
- 2 good handfuls baby arugula, rinsed and dried
- 2 to 3 scallions, thinly sliced

  Salt and freshly ground pepper to taste

1. Combine the vinaigrette, mustard, and seasoning blend in a small bowl and whisk together. Set aside.

2. Bring 2 cups or so of water to a boil in a small saucepan. Add the edamame and cook for 5 to 7 minutes, or until just tender. Add the green beans and continue to cook for 2 minutes longer, or until tender-crisp. Drain and rinse under cool water.

3. Combine the edamame and green beans with the remaining ingredients in a serving bowl. Add the dressing and toss well. Let the salad stand, covered, at room temperature or refrigerated, for at least an hour (or up to several hours). Give the salad a good stirring before serving.

# Bean-Thread Noodles and Asian Vegetables in Creamy Cashew Sauce

**GLUTEN-FREE (make sure the soy sauce is gluten-free)**

**8 SERVINGS**

Crisp vegetables, a rich, nutty sauce, and bean-thread noodles add up to a dish that tastes great warm or at room temperature, making it a good choice for potlucks any time of the year.

## SAUCE

- ⅓ cup cashew butter
- 1 tablespoon dark sesame oil
- 3 tablespoons rice vinegar or other mild white vinegar
- 1 tablespoon natural granulated sugar
- 2 teaspoons grated fresh ginger

## NOODLES AND VEGETABLES

- 8 ounces bean-thread (cellophane) noodles
- 1 large red bell pepper, cut into narrow strips
- 1½ cups snow peas or sugar snap peas, trimmed
- 1 large carrot, peeled and cut into matchsticks or sliced diagonally
- 6 stalks bok choy, sliced diagonally
- 1 15-ounce can baby corn, liquid reserved
- 2 to 3 scallions, green parts only, cut into 1-inch lengths
- 2 tablespoons reduced-sodium soy sauce, plus more to taste
- 1 teaspoon dark sesame oil

**1.** Combine the ingredients for the sauce in a small bowl with ½ cup hot water and whisk together. If the nut butter you're using is rather stiff, place all the sauce ingredients in a food processor; process briefly until smooth.

**2.** Cook the noodles according to the directions on the package, then drain and transfer to a serving dish. Cut them in several directions with kitchen shears to shorten them. Pour in the cashew sauce and toss together.

**3.** Prepare all the vegetables as described before starting to stir-fry. Slowly heat the soy sauce, sesame oil, plus ¼ cup of the reserved liquid from the baby corn in a wok or stir-fry pan.

**4.** Raise the heat to high and add all the vegetables. Stir quickly to coat with the soy sauce mixture, and stir-fry for 3 to 4 minutes, just until the vegetables have lost their raw quality. Remove from the heat. Add the vegetables to the noodles and toss well. Serve at once, passing around extra soy sauce if desired.

# Three-Part Harmony
# Composed Salad Platter

**GLUTEN-FREE**

**SOY-FREE**

Can be made **NUT-FREE** by eliminating walnuts in the carrot salad

**6 to 8 servings**

*This attractive and easily composed salad is a nourishing meal in and of itself. It's impressive served to company or brought to a potluck, but simple and fast enough to prepare for an everyday meal with a warming soup.*

### QUINOA-CORN SALAD

⅔ cup red or regular quinoa, rinsed

1 cup cooked fresh or thawed frozen corn kernels

1 medium red bell pepper, finely diced

3 to 4 scallions, minced

2 tablespoons extra-virgin olive oil

2 tablespoons wine vinegar, or to taste

Salt and freshly ground pepper to taste

**1.** Combine the quinoa and 1⅓ cups of water in a medium saucepan and bring to a gentle boil. Lower the heat, cover, and simmer for 15 minutes, or until the water is absorbed.

**2.** Taste, and if you'd like the quinoa to be more tender, add ½ cup more water and cook until absorbed. When the quinoa is done, remove it from the heat, fluff with a fork, and transfer to a mixing bowl. Stir in the corn kernels and allow the mixture to cool while making the other salads.

**3.** Combine the quinoa with the remaining ingredients for this salad and toss well.

### BLACK BEAN AND TOMATO SALAD

1 15- to 16-ounce can black beans, drained and rinsed

1 cup cherry or grape tomatoes, or ½ cup each yellow and red grape tomatoes

2 tablespoons extra-virgin olive oil

1 to 2 tablespoons lemon or lime juice, to taste

½ cup small green pimiento olives

¼ cup minced fresh cilantro or parsley, or more, to taste

Salt and freshly ground pepper to taste

**1.** Combine all the ingredients for the black bean and tomato salad in a mixing bowl and toss together.

**GRATED CARROT AND WATERCRESS SALAD**

| | |
|---|---|
| 1 | pound baby carrots |
| ½ | bunch watercress leaves |
| ½ | cup parsley leaves |
| ¼ | cup oil-packed sun-dried tomatoes |
| ¼ | cup walnuts |
| 2 | to 3 tablespoons lemon juice, or to taste |
| 1 | to 2 tablespoons agave nectar, to taste |
| 1 | tablespoon oil from sun-dried tomatoes |
| | Salt and freshly ground pepper to taste |

1. Grate the carrots in a food processor fitted with the grating blade. Transfer to a mixing bowl.

2. Combine the watercress, parsley, dried tomatoes, and walnuts in a food processor fitted with the metal blade. Pulse on and off until finely chopped. Don't overprocess!

3. Transfer the watercress mixture to the mixing bowl with the carrots. Add the remaining ingredients and stir until well combined.

4. To serve, mound the carrot salad in the middle of a large platter and arrange the quinoa salad and black bean salad on either side of it. Serve at room temperature.

# Rice Noodles with Watercress and Cilantro

**GLUTEN-FREE**

**SOY-FREE**

Can be made **NUT-FREE** by omitting the optional nuts

**6 SERVINGS**

*I admire people who bring huge platters of perfect, homemade rice paper rolls to parties. I'm jealous of them as well, since all my attempts at rice paper rolls have yielded results that can only be described as wobbly. I love the combination of fresh flavors encased in these delectable rolls—particularly the cilantro, mint, cucumbers, and carrots mingled with the starchy rice paper—so I combined these elements into a salad that's infinitely easier to make and even more fun to eat.*

4 to 5 ounces Asian rice noodles

1 tablespoon olive oil or other healthy vegetable oil

½ good-size bunch watercress, leaves only, rinsed

½ cup cilantro leaves

8 mint leaves, or more, to taste

2 scallions, green parts only, cut into several pieces

½ medium cucumber, quartered and thinly sliced

12 baby carrots, quartered lengthwise

¼ cup rice vinegar, or more, to taste

1 to 2 tablespoons natural granulated sugar, or more, to taste

2 tablespoons sesame seeds (black sesame seeds add a nice accent)

½ teaspoon salt

Freshly ground pepper to taste

¼ to ½ cup finely crushed peanuts or cashews, optional

1. Cook the noodles according to the directions on the package, then drain and transfer to a serving dish. Cut them in several directions with kitchen shears to shorten them, and toss with the oil.

2. Meanwhile, combine the watercress, cilantro, mint, and scallion in a food processor. Pulse on and off until the leaves are very finely chopped, not pureed.

3. Combine the watercress mixture with the noodles and toss well. Add the remaining ingredients and toss again. Taste, and adjust the tart/sweet balance to your liking. Scatter the optional nuts over the top. Cover and chill or serve at once.

**VARIATION:** If you'd like to add a spicy kick to this dish, either add a small, minced, fresh hot chili pepper or dried hot red pepper flakes, to taste.

# Pasta Puttanesca
# (Pasta with Olive Sauce)

**GLUTEN-FREE**

**SOY-FREE**

Can be made **NUT-FREE** by omitting optional pine nuts

**8 SERVINGS**

*The simplicity of this Neapolitan recipe, named for ladies of the night, belies its luscious flavor. Make life easier for yourself by using pitted olives from your supermarket or specialty market olive bar.*

16 ounces pasta, any long shape

1 12-ounce jar roasted red peppers

3 tablespoons extra-virgin olive oil

3 to 4 cloves garlic, minced

1½ cups pitted and chopped brine-cured olives (use a combination of pitted black and green olives)

1 14- to 16-ounce can diced tomatoes

1 6-ounce can tomato paste

¼ cup dry white wine or red wine

¼ cup minced fresh parsley

¼ toasted pine nuts, optional

Salt and freshly ground pepper to taste

1. Cook the pasta in plenty of rapidly simmering water until *al dente*, then drain.

2. Drain and reserve the liquid from the roasted peppers. Cut the peppers into fairly short, narrow strips.

3. Heat 1 tablespoon of the oil in a large saucepan. Add the garlic and sauté until over low heat until golden, about 2 to 3 minutes. Add the olives, roasted peppers and their liquid, tomatoes, tomato paste, and wine. Turn the heat up to medium-high and bring to a simmer, then remove from the heat.

4. Combine the cooked pasta with the olive sauce in a large serving bowl. Add the parsley and optional pine nuts, season with salt and pepper, and toss well. Serve at once.

# Pappardelle with Swiss Chard

**SOY-FREE**

Can be made **NUT-FREE** by omitting optional pine nuts

**6 TO 8 SERVINGS**

*Here's a sturdy, late-summer-to-fall pasta dish to serve as part of an at-home meal for company or to take to a potluck or other gathering. If you're transporting it, put the dish in a large, covered casserole, after allowing it to cool somewhat first. Before serving, set your host's oven to 350° F for 15 to 20 minutes to warm up the dish, or microwave it on high for 5 minutes to reheat.*

- 10 to 12 ounces Swiss chard
- 1 10- to 12-ounce package pappardelle (broad, flat pasta; substitute fettuccine if unavailable)
- 3 tablespoons extra-virgin olive oil
- 3 to 4 cloves garlic, minced
- 1 medium yellow summer squash, quartered and thinly sliced
- ¼ cup white wine or water
- 1 28-ounce can diced tomatoes
- 1 16-ounce can cannellini, drained and rinsed
- ⅓ cup sliced sun-dried tomatoes, oil-cured or not, as preferred
- ⅓ cup dark raisins or currants
- Salt and freshly ground pepper to taste
- ¼ cup toasted pine nuts, optional

1. Remove and discard the stems and thicker midribs from the Swiss chard leaves. Rinse the leaves, then drain and coarsely chop them.

2. Cook the pappardelle in plenty of rapidly simmering water according to the directions on the package until *al dente*, then drain.

3. Meanwhile, heat the oil in an extra-large saucepan or steep-sided stir-fry pan. Add the garlic and sauté over medium-low heat until it begins to turn golden. Add the summer squash and continue to sauté until tender-crisp.

4. Add the wine and Swiss chard. Cover and cook just until the chard wilts down, stirring once or twice, about 3 minutes.

5. Stir in the tomatoes, beans, dried tomatoes, and raisins. Cook until everything is well heated through, about 4 to 5 minutes longer.

6. Combine the cooked pasta with the chard mixture in a large serving bowl. Toss well; season to taste with salt and pepper, and toss again. Top with the optional pine nuts and serve at once.

# ACKNOWLEDGMENTS

It has been said that too many cooks spoil the broth, but a book on holiday meals and traditions wouldn't be as well seasoned without the contributions and involvement of at least a few other cooks—both in the literal and figurative sense. My thanks go to the following for their contributions or assistance:

Anne Atlas, for her long-ago contribution of Marinated Mushrooms, Asparagus, and Artichokes; my son, Evan Atlas, for helping to test recipes in the early stages of this project and for his input, and for contributing one of my favorite new recipes in this book, Plantain Fritters with Black Bean Dip; Jean-Luc Botbol for Moroccan Carrots; Seth Branitz, chef and co-owner of Karma Road in New Paltz, NY, for his great suggestion on how to make vegan matzo balls; Alisa Fleming, of godairyfree.org, for inspiring me to use butternut squash in vegan challah; Wendy and Harry Lipstein, who changed my life by teaching me about massaged kale; Melissa Mandel, for recipe testing, as well as her contribution (via her mom) of Chocolate Mint Bars; Barbara Pollack, for Quinoa Pilaf and Passover Granola; Robin Robertson, vegan author extraordinaire, for the sidebar on Slow-Cooker Vegan Cholent; and Uziel Sason, for Turkish Eggplant Stew. Thanks to family members and friends who willingly subjected themselves to my experimentation; I know it was a tough and thankless job!

A very special thanks goes to Susan Voisin, whose stunning photography graces these pages. Each shot was meticulously thought out and lovingly crafted to reflect the spirit of the recipe depicted. It's not surprising that Susan (a talented recipe developer as well as photographer) has legions of her own fans for her award-winning blog, FatFree Vegan Kitchen (blog.fatfreevegan.com). I also thank her for contributing Apple-Pumpkin Delight, Skinny Figgy Bars, New World Wassail, Chocolate-Orange Cake, and Strawberry Snack Cake.

My agents, Lisa Ekus and Sally Ekus, truly enrich my creative life. I thank them for all they do for me professionally, as well as for being such dear friends. How did I ever live without you?

The editor of lengthy and complex projects deserves the place of pride, which is the last word in the acknowledgments. My editor Jennifer Williams and I have a lot in common, from our birth year to our penchant for finding humor in the mundane. Jennifer, you really are so much fun to work with; let's do so again soon.

# ABOUT THE AUTHOR

Nava Atlas is the author and illustrator of many well-known vegetarian and vegan cookbooks, including *Vegan Express, Vegan Soups and Hearty Stews for All Seasons, The Vegetarian Family Cookbook,* and *The Vegetarian 5-Ingredient Gourmet.* Her first book was *Vegetariana,* now considered a classic in its field. In addition, she has published two books of humor: *Expect the Unexpected When You're Expecting! (A Parody)* and *Secret Recipes for the Modern Wife.* Her latest book of visual nonfiction is *The Literary Ladies' Guide to the Writing Life.*

Nava is also a visual artist, specializing in limited edition artists' books and text-driven objects and installations. Her work has been shown nationally in museums, galleries, and alternative art spaces. Her limited edition books are housed in numerous collections of artists' books, including the art libraries at the Museum of Modern Art (NY), National Museum of Women in the Arts (Washington, DC), National Library at the Victoria and Albert Museum (London), Brooklyn Museum, and Boston Museum of Fine Arts, as well as dozens of academic collections.

Learn more about Nava's work at her various Web sites: VegKitchen.com, navaatlasart.com, and literaryladiesguide.com. Nava has two grown sons and lives in the Hudson Valley region of New York State with her husband.